Levi Rawson Taft

Greenhouse management

A manual for florists and flower lovers on the forcing of flowers, vegetables and

fruits in greenhouses, and the propagation and care of house plants

Levi Rawson Taft

Greenhouse management

A manual for florists and flower lovers on the forcing of flowers, vegetables and fruits in greenhouses, and the propagation and care of house plants

ISBN/EAN: 9783337374464

Printed in Europe, USA, Canada, Australia, Japan

Cover: Foto ©Lupo / pixelio.de

More available books at **www.hansebooks.com**

Greenhouse Management.

A Manual for Florists and Flower Lovers

ON THE

Forcing of Flowers, Vegetables and Fruits

IN

GREENHOUSES,

AND THE

Propagation and Care of House Plants.

BY

L. R. TAFT

Professor of Horticulture and Landscape Gardening, Michigan Agricultural College, and author of "Greenhouse Construction."

ILLUSTRATED

NEW YORK
ORANGE JUDD COMPANY
1911

COPYRIGHT, 1898,
BY ORANGE JUDD COMPANY

PREFACE.

The florist finds that in his profession changes are continually taking place, and if he would succeed he must keep up with the procession. Not only are new and improved methods continually being brought into use, but the plants that he grows change from year to year. A few years ago camellias, tuberoses and bouvardias were among the plants that were most grown, but now, if grown at all, they have but a small place. Not only does Fashion change the classes of plants that are grown, but from year to year the varieties change, and the methods of culture improve.

To inform himself as to the methods that have been found valuable by his competitors, one can, to be sure, look to the horticultural periodicals, which contain much valuable information, but the books to which he can go for advice are few and most of them are out of date. To supply a source from which information as to the methods used by the more successful florists can be drawn, this book has been prepared. As originally written it consisted of about ten chapters, which were intended as a sort of appendix to Greenhouse Construction, but the subject of Greenhouse Management was deemed worthy of a separate volume, and accordingly the copy was withdrawn from the printer and considerably added to.

An attempt has been made in this book to give to florists an insight into the methods that are to-day being used by their intelligent and successful brethren. In nearly every case they have been tried by the author, or be has seen the results of their use in numerous instances, so that they can be used without hesitation. It is hoped that the information as to the best methods of forcing vegetables will be of especial value, as but little attention has been given that industry, which is one that is rapidly increasing in importance. Although this subject has perhaps received less space than it really deserves, we have endeavored to present it in a clear and concise form that can be followed and understood by anyone.

In treating the standard crops of the commercial florist, such as the rose, carnation, violet and chrysanthemum, we have touched upon the time and method of cultivation and the general care required in growing them, but have not deemed it worth while to go into lengthy descriptions of varieties, as they change from year to year; the lists given, however, are those that are to-day deemed most valuable.

Florists are more and more, each year, troubled by injurious insects and fungi. For many of them we have pointed out the treatment, and have added a list of remedies which includes those that are considered most reliable. In the chapters devoted to the care of house plants, we have indicated the methods of growing and caring for the plants that are commonly grown in the house.

Many of the illustrations are from drawings and photographs made under the direction of the author, and for the others we are indebted to the kindness of friends. Several were furnished by the publishers of the *American Agriculturist*, while most of the half tones of the specimen pots, and of specimen blooms, as well as Figs. 47, 91 and 92, were supplied by the publishers of *The Florist's Exchange* and *American Gardening*. We are also indebted to *Gardening* and *The American Florist*. Many of the cuts illustrating the

PREFACE.

interiors of greenhouses used for various crops, as well as the cultural methods used, were supplied by various specialists. Thus, Mr. Alex. Montgomery of the Waban conservatories, Natick, Mass., furnished cuts of their rose houses; Fred Dorner & Son, Lafayette, Ind., and The Cottage Gardens, Queens, L. I., carnations; Pitcher & Manda, Short Hills, N. J., and E. D. Smith, Adrian, Mich., chrysanthemums; Fred Boulon, Sea Cliff, L. I., Hitchings & Co., New York, and Profs. Galloway and Dorsett, Garrett Park, Md., violets; J. C. Vaughan, Chicago, Ill., J. M. Gasser, Cleveland, Ohio, and Cushman Gladiolus Co., Euclid, O., bulbs; W. H. Elliott, Brighton, Mass., asparagus house; and Julius Roehrs, Carlton Hill, N. J., miscellaneous plants. Acknowledgments are also due for the use of cuts and for helpful suggestions to the following officers of experiment stations: Prof. L. H. Bailey, Ithaca, N. Y., Prof. S. T. Maynard, Amherst, Mass., Prof. W. M. Munson, Orono, Me., Prof. L. F. Kinney, Kingston, R. I., Prof. C. S. Plumb, Lafayette, Ind., and Prof. R. L. Watts, Knoxville, Tenn., as well as Prof. B. D. Halsted of New Jersey, for the article on Violet Diseases, and Prof. W. J. Green, Wooster, Ohio, who supplied the article on Sub-irrigation.

L. R. TAFT.

AGRICULTURAL COLLEGE, MICH.

TABLE OF CONTENTS.

CHAPTER I.
The Forcing of Roses,

CHAPTER II.
The Carnation,

CHAPTER III.
The Chrysanthemum,

CHAPTER IV.
The Violet,

CHAPTER V.
Bulbs and their Culture,

CHAPTER VI.
Tuberous Begonias,

CHAPTER VII.
Orchid Culture,

CHAPTER VIII.
Azaleas,

CHAPTER IX.
Calceolarias, Cinerarias and Primulas,

CHAPTER X.
Ferns, Smilax and Asparagus,

CHAPTER XI.
Palms, Pandanus and Araucaria,

CHAPTER XII.
Dracænas and Cordylines,

CHAPTER XIII.
Lettuce Forcing,

CHAPTER XIV.
Cucumbers, Tomatoes and Melons,

CHAPTER XV.
Mushroom Culture,

CHAPTER XVI.
Asparagus and Rhubarb,

CHAPTER XVII.
Radishes, Carrots, Beets and Beans,

CHAPTER XVIII.
Grape Growing Under Glass,

CHAPTER XIX.
Strawberry Growing under Glass,

CHAPTER XX.
Fruit Trees under Glass,

CHAPTER XXI.
Management of House Plants,

TABLE OF CONTENTS.

CHAPTER XXII.
The Growing of Bedding Plants, ...

CHAPTER XXIII.
Propagation of Plants by Seeds and Cuttings,

CHAPTER XXIV.
Propagation by Layering, Grafting and Budding,

CHAPTER XXV.
Insects of the Greenhouse, ...

CHAPTER XXVI.
Diseases of Greenhouse Plants, ...

CHAPTER XXVII.
Insecticides and their Preparation, . .

CHAPTER XXVIII.
Fungicides, their Preparation and Use, . .

CHAPTER XXIX.
Soil, Manures and Watering, ...

CHAPTER XXX.
Fuel—Coal, Oil and Gas, ...

LIST OF ILLUSTRATIONS.

Fig.		Page
1.	Pres. Carnot rose,	13
2.	House of Bridesmaid roses,	15
3.	Wire trellis for roses,	20
4.	Hybrid roses pruned and tied down,	23
5.	Bed of hybrid roses in bud,	25
6.	Types of carnation cuttings,	28
7.	Carnation house, short span to south,	33
8.	Carnation supports,	41
9.	Carnations supported by chicken netting,	43
10.	Carnations supported by meshes of cotton twine,	45
11.	Carnations supported by wire lathing,	47
12.	Daybreak carnation,	50
13.	Mrs. Geo. M. Bradt carnation,	52
14.	Chrysanthemums trained to stakes,	59
15.	Chrysanthemums supported by wire and twine,	61
16.	Chrysanthemum crown bud,	64
17.	Chrysanthemum terminal bud,	65
18.	Chrysanthemum, Eugene Dailledouze,	72
19.	Chrysanthemum, Mayflower,	73
20.	Chrysanthemum, Mrs. Perrin,	74
21.	Chrysanthemum, Iora,	75
22.	Narrow violet house,	76
23.	Hitchings violet house,	79
24.	Narrow violet house, improved,	81
25.	Single violet, Princess de Galles,	87
26.	Box of Roman hyacinths,	89
27.	Double Dutch hyacinths,	91
28.	Improved hyacinth glass,	91
29.	Single early tulips,	92
30.	Freesia refracta alba,	94
31.	Lilium Harrisii,	96
32.	Forcing lily of the valley,	97
33.	Cyclamen plant,	100
34.	Gladiolus May,	102
35.	House of tuberous begonias,	104
36.	Single tuberous begonia,	105
37.	Double tuberous begonia,	106
38.	Gloxinia,	110
39.	House of gloxinias,	111
40.	Fancy caladium,	114

LIST OF ILLUSTRATIONS.

Fig.		Page
41.	Orchids in bloom,	118
42.	Cypripedium Spicerianum,	120
43.	Cattleya trianæ,	122
44.	Orchid baskets,	123
45.	Aerides Savageanum,	124
46.	Phalænopsis grandiflora,	126
47.	Potting and cribbing orchids,	127
48.	Azalea in compact form,	132
49.	Azalea with open head,	134
50.	Hydrangea Otaksa,	135
51.	Cytisus,	137
52.	Bench of lilacs,	140
53.	Kalmia latifolia,	142
54.	Specimen calceolaria,	144
55.	Cineraria hybrida,	145
56.	Single Chinese primrose,	147
57.	Machet mignonette,	151
58.	Adiantum Farleyense,	155
59.	Boston fern,	156
60.	Asparagus Sprengeri,	157
61.	Asparagus house,	161
62.	Fan palm,	163
63.	Dwarf rattan palm,	164
64.	Variegated aspidistra,	167
65.	Group of anthuriums and alocasias,	176
66.	Alocasia metallica,	178
67.	Aglaonema pictum,	179
68.	Even-span lettuce house,	183
69.	Lean-to lettuce house,	185
70.	Lettuce pot plant,	187
71.	Pot plant ready for market,	188
72.	Interior of lean-to lettuce house,	190
73.	Lettuce packed for local market,	193
74.	Cucumber house, interior,	200
75.	English forcing cucumbers,	204
76.	Interior of tomato forcing house,	207
77.	Growing mushrooms on greenhouse benches,	210
78.	Crop of mushrooms under a bench,	212
79.	Brick spawn,	218
80.	French mushroom spawn,	219
81.	New mushroom in a cold frame,	224
82.	Black Hamburg grape,	238
83.	Grape house in fruit,	240
84.	Eye cutting of grape,	246
85.	Short cutting of grape,	246
86.	Bench of strawberry plants,	250
87.	The crop gathered,	251
88.	Fruiting strawberry plants,	251
89.	Pear tree in pot,	254
90.	Plum tree in fruit,	255
91.	A window garden,	260
92.	A well arranged window box,	270

LIST OF ILLUSTRATIONS.

Fig.		Page
93.	Epiphyllum truncatum,	285
94.	A collection of cacti and aloes,	286
95.	A house of pedigree violets,	292
96.	Showing condition of stem for cuttings,	293
97.	Soft cutting of coleus,	294
98.	Geranium cutting,	296
99.	Cutting of Arbor Vitæ,	298
100.	Long cutting of grape,	299
101.	Tongue or whip grafting,	302
102.	Cleft grafting,	303
103.	Side grafting,	304
104.	Budding,	306
105.	Wingless female aphis,	309
106.	Winged male aphis,	310
107.	Fuller's rose beetle,	311
108.	Red spider,	312
109.	Thrips,	313
110.	Mealy bug,	314
111.	Fumigation of a violet house,	322
112.	Rose spot,	324
113.	Spores of black spot,	325
114.	Carnation rust,	329
115.	Spores of carnation rust,	330
116.	Spot disease of carnations,	332
117.	Effect of spot on carnations,	333
118.	Anthracnose of carnations,	334
119.	Fairy ring spot of carnation,	335
120.	Spores of fairy ring spot,	335
121.	Carnation leaf mold,	336
122.	Botrytis or rot of carnations,	336
123.	Bacteriosis of carnations,	337
124.	Violet leaf spot,	339
125.	Bermuda lily disease,	343
126.	Leaf blight of mignonette,	346
127.	The Kinney pump,	366
128.	Crude oil burner,	377

GREENHOUSE MANAGEMENT.

CHAPTER I.

THE FORCING OF ROSES.

While other departments of floriculture have made wonderful progress during the past ten years, in none of them has it been as great as in the winter forcing of roses, and to-day hundreds of large establishments are almost entirely devoted to this work, while every small florist has his rose house, and the sale of cut bloom generally equals the amount received from all other flowers combined.

Although it is true that roses, to be successfully grown, require careful attention, it is not true that there is any wonderful secret that one must acquire in order to grow them, and, while the inexperienced rose grower cannot expect the highest success, it is hoped that if the directions here given are carefully followed many mistakes may be prevented. The work of the rose grower generally begins with the propagation and growing of the plants, and therefore we will commence with that operation and follow along with the various steps as the season advances.

PROPAGATING THE PLANTS.

Rose plants for forcing purposes are generally grown from cuttings of the new wood made any time from November to February, but for most purposes the earlier date is preferable. The rule generally given for learning if the plants are in proper condition to be used for cuttings, i. e., when in bending a branch the wood snaps, does not hold for roses, as cuttings should not be made until the buds in the axils of the leaves have become firm and hard. Some consider that the lower buds on a stem are in good condition when the flower buds are ready to be cut, while others believe that the best time for making the cuttings is when the buds begin to show color. At any rate, the cuttings should be made before the leaf buds begin to swell. The cuttings made as soon as the buds have formed and the wood has lost its succulent nature, will root quicker, and a much larger per cent of them will form roots, or "strike," as it is called. If the variety is a new and choice one, the blind shoots, or those that have not formed flower buds, are often used for making cuttings. While it may be done occasionally without marked injury, if persisted in the tendency will be to develop plants that form few flowering stems, and the results will not be satisfactory, so that the continued use of the blind shoots for cuttings is not to be recommended.

When the stems have long internodes, and particularly if it is a new sort, a cutting should be obtained from every good bud, but those at the lower part of the stem, and all at the upper portion that are to any extent soft and succulent, should be rejected. The cuttings of American Beauty, and other varieties with short joints, should contain two or more buds. Cuttings should be from one and one-half to three inches long, with one bud near the top, at any rate, and with the lower end cut off smoothly at right angles, with a sharp knife. If the upper leaf is large, about one-half of it should be cut away, and the other leaves, if any, should be rubbed off.

The cuttings should be dropped into water to prevent their drying out, and as soon as possible should be placed in the propagating bed. This should contain about four inches of clean, sharp sand of medium fineness, and should have heating pipes beneath, to give bottom heat. Set the cuttings in rows, about two inches apart and three-fourths of an inch in the row, and press the sand firmly about them. At once wet them down thoroughly, and if the weather is clear and bright the beds should be shaded during the middle of the day for the first week. The propagating house should be kept at a temperature, at night, of fifty-eight or sixty degrees, with about ten degrees more of bottom heat. During the day, it should be well ventilated to keep up the bottom heat and thus promote root development, and to admit fresh air, but a temperature ten degrees higher than at night is desirable.

In about three or four weeks, with proper care, every cutting should be rooted. The requirements for success, as noted above, are, good cuttings, clean, sharp sand, a proper temperature, shading when necessary, and an occasional wetting down of the bed, in order that the cuttings may not at any time become dry. If the house is inclined to dry out, or if the weather is bright, the cuttings as well as the walks should be sprinkled occasionally, and the ventilation should have careful attention. It is best to use fresh sand for each batch of cuttings.

POTTING AND CARE OF THE PLANTS.

When the roots are three-fourths of an inch long, the cuttings should be potted off into two or two and one-half inch pots, pressing the soil firmly. The best soil for the potting of rose cuttings is made of equal parts of leaf mold, or decayed pasture sods, and garden loam, with a little cow manure and bone meal, and sand in proportion to the heaviness of the soil. After being potted the cuttings should be placed in a house with a night temperature of a little less than sixty degrees. They require the same care as other plants, careful watering, with an occasional syringing to keep down the red spider, proper ventilation, and an avoidance of drafts and direct sunlight for a few days, being the main things desired.

Unless tobacco stems are strewn on the beds, it will be necessary, once or twice a week, to burn tobacco stems in the house, or syringe them with tobacco water. From the time the cuttings are potted off until they have finished flowering and are ready to be thrown out, or rested, they should be kept growing, every precaution being taken to avoid a check, if the best results are desired. Some, however, prefer to grow the plants rapidly until they are in four-inch pots, and then give them a short rest. As soon as the roots have filled the pots, and before the plants become pot-bound, shift to three or three and one-half inch pots. By the last of April, if they have had good care, the first batch will have filled four-inch pots and will be strong enough to plant in the beds for early flowering, while the others, as they come on, can be repotted, and will soon be large enough to be transferred to the beds. Only strong, well-grown plants should be used, and if possible all should be planted out by the first of July. By this early planting not only can a large crop of blooms be secured during the summer, when there is a good demand at a fair price, but the plants will be so strong that they will be able to give large crops during the fall and early winter, when they are most needed. Planting some of the beds by the first of April, for summer use, will often be desirable.

SOIL FOR ROSES.

While the different varieties will not always thrive with the same kind of soil, it is generally admitted that, at all events, a soil for roses should contain decomposed pasture sods and cow manure. The sod should be obtained during the previous summer from some old pasture with a thick, fibrous sod, if possible, and should be piled up with alternate layers of cow manure, using one part of the manure to from four to six of the sods, according to the character of each. The sods should be cut just thick enough to remove the thick, fibrous portion, and if from an average loam soil, neither very heavy nor light, but with a good admixture of clay, the compost prepared as above will be of a suitable character for the rose benches, but if the sods come from a sandy loam soil the addition of one part of clay to five or six of the mixture will be desirable. On the other hand, if the soil is inclined to be heavy, an equal quantity of sand should certainly be added. While considerable clay is desirable in soil for roses, there is danger of its being too heavy, as, even in shallow benches, if the soil at any time becomes too wet, particularly in the fall before the fires are started, or during a cloudy period in the winter, it will not only be longer in drying out than a lighter soil, but "black spot" and other diseases will be much more likely to follow.

Early in the spring the compost pile should be worked over and the coarser sods broken up. After lying in the pile for two or three weeks more it will be ready to place on the benches. When the houses are long, it will be convenient to have openings in the side walls, through which the soil can be thrown upon the benches, and if there are side ventilators this can be readily done. If it is not feasible to have openings in the sides of the houses, it will be a great convenience if a small car can be run along the edges of the benches. As an entire chapter was devoted to "Rose Houses" in the companion volume, "Greenhouse Construction," in which the form and width of house best adapted to the crop was discussed at length, it is not thought necessary to devote space to it here. By reference to the other book, full information regarding these points, and upon such important matters as the pitch for the roof, arrangement of the ventilators, the method of estimating the amount of heating pipe required and the best way of arranging it, will be obtained.

SOLID BEDS VERSUS RAISED BENCHES.

For many years solid beds were almost universally used for growing roses and similar plants. They admit of supplying a full amount of plant food, but while they lessen the danger of injury from neglect in watering, they frequently do great harm if the plants are overwatered, particularly if the sun does not show itself for a number of days, as they are a long time in drying out. For this reason they fell into disrepute, and were replaced, in most establishments, by shallow raised benches, as it was found that roses grown upon them, in four or five inches of soil, were less likely to receive a check during the dull days of early winter, when they are most in demand and bring the best prices. Upon solid beds, however, with good drainage, large crops are secured as the bright, sunny days of spring come on, and, what is of much importance, the plants can be grown for two or more years before they are thrown out, while upon shallow benches it is generally advisable to renew the plants each year.

A method has now come into use that provides both for the thorough drainage and the aeration of the soil, as well as warming it up and drying it out. The solid beds are generally about seven feet wide, with two beds and three walks in a house twenty feet in width. The drainage is provided, in some cases, by means of common drain tile laid across the beds at intervals of from one to three feet, while in others a foot or more in depth of stones, or broken brick, is placed in the bottom and covered with eight inches of soil. A few of our most successful growers secure bottom heat by running one or more steam pipes lengthwise of the beds at about the center of the layer of stones; the heat distributes itself through the bed, and is of marked advantage in wet, dull weather, in drying out the surplus water and warming up the soil. Another favorite arrangement is to have three beds, each five feet wide, and four walks, in a house twenty-two feet wide. These beds have all of the advantages of the old solid bed, with none of the disadvantages, and are equally well adapted to carnations, violets, lettuce and other crops. The watering of the plants by what is known as sub-irrigation has many advantages, and is treated in another chapter.

PLANTING THE HOUSES.

Before the beds are filled with soil, ample drainage facilities should be provided, and if raised, wooden benches are used there should be cracks of nearly one inch between the bottom boards, which should preferably not be more than six inches wide. When tile bottoms are used the cracks can be somewhat smaller. To prevent the soil from falling through the cracks, or from filling up the openings between the stones in the solid beds, it is well to first put down a layer of sods with the grass side down, and upon these four or five inches of the prepared soil for a raised bench, or seven or eight for a solid bed, should be placed. This should be leveled off and firmly packed down.

The beds are now ready for planting, and this should not be long delayed, as the thin layer of soil will soon dry out and will be in an undesirable condition for setting out the plants. The rows are generally twelve inches apart lengthwise of the house, so that a bed will hold as many rows as it is feet wide, and the plants are set twelve to sixteen inches apart in the rows, according to the strength of the variety and whether designed for one or two years' growing. Assort the plants, and use the smaller ones next the walk. Dig holes for the plants with a trowel, and set the plants about as deep as they grew in the pots, taking care not to break the "balls," unless the plants have become pot-bound, when it is well to loosen the roots. While it is always desirable to work the soil carefully into place and to press it firmly about the roots, the soil between the plants should be smoothed off and the surface left light. Upon sloping benches, in particular, it is an excellent plan to have depressions about the plants to hold water and cause it to sink down to the roots, for the first few waterings, until the plants become established. If weeds start, as they probably will in a week or ten days, the soil should be stirred as soon as they appear, and this should be repeated whenever necessary to keep the beds clean, until the roots fill the soil, when it should be discontinued, as it is likely to check the growth of the plants by breaking the roots.

WATERING AND VENTILATING.

From planting time, every detail of watering and ventilating should be carefully performed, as any check now would seriously injure the prospect of a paying crop of flowers. As soon as planted, and every bright morning thereafter until established, the plants, and also the walks, should be thoroughly syringed, and the beds should be watered whenever they show signs of drying out, but while they should not suffer from lack of water, even greater pains should be observed that they are not saturated. This will also aid in keeping down the red spider, which only flourishes in a dry atmosphere. No plant requires more care than the rose, about ventilation. Drafts of cold air upon the foliage should always be avoided, and it is generally a good thing, in a rose house, to have the ventilators arranged with this idea. If there is but a single row, they should be on the side from which the prevailing winds come, if hinged at the bottom, and on the opposite side if hinged at the top.

While either extreme of temperature should be guarded against, it is quite as desirable to give the plants fresh air, at least for a short time, each day. In hot weather give all of the air possible, and leave on some even at night, at the ridge. Exposing the plants to great extremes of temperature is especially likely to bring on an attack of the mildew, and if it should appear, as it often does, without apparent cause, the house should be kept somewhat closer than usual for a few days, and after syringing them the plants should be dusted over with sulphur. As the weather becomes cool in September, it is well to furnish a little artificial heat, to keep the temperature of the house above fifty-five degrees. One or two steam pipes, or a low fire in the hot water heater, will secure this and often prevent a serious check of the plants. With this care, firm, short-jointed wood should be secured, which will give an abundance of bloom. While fifty-eight degrees is given as desirable for a rose house, in order to secure the best results, with the various sorts some little deviation is advisable. The Meteor, among other kinds, needs a few degrees higher than that, while the Perle, Bride and Mermet, and others of the old varieties, should have a temperature a little lower than fifty-eight degrees, if the plants have been properly grown.

It will generally be found best to do the watering early in the morning, and, on the warm, bright days when syringing is necessary, it should be done early enough so that the plants will dry off before night. In ventilating, care should be taken to avoid extremes, and it is best to give a little air as soon as the sun begins to warm the houses, and the amount should be gradually increased, so that during the warmest and brightest part of the day it will be ten or fifteen degrees higher than at night. When the temperature is allowed to run up ten or fifteen degrees before the air is let on, and then the ventilators are opened wide, it will be almost sure to bring on mildew. Plants grown with a judiciously regulated supply of air will be in a much healthier condition than those grown where extremes prevail.

LIQUID MANURES AND FERTILIZERS.

After the roses have started into growth, it will be well to give them an application of liquid manure once in two weeks. It will generally be advisable to pinch off the first flower buds that form, that the plants may throw all of their vigor into the development of stems and leaves.

From the first benches planted, cutting can begin in July, and as soon as the crop is off the bed should receive an application of ground bone, at the rate of one pound to twenty-five square feet. This should be slightly worked into the soil, and the bed covered with manure. A half inch of sheep manure will be preferable, but if this cannot be obtained three-fourths of an inch of cow manure will answer. Unless mineral manures are relied upon, the application should be repeated once in two months. During the dull weather from November to January, the mulching should be thin, but by February the amount used may be slightly increased.

It is believed by many growers that the diseases like "black spot," and mildew, and the other troubles, such as blind shoots, and imperfect flowers, may be attributed, at least in part, to the stimulating effects of stable manure. While they are not caused directly by its use, there can be no doubt but that the large quantity of sheep and cow manure used by many florists promotes a soft, watery growth that is particularly susceptible to disease, and, what is more to be dreaded, that a slight neglect, such as an improper temperature, or the application of too much water, will give the plants a check that will result seriously to them. The use of mineral fertilizers, on the other hand, tends to develop earlier, larger and better flowers, and the plants will be stronger, and with firmer stems and foliage, that will be less likely to be injured by neglect and disease.

For these reasons it is a growing practice with many of our most successful rose growers to rely largely upon mineral manures, beginning as early as November upon old plants, although January will be safer for young ones. These fertilizers can be broadcasted either in a dry state or in water. For roses, a good mixture will consist of one part of nitrate of soda, two parts of sulphate of potash, and ten parts of ground bone. These should be thoroughly mixed and applied broadcast at the rate of one pound to twenty-five square feet of bench, or at the rate of one pound up to four pounds, according to the size of the plants, in fifty gallons of water. When roses are growing rapidly the broadcast application can be repeated once a month, but a less frequent application will be better for small plants, or if there is but little growth. The liquid applications can be made much more frequently, but care should be taken not to use too large a quantity of nitrate of soda, or sulphate of potash, as, if applied in excessive quantities, they will check the growth and even kill the plants. When the ground bone has been scattered upon the surface and mixed with the soil, an excellent liquid fertilizer is made by placing one pound each of the nitrate of soda and of sulphate of potash in two hundred gallons of water, for young plants, which amount may be decreased to one hundred gallons of water when the plants become full grown, applying at intervals of from two to four weeks. The best time to apply liquid manure is in the morning, when the beds are a little dry, as it will then be more evenly distributed through the soil. When nitrate of soda and sulphate of potash are used as a top-dressing, one pound of each to two hundred square feet of bed will be ample.

Unleached wood ashes afford a desirable source for potash and phosphoric acid, and may be used at the rate of a bushel to two or three hundred square feet of bed. The potash will promote the development of firm, short-jointed wood, and, combined with the phosphoric acid, will favor the production of flowers. Many florists still cling to the use of liquid fertilizers made from animal manures, and one of the best mixtures is composed of a peck of hen manure and a half bushel of sheep manure in one hundred gallons of water. The food contained in the few inches of soil in which roses are grown is soon exhausted, and it must be replaced in some way. The top-dressing of sheep or cow manure answers fairly well for this purpose, as well as for a mulch to keep the weeds down after the roots of the roses have filled the soil so that stirring the surface will injure them, but it is unsightly, and keeps the surface wet and sour and prevents the ready access of the air to the roots, so that, although it is of much benefit during the summer months, it is a positive drawback during the winter.

All fallen and diseased leaves should be removed and burned, and the surface of the bed should have an occasional stirring, to admit the air and to prevent the baking of the soil, but care should be taken not to disturb the roots. In addition to the other work mentioned, it is desirable to be prepared at all times to fight insects and diseases. A description of the most troublesome forms, and the treatment for them, will be found in another chapter.

VARIETIES FOR FORCING.

The varieties of roses that will be most profitable will depend, to a large extent, upon the character of the market, as well as upon the character of the soil available for growing them in. To be profitable, a variety should have a good constitution; it should be a vigor-

FIG. 1. PRESIDENT CARNOT.

ous grower, with strong, upright stems; the foliage should be of rich color and good substance, and free from any tendency to disease; the flowers should be large and single on the stems, of a clear color, and in the case of the red sorts without any tendency to turn purple. They should be double enough not to show the center, and the plants should have a long and steady season of flowering.

Among the varieties that are most commonly grown are Bride, Perle (des Jardins), Catherine Mermet and American Beauty. To these should be added Mad. Caroline Testout, Kaiserin Augusta Victoria, Bridesmaid, Mrs. W. C. Whitney, Pres. Carnot (Fig. 1) and Meteor, of more recent introduction, which are fast coming into favor.

American Beauty has no rival in its class, and its flowers are always in demand at good prices. Its flowers are rather small in summer and the petals soon take on a purple color, but when well grown it is a grand rose. Many growers who are successful with most sorts fail with this variety, which will only succeed with the very best of care. It needs a strong, stiff soil, and a temperature at as near sixty degrees as can be secured.

Bride is the favorite white variety. It also needs a rather heavy soil, and should be started early. The temperature for this sort is fifty-six degrees, or a little below. With close attention to ventilation, this is a very desirable sort.

Mermet was for many years the best pink variety, but the fact that it is of a very light color during the dark days of winter, and, like the Bride, which is a sport from it, quite subject to mildew, has lessened its popularity. It requires the same care as Bride, and if given a low temperature at night, careful ventilation during the day, and if sheltered from cold drafts of air, it is still a desirable sort. Bridesmaid (Fig. 2), a recent candidate for a place in the list of commercial varieties, is a little deeper pink than Mermet, and has the marked advantages of holding its color and being comparatively free from the attack of mildew. Wherever it has been planted it is

THE FORCING OF ROSES. 15

FIG. 2. HOUSE OF BRIDESMAID ROSES, GROWN AT WABAN CONSERVATORIES, NATICK, MASS.

the most popular pink sort, and it is rapidly supplanting Mermet. It thrives at a medium temperature.

Testout is another variety with large flowers of a pure pink color. It is rather particular as to soil and care, and although a fair variety for winter when well grown, it is too single for summer use. Valuable for the amateur. It should have not less than sixty degrees and it likes a yellow loam soil.

Meteor is one of the best red, everblooming roses, but to be successfully grown it should have a house where a temperature of at least sixty-three degrees can be given, while it will luxuriate at sixty-five to sixty-eight. It is naturally quite likely to be attacked by mildew and red spider, unless great care is taken with the ventilation and syringing.

Kaiserin is a good summer variety and has a long season of flowering, but is generally considered a failure as a variety for winter flowering, as it is likely to take on a greenish-white color.

Mrs. W. C. Whitney is an early and a free flowering variety. It has an excellent foliage, is a vigorous grower and has long stems. Its flowers are large and full and of a pure, deep pink.

American Belle is a sport from American Beauty, and where a sufficiently high price can be obtained it is a favorite variety. The flowers are very full and have a deep pink color with a carmine shade.

The new rose, Souvenir de Pres. Carnot, is making a very good impression. It is a very strong grower, with long, stiff stems. The flower is of a distinct shade of pink; it is of a large size and has a sweet odor. It is claimed to flower freely, both indoors and out, and to be particularly valuable on account of its excellent keeping qualities.

Of the other recent sorts that are being largely planted are Belle Siebrecht and Mrs. Pierpont Morgan.

Although it is claimed by some that the former is subject to black spot in the summer and fall, with us it has very handsome, clean foliage, and the flowers are large, full, very fragrant, and of a rich, deep pink color. Its petals are rather thick, and it is a good keeper. With some growers the stems are inclined to be short and weak.

Mrs. P. Morgan is a promising sport from Mad. Cusin. It is a stronger grower, a freer bloomer, and the flowers are larger and darker. They are inclined to be irregular in shape and variable in color. Both of these roses will do well at about fifty-eight degrees. The latter is injured if the house is damp, and if dull weather comes when the house is wet from recent syringing, the results to the flowers may be serious unless the air can be dried. For this reason a steam heated house is desirable.

For growing at low temperatures, among the best of the old kinds are Wootton for red, Perle as yellow, Bridesmaid as a large pink, and Mad. Cusin for small, with Bride, or Niphetos for white.

Perle is perhaps more extensively grown than any other variety, and has no rival as a yellow sort. It requires a moderately light soil, not too rich in undecomposed manure, and an abundance of sunlight, with a temperature of about sixty degrees. If the soil is heavy, the houses should be at least two or three degrees warmer than this. If any or all of these conditions are not given, this variety is very apt to furnish what are known as "bullheads," and on this account many growers have become dissatisfied with it, but can find no other variety to compare with it. Care in securing a soil that is not too rich, and in keeping up a temperature a little higher than is required by most of the other sorts, will generally give satisfactory results.

Niphetos is an old white sort, but, excepting Bride, it has no equal, as it thrives and gives large numbers of flowers under conditions that would be far from suitable to most of the new sorts. It is a rather weak grower, and is well adapted for planting on the side benches. While it does well at quite a range of temperature, the largest and best flowers are obtained at rather less than fifty-eight, although the number will be increased at sixty to sixty-five degrees.

La France was formerly a favorite, disputing with Mermet the right to first place as a pink sort, but both have, in most establishments, had to give way to Bridesmaid. It is quite subject to black spot, but with careful handling can be grown with success.

Among the older sorts that are still much grown, where the market does not call for high priced flowers, are Bon Silene and Papa Gontier, carmine; Sunset, a strong-growing buff variety, and Duchess of Albany.

Where the prices will not warrant the growing of Beauty, Papa Gontier may be used instead. It does best on shallow, raised benches, with fifty-five degrees or less at night, and with plenty of air on mild days. Larger buds are obtained on solid beds, but the number will be much less. After flowering, apply water sparingly, as otherwise the plants may drop their leaves.

Souvenir de Wootton is also highly regarded by many who do not succeed with American Beauty.

Of the other sorts, Madam Cusin and Madam de Watteville and Madam Hoste are still favorites in many establishments.

In nearly all cases where raised beds are used, it is customary to throw out the plants after cropping them for one season, but if they have been planted late and have not been forced, some of the smaller sorts may be dried off and rested, and after a few weeks taken up, placed in small pots and kept in a shaded place until the roots have filled the pots, when they may be repotted, or at once planted out in fresh soil upon the beds. As a rule, it will be better to replant with well-grown, young plants.

When grown in solid beds, the same result is secured without taking them from the bed. The plants are dried off in May, so that they will rest, but not enough so that they will shrivel, and kept in this condition for six weeks or two months. The small wood should then be cut out, and the remaining branches headed back. A little of the surface soil can then be removed, if it can be done without disturbing the roots, and a rich mulch applied to the bed. Water should then be applied, but rather sparingly at first, so as to avoid saturating the soil before the growth has started. If properly handled, a heavy cut should be secured during the fall, and the results for the season will oftentimes be as great as could be obtained from new plants, while there will be quite a saving in the expense for the plants and for renewing the soil. Some of the most successful growers make a practice of carrying over about one-half of the plants each year.

If they are to be replaced, as soon as they are past the period of profitable flowering, or when the beds are needed for replanting, the plants should be removed and burned and the soil taken from the table. The benches should at once be repaired and made ready for new plants. It is well to paint all the woodwork of the benches and walls each year with a hot wash composed of equal parts of lime and cement, to which a small quantity of salt has been added. This can be applied rapidly with a whitewash brush, and will help to preserve the lumber and destroy insects, besides improving the appearance of the interior of the house. If the plants have been troubled with fungi and insects, it will be well to burn a small quantity of sulphur, but it should not be done while there are plants in the adjoining houses, as it will prove fatal to them as well as to the insects and the germs of the diseases. Nearly as good results can be obtained, however, without injury to the plants, if the sulphur is slowly evaporated over an oil stove.

STAKING AND TRELLISING.

When the plants have been in the beds for six weeks or two months, the growth will generally be sufficient to require staking. Most growers still tie with raffia to stakes of wood or bamboo, and by an occasional re-tying keep the shoots in place. The use of wire is, however,

FIG. 3. WIRE TRELLIS FOR ROSES.

becoming quite common, and rose growers have devised a variety of trellises for the purpose. One of the simplest of these consists of a No. 12 wire stretched about three feet above the bed over each row of plants (Fig. 2), to support stakes of No. 6 or No. 8 wire, to which the plants can be tied. Sometimes another wire is run lengthwise of the house along each row of plants, near the soil, and a smaller wire, fastened to this at the bottom and to the other wire at the top, can be used as a support for each plant. Still a third method is to run about three wires (No. 12 galvanized) lengthwise of each row and one above the other at intervals of about one foot, the lower wire being about the same distance from the soil. The wires will need to be stretched and fastened at each end to a gas-pipe framework (Fig. 3), and supported at intervals of twenty-five feet with a lighter framework.

Although there is considerable expense at first for the wires, it will be found very satisfactory, and in the end perhaps less expensive than any of the old methods. If desired, it will be a simple matter to so arrange the long wires that, when refilling the beds, they can be drawn up out of the way.

FORCING HYBRID PERPETUAL ROSES.

When they can be brought into flower by Christmas or New Year's, the large flowers of this class of roses bring a large price, and they are then quite profitable. The care required is different than for teas and for most hybrid teas, as the plants must make their growth and have a period of rest before flowering. They are generally grown in solid beds, but sometimes boxes or pots are used. When grown in beds they should have thorough drainage with tiles, stones, or broken brick, arranged in the same way as described for tea roses, and provided with eight or nine inches of rich compost. Although cuttings are often used, the largest blooms can be obtained when they are either budded, or grafted upon Manetti stocks.

The plants should be set early enough so that they will complete their growth by the middle of July. They should be ripened off by gradually withholding water, and only giving them enough to keep the plants from wilting and shrivelling. By syringing morning and evening, the plants can often be kept from wilting without wetting the soil. During rains the beds should be kept dry, as, if the soil becomes saturated, rest will be prevented and the crop will be a failure. If in pots or boxes, they should be turned upon their sides during rains. From four to six weeks will generally be rest enough, and when growth has stopped, and the shoots have taken on a lighter color, they should be pruned, removing the weak shoots and cutting the strong ones back to sound wood and plump buds. After a few days, scrape off the top soil and replace with a fresh compost of equal parts of rotten sods and cow manure. Water thoroughly, and repeat when the soil becomes dry. Syringe every pleasant morning and give thorough ventilation, keeping the house at forty-seven to fifty degrees at night until the buds start. The temperature can then be raised at the rate of one or two degrees a week, with less ventilation after the leaves show. By the time the flower buds appear it should have reached fifty-four degrees, and should then be raised to fifty-five or fifty-six degrees, at which temperature the house should be kept until the plants are through flowering. Ventilate at sixty-two to sixty-five in the morning, but let the temperature run up to seventy-five degrees at noon. After the buds appear, the beds should be given a watering with liquid manure once or twice a week. If started by the first of October, they will flower for Christmas and New Year's. The later sorts can best be grown in pots or boxes, as they can then be left outside until the weather becomes severe, when they should be placed in a cool greenhouse and brought into heat as desired.

Beds of hybrids are generally carried for several years, and require about the same care as the first year, except that the shoots are left somewhat longer and are bent over to promote the starting of side branches (Fig. 4). They can be held in place by stretching No. 14 galvanized wire over each row at the hight of from one or two

THE FORCING OF ROSES. 23

FIG. 4. HYBRID ROSES PRUNED AND TIED DOWN, WABAN CONSERVATORIES, NATICK, MASS.

feet, according to the size of the plants, and tying the shoots to it.

For the successful growing of hybrid roses in solid beds, the houses should be so arranged that the glass upon at least one side of the roof can be taken off. This should be done by the first of July, to assist them in ripening off, and if rain comes the roof should at once be replaced. As soon as the plants are pruned the glass should be replaced and a regular temperature maintained, if the plants are to flower at Christmas.

ROSES IN POTS AND BOXES.

If only a few plants are used for forcing, they may be grown in nine-inch pots, or in long boxes six inches wide, and about the same depth. This method is particularly desirable for hybrid perpetuals. The small plants should be grown the same as for the beds, and should receive their final shift not later than the first of July. The tea roses will do best if kept growing in the house, although some florists think it well to harden them by placing them out of doors when they are in eight- or nine-inch pots and plunging them to their rims in sand or coal ashes, the same as should be done with the hybrids. They will need frequent syringing, but care should be taken not to give enough water to the soil to admit of their becoming water-soaked. By the middle of August, the pots will be filled with roots, and the teas should be removed to a cold frame, or a cool house.

The hybrids should be dried off, and will need the same attention as those in solid benches, until the wood becomes hard, when they should be pruned, and after being first placed in a cold frame, should be gradually brought in to heat. With the same care in watering, syringing and ventilating as is given the roses in the beds, they will bloom by Christmas. A house of hybrid teas in bud is shown in Fig. 5.

FIG. 5. HYBRID TEAS IN BUD, WABAN CONSERVATORIES, NATICK, MASS.

For early blooming, the best sorts are the well-known Gen. Jacqueminot, Anna de Diesbach, Mrs. John Laing and Magna Charta. For late sorts, in addition to the above, Gloire de Margottin, Ulrich Brunner and Baroness Rothschild can be used, and with good care will give satisfaction.

CHAPTER II.

THE CARNATION.

Although the old garden pink and the carnation, or gillyflower, as it was called, have long been grown, there being over three hundred varieties as far back as 1676, the florist's carnation of to-day is comparatively a modern creation. The first real step in its development was made by Dalmais, of Lyons, France, some fifty years since, and they were further improved by Alegatiere, who, in 1866, developed varieties with stiff stems.

The origination of new varieties has been taken up by quite a number of American florists, and they have met with remarkable success. The method pursued is by careful and systematic cross-fertilization. When skilfully performed, perhaps fifty per cent of the seedlings will give double flowers, and five per cent may have enough promise to warrant their further trial. The improvement is along the lines of size, shape, fragrance and color of the flowers, the vigor and freedom of bloom in the plant, the length and stiffness of stem, and the perfection of the calyx; and although much has been achieved, there is promise of great progress in the future.

Within the past ten years the demand for carnation flowers has greatly increased, and this has led to the erection of many large establishments devoted almost entirely to growing them. We also find a considerable number of florists whose principal business is the growing of hundreds of thousands of rooted cuttings and plants, for sale to other florists. The reason for the demand need not long be sought for, as it is very evident that the carnation, as a flower available the year round, has few, if any, equals. It is showy and attractive, its colors are well adapted for use in decoration and for personal adornment, it has a pleasing fragrance, and the flowers are far more lasting than those of the rose and most other plants, and these points in its favor, together with the fact that they are sold at a comparatively low price, have made it the people's flower, and led to the great growth in carnation culture.

PROPAGATION.

For ordinary greenhouse cultivation, the plants are generally started from cuttings as early as November or December, although with a favorable summer for their growth, strong plants can be obtained by the last of August from cuttings struck as late as March. If desired for summer blooming, they should be struck as early even as October, and if flowers are desired in the early fall, the making of the cuttings should not be delayed after November. Another reason for making the cuttings so early is that at that time the plants are strong and vigorous, while later on they will be weakened by flower production, and by the forcing process to which they are subjected during the winter.

As often propagated, it is not strange that varieties run out, but with proper care much can be done to prevent it, if the cuttings are rightly selected. Above all, they should not be made from plants that are in any way diseased or that have been flowering freely for a long period. The best cuttings are made from side shoots of flowering stems, and it is a good plan not to pull them until the flowers have opened, as one can then tell what the flowers of the cuttings are likely to be.

The portions used for cuttings should be firm rather than soft and watery, but should not be the weak, puny stems that weak plants often send out. While the best results can be secured from the suckers that form around the base of the plants, the strong pips along the sides of the stems may be used and will make good plants. These shoots may be pulled from the plants, and by removing some of the lower leaves the cuttings may be

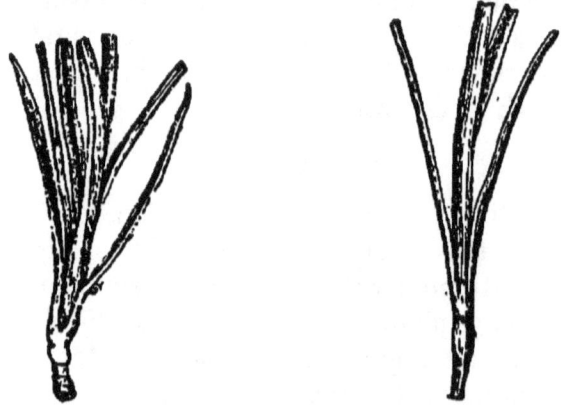

FIG. 6. TWO TYPES OF CARNATION CUTTINGS.

prepared without the use of a knife. The terminal leaves, if very long, may be cut back (Fig. 6).

Cuttings may be rooted either in propagating beds or in boxes of sand. The bottom of the bed should be covered with a thin layer of cinders, or gravel, and about three inches of clean, sharp sand should then be put on. While it is not desirable to use sand that is very coarse or very fine, the character of the sand makes comparatively little difference, provided it is not of a quicksand nature and is free from organic matter. The sand should be compacted and thoroughly wet down.

and the cuttings set in rows about two inches apart and three-quarters of an inch between the plants in the rows. After a row is in place, the soil should be firmly pressed about them, and a narrow groove made for another row.

The cutting bed should be in a temperature of fifty to fifty-five degrees at night, while five to ten degrees of bottom heat are desirable but not necessary; during the day the house should be thoroughly ventilated and the temperature kept as near sixty degrees as possible. Unless the cutting bed is in a north-side house, into which no direct rays can enter, the cuttings will require shading from nine until three o'clock on sunny days, and should be kept rather close for at least the first week. The cuttings should not be allowed to get dry, as, if the lower ends of the cuttings become parched, they may as well be thrown out. The beds should be sprinkled on bright mornings, and under favorable conditions roots will form in three or four weeks.

POTTING OFF.

As soon as the roots have developed, the plants should be placed in flats of good soil, or in beds, at intervals of two inches each way. Some growers find that it pays them to pot off the cuttings, using two-inch rose pots, while others greatly reduce the labor by keeping them in the cutting box until they are planted in the field. Very good results can be obtained by this method with late-struck cuttings, provided an inch of rich soil is placed in the bottom of the box, and covered with two inches of sand. After the roots have been formed in the sand, they will find their way into the soil below, and thus obtain nourishment until they are planted out. After being boxed or potted off, the young plants should be kept at a temperature of fifty degrees until they have become well established. If, during this time, any of the plants start to throw up a flower stalk, the center bud should be pulled out, or the plant pinched back, and all future attempts at flowering should be checked by pulling out the terminal leaves from any plant that shows the least tendency towards it.

As soon as the plants begin to thicken up, it is well to remove them to a cool house, or cold pit, where the temperature will be thirty-five to forty degrees. In the case of the December-struck cuttings, this will give them an opportunity to rest, and the plant will be less subject to disease than if kept growing continuously throughout the winter. At any rate, it is desirable that the young plants be established in the boxes by the first of March, that they may be removed to the cold frame early in April and become sufficiently hardened to be planted out between the 20th of April and the first of May. The planting time should be as early as the ground can be worked, and danger of severe frost is over. If taken at once from a greenhouse, they would be injured by the least frost, but if gradually hardened in a cold frame, a slight frost will not injure them.

SOIL FOR CARNATIONS.

Although in selecting a soil for planting out carnations, very light sand, heavy clay, or muck, should be avoided, almost any average loam soil adapted to the growing of vegetables will be suitable for the purpose. Given a congenial climate, and a medium heavy loam soil, with a proper supply of plant food, and an abundance of moisture, but with good drainage, there will be little trouble in growing carnations. The land should be well enriched with decomposed manure, and deeply plowed the previous fall, and in the spring plowed and dragged smooth. If manure cannot be readily obtained, one thousand pounds per acre of ground bone, or dissolved bone black, will help out. The rows may be as narrow as one foot, or as wide as two and a half, or two feet and ten inches. If the smaller distance is used, every ninth row should not be planted, and the soil worked with a hand cultivator, while the larger spaces between the rows will admit of cultivation with a horse, which will greatly lessen the amount of hand labor required, and where land is not high priced, this practice should be employed whenever possible.

PLANTING OUT AND CULTIVATION.

Having marked out the rows at the distance fixed upon, the ground should be cross-marked at intervals of from ten to twelve inches, for the plants. In planting the carnations, they should be set deep enough so that they are held firmly in place. If this is neglected, the plants may be blown about and perhaps ruined, but care should be taken that they are not too deep, as, particularly if on wet, heavy soil, and in a wet season, they will be apt to rot at the collar. Among the other causes that may produce stem rot is injury in the cutting bed, and if at planting out time any of the cuttings appear injured, as often happens from too much water with too high a temperature and too little air, they should not be planted.

During the summer the plants should be frequently cultivated, thus both keeping the weeds down and, by breaking the crust, forming a mulch conserving the moisture. It is a good plan to stir the soil as soon as it is dry after every rain, and even if no rain has fallen and no weeds are in sight, a shallow cultivation once in four or five days during the summer will be of benefit to the plants. If the soil is poor, an occasional application of liquid manure, or bone meal is often desirable.

The only additional care that they require is the pinching out of all flower stalks that start, as soon as four or five offshoots form at the base of the stem; this should be discontinued by the middle of July on plants designed for early blooming, but on others may be kept up until the middle of August.

On light soils and in dry seasons irrigation will be of great value, but the mere wetting of the surface soil will often do more harm than good. If irrigation is used at all, it should be sufficient to wet the soil to a depth of four or five inches, and the land should receive a shallow cultivation before the surface has had time to bake.

CARNATION HOUSES.

Although the character of the house in which carnations are grown has less to do with the success obtained than with the rose and some of the other crops, it will always be well to have the houses planned in such a way as to secure for the plants the most favorable conditions. While almost any shape of house will answer, it will be found of advantage to consider the conditions under which the plants are to be grown before making a selection. The principal demand and the highest price for the flowers is during the dark, dull weather of winter, and to secure blooms at that time it is desirable that the house be constructed with a light framework and large glass, and with such a pitch of the roof as will secure the most light and heat from the sun. This will generally be secured in a three-quarter span house running east and west, and good results can be obtained either with a long slope, or with the short slope of the roof to the south (Fig. 7). Where a suitable location can be secured, a form of house that was first designed for growing vegetables, with a lean-to roof and a width of from thirty-five to fifty feet, will be found well adapted to the carnation. If a slope to the south of about fifteen degrees can be secured, the roof can be given a slope of about twenty degrees, and the north wall will not be unduly high at the least width mentioned, but for greater widths the house can be built of a two-thirds span, or less, with from one-fourth to one-eighth of its roof sloping to the north. **If the**

FIG. 7. SHORT SPAN TO THE SOUTH, CARNATION HOUSE, FRED DORNER & SON, LAFAYETTE, IND.

three-quarter span, with about one-third of the roof upon one side of the ridge, and the remainder on the other, is used, it will seldom be desirable to have the house much less than twenty feet wide.

When the flowers are desired during the fall and early winter, it becomes necessary to plant the house early in the summer; and to grow them successfully during the hot weather it is desirable that provision be made for the removal of part or all of the glass. Some houses for this purpose have the roof formed of hotbed sash, that can be quickly taken off and replaced, while others have permanent sash bars, with butted glass held in place with wooden caps, that permit a part of the glass to be removed during the summer. Other growers find it well to provide for a supply of blooms during the spring and early summer, and unless the plants are flowered in the beds from which chrysanthemums have been removed, as mentioned in another chapter, special houses will be needed. It will generally be well to get them well established in the fall, and to carry them through the winter in a state of rest, at a low temperature. For this purpose, a north and south even-span house is desirable, and if one has an old style house with small glass and heavy framework, it can be put to no better use.

If one is to build a house for carnations, it will be best to construct it after some of the forms first described, as, if at any time it is no longer desired for carnations, it will be well adapted to a number of other crops. As the crop requires thorough ventilation, it will be well to have a continuous row of ventilators in the south wall, and at least one row at the ridge.

GROWING THE PLANTS IN THE HOUSES.

Some of the growers have adopted, with good success, the plan of growing the plants during the summer in the houses in permanent beds, thus saving the trouble of transplanting, and they claim that, as seems quite probable, the plants being saved from any check, they are less likely to be attacked by the various diseases to which this plant is subject. As the plants are more closely under the eyes of the florist, they are less likely to be neglected and a better growth can be secured, provided the air can be kept sufficiently cool during the hot weather of summer.

For growing plants in this way, it is desirable that the houses should be large and airy, and unless the sash can be removed from at least one side of the roof during the summer, abundant side ventilation should be provided. The short-span-to-the-south houses seem well adapted for this purpose, while the even span is preferable to the ordinary three-quarter span form. It is almost necessary that the benches be deep and solid. For a house twenty feet wide, no better arrangement can be made than that shown in Fig. 7, with two benches, each about seven feet wide, with walks at the center and at each side of the house. Sub-irrigation is especially desirable for the house-grown plants, and this can be readily arranged, according to the methods explained elsewhere in these pages.

It is even more desirable that proper soil should be provided than when they are first grown in the field. It should be not less than eight inches thick, and should consist of from one-half to two-thirds rotten sods, the balance being decomposed manure and sand, in proportion according to the character of the sods. The plants may, if desired, be given one shift before they are planted out, but it is desirable that they be placed in the beds by the first of June. When there is a demand for flowers in the fall it is a good plan to plant in the open ground some of the early varieties, so that they can be covered with a frame when cold weather comes in the fall. They will bloom freely for several months and the slight expense will be well repaid.

BEDS AND BENCHES.

The plants can be grown either in raised benches or in solid beds, which in either case will be about the same as described for the rose. If the latter are used, care should be taken to secure thorough drainage, but even then, unless great care is taken in watering, the crop will not be as early as on raised benches, although the flowers will be larger and have better stems, and the plants will give more blooms during the spring and summer. The bed can have its sides formed of plank, but it will be neater and cheaper in the end if cement or brick is used. Being near the level of the walks, it will be easier to get the soil upon them than on the benches, as the wheelbarrow can be run upon them. The bed also has the advantage of permitting the holding of the flowers for several days; the shallow bench, on the other hand, renders possible the forcing of the flowers for a certain occasion.

Unless there is some reason for wishing early flowers, the solid bed will be generally preferable, although it is a good plan to have a solid bed in the center of the house, with raised side benches. For the solid beds, about eight inches of soil will be required, while four or five inches will answer for the raised benches. The soil may vary, according to circumstances, but a good mixture is prepared from six parts of good garden loam and one part of decomposed manure. To this, if the soil is inclined to be heavy, may be added one part of sharp sand. For the shallow benches a larger proportion of manure is desirable. Another method of preparing the soil for the benches is to top-dress a piece of land early in the summer and turn it under, sowing upon it, in July, crimson clover at the rate of ten quarts to the acre.

In severe climates rye may be used instead. They should be turned under early in the spring, before they have formed their heads, and will supply the needed fiber to the soil. The land should be worked during the summer, and will be ready for filling the beds. A similar preparation of the soil, where the plants are to be set in the field, is a good practice.

Our experiments with greenhouse sub-irrigation show that it has many advantages, which are explained under that heading. If early flowers are desired, they should be benched from the middle of July to the middle of August, but to be successful the house should have ample ventilation. The first of September is as late as the benching of any of the plants intended for early winter use should be delayed, but good results may be secured from late flowering kinds if they are boxed off before severe frosts come, and are kept in deep cold frames until the chrysanthemums are out of the way, when they may be set in the beds, or if the boxes are deep the plants can be left in them. This is an excellent way of handling Hinze's White.

It is desirable to have the planting ground near the houses, so that the plants may be placed in hand-barrows and carried to the houses, but if the soil near by is not suitable it is better to go to some distance, as the plants can then be readily handled if placed in boxes, loaded on a wagon and drawn to the houses. If the soil will fall from the roots without breaking them, no attempt should be made to retain it, but if it clings to them it will be better to take up a ball of earth and place it in the bed, provided it is not unsuitable for use in the house. If the plants are growing in soil that has become baked, unless the land can be irrigated it will be necessary to delay planting until a rain comes to soften it.

PLANTING THE HOUSES.

Having filled the beds with soil, when the proper time comes for planting it is well, if one has but a few plants, to select a dull day for the planting, or, if it does not come, the plants may be dug in the early morning and placed away in the flats in some cool place until towards evening. With large numbers of plants this will not be possible.

The distance required by the plants in the houses will depend upon the variety, the size they have attained in the field, and on whether a large number of comparatively small flowers is preferred to a smaller number of large ones. For the former, plant so that they will touch, or eight or nine inches each way, while for large flowers have them at least a foot apart. Many growers prefer to have the long rows eight to ten inches apart, and those across the beds from ten to twelve or more, thus giving a better chance to work the soil.

Dig a good-sized hole with the hand or trowel, and set the plants about as deep as in the field, carefully spreading out the roots and pressing the soil firmly about them. As soon as planted they should be thoroughly watered, and in bright weather shaded for several days, but as soon as the plants have become established some or all of the shading should be removed, using a stream of water and a scrub brush if whitewash has been used. As a temporary shading, nothing is better than to spray over the roof a thin mixture of water and clay, which can be readily removed. During hot weather it is well to leave every other row of the shading upon the roof.

The houses will need thorough ventilation, although, upon the newly set plants, drafts of hot, dry air should be prevented. Even in severe winter weather, unless the houses are very open, a little air should be given for a short time each day. It is possible that one reason why such fine flowers are often grown in old, tumble-down houses, is that the cracks admit fresh air and let out the heat when the houses are neglected and are not opened.

WATERING AND VENTILATING.

Most carnations thrive best in a temperature at night of about fifty degrees, and although they will give quicker results at sixty degrees, the blooms will be small and the plants will be quickly exhausted, so that in the course of the season the number of the flowers will not be half as great as in the cooler house. On the other hand, when kept at forty or forty-five degrees the plants will flower later, but as few will be produced during the winter, they will be able to give quite a crop as the warm weather of spring comes on, at which time, however, there is less call for them and the prices rule much lower than during the winter. During the day the temperature will be determined largely by that of the air outside and the amount of sunshine, but in a clear day it can run up to sixty-five or seventy-five degrees with advantage, provided the air is on the houses. It will probably be well to hold down to those temperatures, if it can be done by ventilating the houses and not secure too much of a draft of cold air. Air should be given at fifty-five or sixty degrees, and this is high enough for the day temperature in dull weather.

Until the plants have become established, they will take but little water from the soil, and, after the first wetting down of the bed, care should be taken not to add more until examination shows that it has become slightly dry, when another watering should be given, sufficient to wet down through the soil. This will be a good rule to follow throughout the year. After the plants are established, during the hot weather of September and October, and during the spring, careful watching is often necessary to prevent the suffering of the plants from lack of water, as, particularly when the heating pipes are under the benches, the roots may be in soil as dry as ashes, although the top soil may be quite wet. On the other hand, serious injury may occur when too much water is used, particularly on solid beds during the dark days of winter, but if the above rule is observed, the danger of injury will be greatly reduced. The use of too much water, especially if accompanied by a high temperature, without ventilation, is likely to cause the development of galls upon the roots, and if numerous, the entire crop may be ruined, and it will often result in the rotting of the stems and lower leaves, even though the galls do not appear.

On the other hand, water should be used freely in syringing the plants, wetting the soil as little as possible, for the first few days after planting, repeating whenever the foliage becomes dry, and upon warm, bright days throughout the season, but it should only be done early in the day, in order that the foliage may dry off, as, if it remains moist over night, it will invite the presence of the rust and other fungi. During dull weather the plants should not be syringed, and care should be taken, when it becomes necessary to apply water to the soil, that it does not wet the foliage. If there is danger of the air becoming so dry as to invite the appearance of the red spider, water can be used freely on the walks and about the house, and in this way the needed moisture will be provided.

STAKING AND TRELLISING.

As soon as the plants have become established, arrangements should be made for supporting them. Formerly wooden or cane stakes were used for the purpose, but they were not firm enough in the soil of shallow beds, and the ends quickly rotted off. In tying the stems to the stakes, they are generally so drawn together that growth is hindered, and when it comes to cutting the flowers it often becomes necessary to cut the ties, in order to get the stems out unbroken. The same objections, except the decay of the stakes, apply to the use of

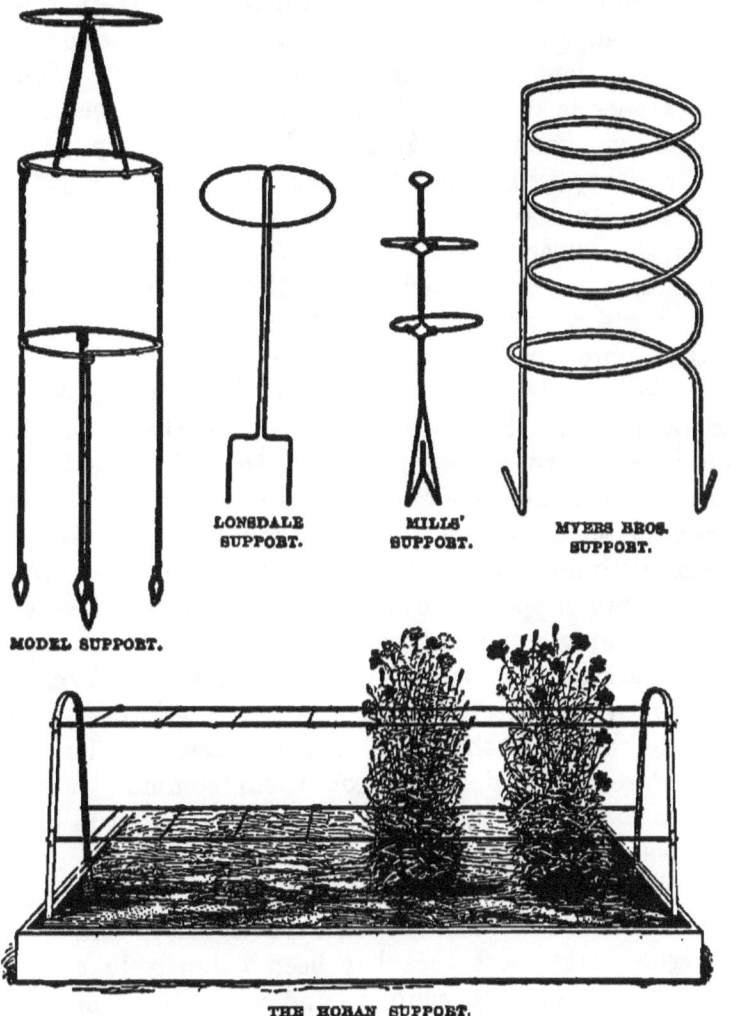

FIG 8. CARNATION SUPPORTS.

rods of galvanized wire, but with the rods firmness can be secured by fastening them at the upper end to wires stretched above the bed, while the plants can be tied more loosely if two stakes are used to each plant, or, better yet, by bending No. 9 galvanized wire into the shape of a hairpin, a support will be formed that answers fairly well. There are also a number of individual supports that have been brought out, and in several instances patented, during the last two years. Their appearance is shown in Fig. 8. Several of them are of simple construction and are sold quite cheaply, so that in time they will be no more expensive than the perishable wooden stakes. In most cases they are designed to keep the lower leaves off the soil, and also to support the flower stalks. Nearly all of them are preferable to the single stakes, but most of them confine the stems rather more closely than is desirable.

The Lonsdale stake, with a single ring, is only adapted to small-growing, slender varieties, but this stake with two rings, or some of the other kinds with two or more, answers fairly well except for the strong-growing sorts, where some method that will support them without confining them so closely will be better. The Horan support shown in Fig. 8 has the disadvantage of being expensive and of being easily disarranged, but it serves its purpose well. A home-made form, designed by a Detroit florist, has heavy galvanized wire for the bows at the ends, and to these smaller cross wires are fastened. Between them common twine is woven to support the leaves and stems, so that in a general way it is much like the Horan support.

Among the first to experiment with carnation supports was Fred Dorner, of Lafayette, Ind., who finally designed a support that has been extensively used by florists all over the country, and with slight modifications has been found adapted to houses of strong-growing varieties. He used, to support the lower leaves, galvanized wire chicken netting with a fine mesh (Fig. 9), cut into strips eighteen or twenty inches in width.

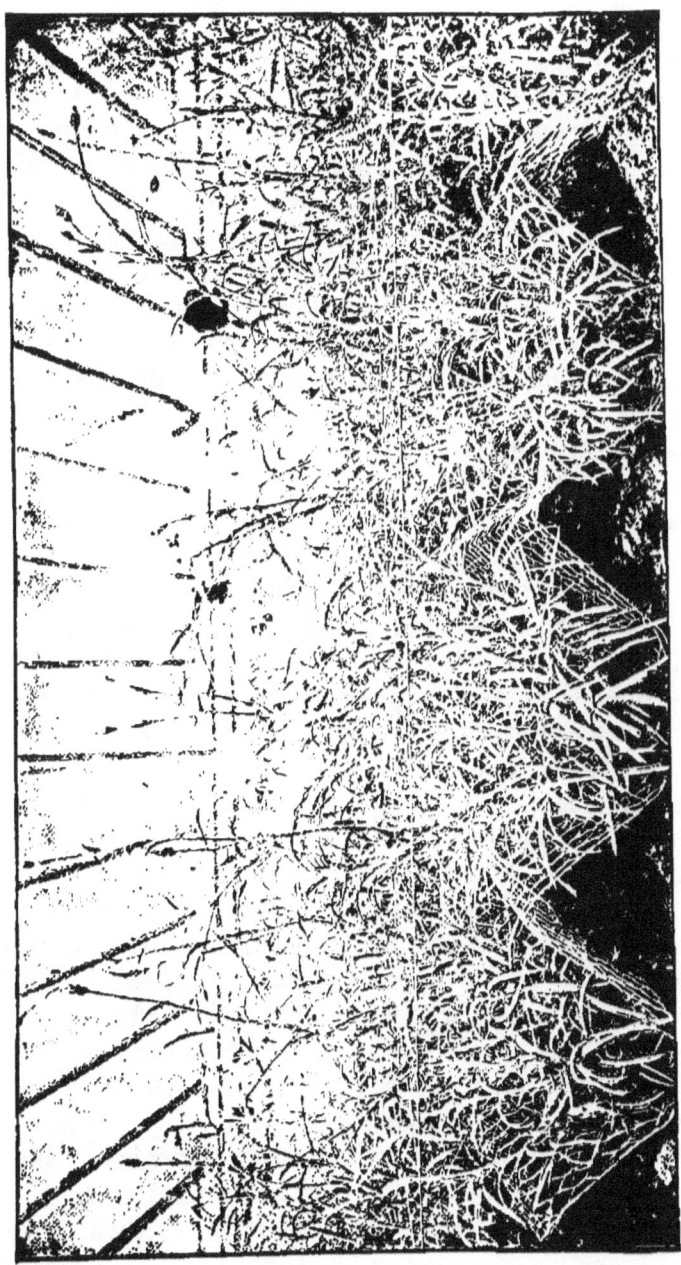

FIG. 9. CARNATIONS SUPPORTED BY CHICKEN NETTING, AS USED BY F. DORNER & SON, LAFAYETTE, IND.

These are bent into an inverted V shape, well rounded over the top, and are placed between the rows of plants crosswise of the bed. To support the flower stems, he stretches No. 12 galvanized wire lengthwise of the beds about a foot apart, and upon these weaves a diamond-shaped mesh with cotton twine, as is shown in the illustration (Fig. 10). Two men on opposite sides of the bed can pass the twine back and forth quite rapidly, at the same time giving it a twist about each of the wires.

The principal objection to the wire netting is that the meshes are so large that the stems often become tangled in them and are much crowded, and that it is somewhat lacking in stiffness to stand up well. To correct these failings, several have tried galvanized wire lathing, which has a half-inch square mesh (Fig. 11), and find that it answers much better in both respects. Another modification is in the weaving to support the stems, where, instead of the diamond-shaped mesh with wires a foot or so apart, there is a No. 18 wire stretched lengthwise of the beds each side of every row of plants, and to hold the stems in place the other way, across the beds other wires or twine are placed, so as to form meshes from four to six inches square, through which the stems will grow. If this is placed six or eight inches above the top of the A-shaped lathing, it will hold the stems so loosely that it will be little hindrance in gathering flowers or cuttings. One of the advantages of the A-shaped lathing is that it keeps the leaves from resting on the damp soil, and as the hose, when watering, can be held beneath it, there is little need of wetting the leaves, and thus the danger for disease is greatly reduced. By lifting the leaves from the bed it also permits the air to circulate and aids in the drying out of the soil.

Whether the individual rings or the wire lathing are used, the best results can only be secured when they are in place before the flower buds form, as then it will

THE CARNATION. 45

FIG. 10. CARNATIONS SUPPORTED BY MESHES OF COTTON TWINE.

be but little trouble to induce them to enter the rings or meshes as desired, while if they have fallen over and sprawled out over the bed before the supports are in place, it will be more difficult to secure stout stems and the desired straight upward growth. If they are early in place, little time will be required in training the stems, and the houses will present a very neat appearance. Before one decides what method of training to adopt, it will be well to visit houses in which the different forms are in use, or to experiment upon a small scale before investing largely in any of them. The best support is the one that offers least obstruction to handling the plants, cutting the flowers and working the soil. Their cheapness, durability and simplicity should also be considered. As stated above, the slender, upright-growing varieties will be best supported by some of the methods first described, while the strong, rank-growing varieties will do better with the lathing and overhead mesh. If desired, the A-shaped netting can be used with the individual wire supports.

DISBUDDING.

While it will not pay for all localities and with all varieties, disbudding is almost essential for large markets where there is strong competition and a demand at a good price for large, single flowers, on long and strong stems. Disbudding consists in the removal of all the flower buds upon a stem except the strongest one at the tip, or, as carnations are now used, a spray of three or four slightly smaller flowers is also desirable, and we can aid in its formation by pinching out the terminal bud and thus favoring the development of the side buds. If disbudding is to be practiced, the plants should be looked over once in two weeks at most, and at the same time all needed tying and training of the shoots should be done. As a rule, growers who market their crops

THE CARNATION. 47

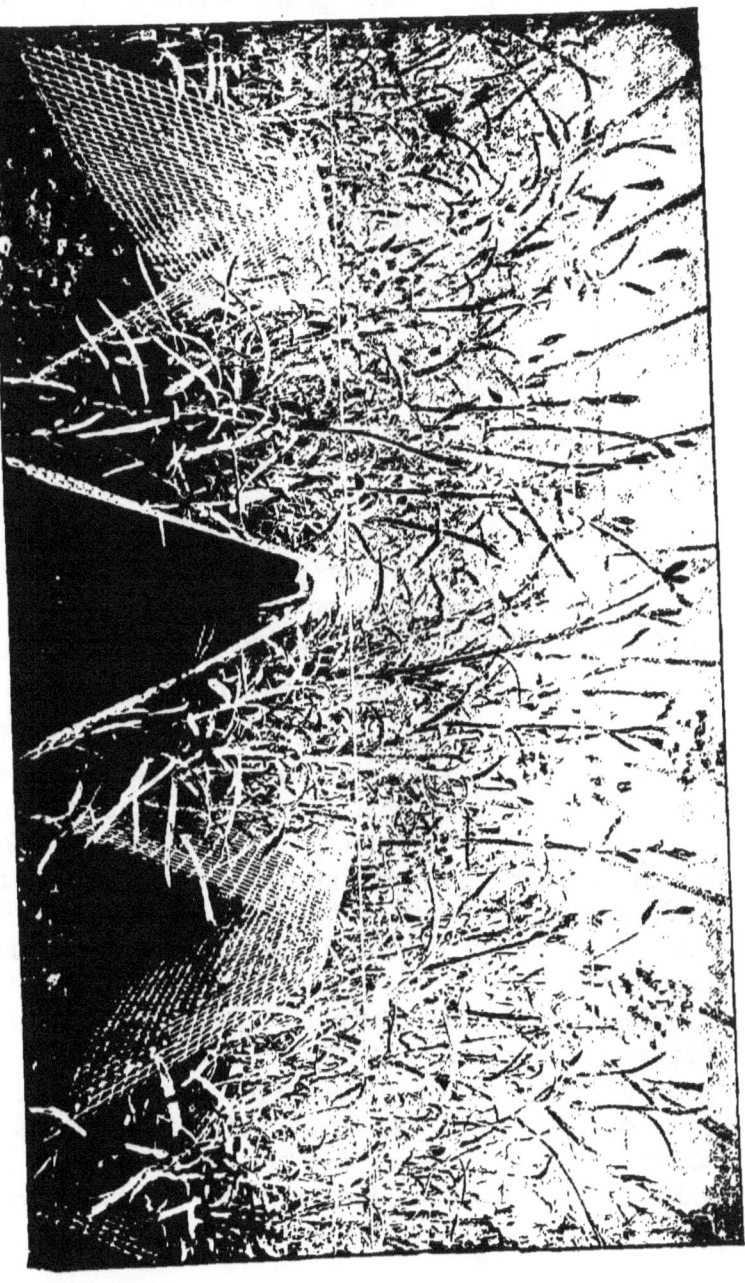

FIG. 11. CARNATIONS SUPPORTED BY WIRE LATHING, AS USED AT COTTAGE GARDENS, QUEENS, N. Y.

near home can grow their plants under high culture and secure large flowers and long, stout stems, but if to be shipped long distances they will need to be grown with a firmer texture, that they may withstand hard usage.

TOP-DRESSING AND LIQUID MANURING.

The requirements of the crop will depend upon the character of the soil used for the beds. If composed of loam, stable manure and ground bone, the plants will be able to obtain food for several months, but by the first of November it will generally be well to apply ground bone to the surface of the bed, and from that time on to give the plants an application of liquid manure once in two weeks. The application of a peck of wood ashes to each hundred square feet of bed once in six or eight weeks will be especially desirable in giving strength to the stems. For the further discussion of the use of manures and fertilizers for carnations and other crops, the reader is referred to the chapter on that subject.

GENERAL CARE OF THE HOUSES.

As soon as the plants have become established, the surface of the beds should be stirred, to keep down the weeds and to loosen it, that the growth of the roots may be stimulated and the food supply increased. This should be kept up during the season, but it should not be deep enough to injure the roots. All dead and diseased leaves should be picked off, and all litter removed from the beds.

The carnation is less troubled by insects than most flowers. The green fly is about the only one that will require especial treatment, and for this the usual remedies can be used. The danger of the appearance of insects and fungous diseases will be greatly reduced, provided the conditions under which the plants are grown are suited to them; and if they are so handled that they receive no check, the need of making use of insecticides and fungicides will be greatly lessened.

The soil upon the shallow beds should be replaced each year, but upon deep, solid beds only the surface need be removed, as, unless it has become wet and sour, it will only require the addition of manure and a little fresh soil to grow another crop. If soil is hard to obtain for the beds, the old soil may be used again, if it is spread out thin and seeded with rye in August. By turning this under, and adding a good dressing of manure in the spring, it will be sweetened and supplied with the needed fiber and plant food.

Among the trials of the carnation grower are the troubles known as the "bursting of the calyx," and the "sleep of the carnation." The former is most common when the plants have been stimulated by high feeding, or grown at a high temperature and in a moist air. It is particularly likely to occur if the plants have previously been kept quite cool. What is commonly known as "sleep" in carnations may also be due to a variety of causes. Among them are sudden and extreme changes of temperature, too close, too hot, or too dry an atmosphere, too much smoke, gas, lack of water, some injury to the roots, too much fertilizer, and anything else that can disturb the nutrition of the plant.

VARIETIES.

With the large number of seedlings that are brought out each year it is not probable that any list can be given that will be of permanent value, although in the points that go to make up a good carnation the following varieties stand quite high, and will probably be found valuable for several years. The commercial grower will do best to confine himself, for the most part, to a few standard sorts that he has tested, and which do well with his soil and care, but in order that he may keep up with the times and be ready to compete successfully, he should, each year, test a few of the more promising new varieties, to learn if they will be better for him than his old kinds.

Of the older sorts, those most grown are the Lizzie McGowan and Silver Spray, white; Daybreak and Wm.

FIG 12. DAYBREAK CARNATIONS.

Scott, pink; Portia and Stuart, red; and Goldfinch and Bouton d'Or, yellow. Formerly, the white sorts were grown in larger numbers than all other colors put together, but the increased use of the carnation, for purposes of decoration, has caused a very large demand for the varieties of the various shades of pink, and, as a result, the varieties of that color are now grown very extensively. Lizzie McGowan is the standard sort of its color; it likes a light house, but does well on either beds or benches. The temperature should not be much below fifty degrees at night. As the plant is a slow grower, it should be planted early. It is a rather slender, upright grower, with large, regular, pure white flowers. Silver Spray is a desirable, early flowering, white sort, coming in before the chrysanthemums. It sometimes produces defective flowers, but, as a rule, they are quite perfect, upon long, stout stems. The plants bear freely, and the flowers keep well.

Among the new sorts, the Ivory is particularly promising. The plant seems to be vigorous, productive and quite free from disease; the flowers are a clear, ivory white, regular, and of a delicate fragrance; the petals are large, well-fringed, and supported by a strong calyx and a stout, long stem. Among the other new sorts are Storm King and Alaska.

Of the pink varieties, none have been more successful than Daybreak (Fig. 12). It is quite healthy, flowers freely, and the plants are strong and vigorous. It does best on a rather heavy soil and in solid beds, as it is less likely to burst its calyx and form side buds than when in shallow beds. The flowers are large, well-formed, of good color, and generally sell at the highest price. Wm. Scott is a good companion for the last variety. It has strong and healthy plants, and the flowers are large, regular, and even in color, and are borne on long, stout stems. The flowers are produced freely and have good keeping qualities. Of the other sorts, Mad. Diaz Albertini is one of the best. The flowers are larger than Daybreak, very double, and with less tendency to fade. The growth is strong, close, and healthy, the stems are strong, the calyx seldom bursts and the flowers are very sweet scented, but in the hands of many growers it has the serious drawback of being a shy bearer. Of the other pink sorts, Grace Darling and

FIG. 13. MRS. GEO. M. BRADT CARNATION. INTRODUCED BY FRED DORNER & SON.

Annie Pixley may be spoken of as having desirable features.

Of the red or scarlet varieties, few stand better with most growers than Portia, which has a very strong and vigorous plant, and the flowers are of a good color and substance, on stout stems. While Stuart is perhaps not as productive as Portia, the plants are very vigorous and healthy, and the increased size of the flowers adds considerably to its market value. Emily Pierson is a promising late scarlet sort, and as the flowers, when well grown, are very large, they bring a high price.

Of the yellow sorts, Goldfinch has a splendid plant, and has generally superseded Bouton d'Or and the older kinds. Mayor Pingree is a promising new variety

Helen Keller is one of the best of the variegated varieties, but it frequently is nearly a failure, and at best is not much in demand. Among the variegated kinds recently introduced, Mrs. Geo. M. Bradt (Fig. 13) is particularly worthy of trial.

In addition to a long list of comparatively untested varieties, there are several sorts that are being largely planted, and which thus far seem very promising. Among them are Rose Queen, Bridesmaid, Meteor and Lizzie Gilbert. Uncle John, although very successfully grown by its originator and many others, has not been generally successful, and its culture is even now given up by many growers. Morello is a new dark red or maroon variety, with large, firm flowers on long, stout stems. It has a rich odor, and the plants seem healthy and prolific. Of the older varieties, Tidal Wave, Garfield, Mrs. Fisher and Hinze's White are still grown extensively.

CHAPTER III.

THE CHRYSANTHEMUM.

For hundreds, if not thousands, of years, this plant has been held in high esteem by the inhabitants of China and Japan. In the latter country, a festival is held in honor of this, the national flower, and the nobles, as well as the peasants, enter into the festivities. The highest of all Japanese decorations is the Imperial Order of the Chrysanthemum, which is only conferred upon persons of royal birth, or, in rare instances, upon the nobility, and is regarded as a high distinction, even by foreigners.

The chrysanthemum was introduced into Europe about two hundred years ago, but was not generally esteemed until the first part of the present century. The first European seedlings were grown in 1827, and the interest excited at that time has been kept up, by the curiosity and admiration over the developments that have from time to time been made. The present century probably covers the history of the chrysanthemum in America, and it is said that the first American seedlings of any value were raised as recently as 1879, by Dr. Walcott, of Cambridge, Mass. Since that time the interest has rapidly increased, until it is now the favorite flower of its season. The attention given to developing new varieties from seed has given us hundreds of kinds, many of which excel in size, color, and form the best that have been imported. Among those who have done most to popularize the chrysanthemum by importation of the best Oriental and European seedlings, or by growing seedlings themselves, are Dr. H. P. Walcott of Massachusetts, H. Waterer, Wm. K. Harris and Robert Craig of Pennsylvania, T. H. Spaulding, John N. May and Pitcher & Manda of New Jersey, John Thorpe and V. H. Hallock & Son of New York, Fewkes & Sons, and Wood Bros., of Massachusetts, E. G. Hill & Co., F. Dorner and H. W. Rieman of Indiana, and Nathan Smith & Sons of Michigan.

PROPAGATION BY SEEDS.

New varieties are obtained by planting the seeds of the most promising sorts, and if the flowers have been cross-fertilized with pollen from plants of other desirable varieties, it is probable that some of the seedlings will show characteristics that will make them equal, or superior, to the parents. The per cent of plants that will show any value will be quite small, however, and perhaps nine-tenths of them will be discarded after one year's trial. The plants designed to be used as parents should be grown in small pots, and when the flowers develop, they should be placed in a dry room, where there will be an abundance of sunlight and air. The largest and most perfect flowers should be selected, and all others removed as they develop. When the flowers are fully open, the rays should be cut with a pair of shears, just above the stamens and pistils. As soon as the pollen has ripened, it should be conveyed upon a camel's-hair brush, or a toothpick, to the stigmas of another plant. To secure the best results, this should be repeated for several days. It is thought by some that the flowers farthest from the center are most likely to produce good flowers.

In selecting the parents, the objects to be attained should be kept in mind, and the choice should be carefully made. If it is desired to know the exact parentage, it is well to cover the flowers with paper or muslin sacks, for a few days before and after pollinating. While the seed is ripening, the plants should be kept quite dry, and if proper surroundings cannot be given to the plants, the stems may be cut off and placed where they will not be in moist air. The seedlings are grown much the same as those of other plants, and require after being potted off, about the same care as those grown from cuttings.

PROPAGATION BY CUTTINGS.

The usual method of propagating chrysanthemums is by means of cuttings. If large plants are desired, they are started in January or February, but when large blooms are wanted for exhibition purposes, the cuttings are often started as late as May or June, and the plants are grown to single stems and allowed to develop but one flower.

In order to grow healthy plants that will give large and fine flowers, strong and vigorous cuttings will be necessary, and they will be best if they are taken from plants that have not been forced. It is a good plan to select strong plants in the spring and plant them out of doors as early as it is safe. From these stock plants, cuttings can be taken that will give good plants for single flowers. In the fall, take up the old plants, place in boxes, and keep until midwinter in a cold frame where they will not freeze. Then take into the house, and a large crop of excellent cuttings can be obtained. The earlier ones will be just the thing for pot plants and for planting out as stock plants.

In April, another crop of cuttings should be taken. These will answer for six-inch pot plants, and for either single stems or "sprays," to be planted in the houses for cut flowers. Another crop of cuttings can be taken in June, but it will be better to take them from plants set in the open ground, as recommended above. While most of the cuttings for late blooms should be struck about the first of June, the first or even the fifteenth of July will not be too late to secure good results, if they are properly handled.

CARE OF THE PLANTS.

Chrysanthemums are grown by florists, either in beds or benches, when the flowers alone are desired, but are to some extent grown in large pots, both as standard and bush plants, for purposes of decoration and for specimens, and in small pots for sale. The treatment required for each kind of plant is somewhat different. The bench and the bed both have their advocates for growing the flowers, but while some varieties seem to do better in one than in the other, it may, perhaps, be truly claimed that the plants in the benches are least likely to suffer from over-watering, while they will need greater care if they are to escape injury from neglect to water often enough, and good blooms can be obtained in either bench or bed.

Unless top-dressing and liquid manuring are depended on to supply most of the plant food, the soil should be composed of about one part half-rotted cow manure and three parts thick sods, prepared as recommended for roses. If the soil is at all stiff, a small amount of sand should be added. At the bottom of the solid beds it is customary with many growers to place a layer of sods, with the grass side down, and cover them with about eight inches of the compost, while the bottom of the benches often has an inch of rotten cow manure upon it, with from four to six inches of the prepared soil. The same objections hold with this crop as with the rose, as to the excessive use of stable manure, and several growers are even now dispensing with the manure and relying upon commercial fertilizers, prepared after special formulas, for the plant food needed by the crop. Their success has induced a very great interest in the matter.

During the early part of the season, the flowers are grown either singly on the plants or as "sprays," but later on the plants are trained to a single stem with one flower at the top. The cuttings for early flowers should be struck as soon as the first of April, and other batches should follow at intervals up to the first of July, when the cuttings for the single stem plants can be struck. The best cuttings are obtained from shoots that are firm and that have short internodes. Slender and wiry shoots, and also the weak and watery ones, should be avoided. The cuttings should not be over three and a half inches long, with the leaves on the lower half removed and the others reduced one-half in size. They may be rooted in small pots, pans or boxes, although if many are grown a cutting bed is desirable. The cuttings are inserted about half their length, in rows two inches apart, and about one inch in the rows. While bottom heat will hasten their rooting, it is not necessary, and good results will be obtained if placed near the glass, at a temperature of fifty degrees, even without bottom heat. If particularly fine plants with large blooms are desired for exhibition purposes, the cuttings should be placed singly in small pots containing a mixture of sand and compost at the bottom, and sand at the top.

When the roots are half an inch long they should be potted, as they will be less likely to wilt than if the roots have become longer and are broken in potting. Place in two and one-half-inch pots, using a compost of rotten sods, loam and sand. Keep at fifty to fifty-five degrees, and from this time never allow the plants to suffer for lack of water, food, air, or room. When the roots show through the soil, repot into the three and one-half-inch size, using a little richer compost, and when the roots have filled the pots, have the beds or benches

THE CHRYSANTHEMUM. 59

FIG. 14. BENCH OF CHRYSANTHEMUMS TRAINED TO STAKES, PITCHER & MANDA, SHORT HILLS, N. J.

ready and plant out at once, which, for the first batch, should be the last of May or the first of June. Have the soil firmly pressed down upon the beds and just moist enough to work well. The distance for planting will depend something upon the number of flowers to be grown upon a plant. If more than one variety is grown in a bed, place the taller ones at the north end in a north and south house, so that they will not shade the others. As a rule, the rows across the beds are ten or twelve inches, and the plants eight inches in the rows when three or more flowers are grown to a plant, or six inches each way if the plants are to be grown to single stems.

Water the plants thoroughly, and until they become established syringe them often, and shade the roof, using whitewash, or better, white lead and naphtha, mixed so as to make a thin wash. Until the roots have taken hold, care will be necessary to keep the soil from becoming saturated. In about a week, give the surface a good stirring and if more than one flower is desired from a plant, pinch out the tip buds to make them branch. As the side buds push out, rub them off at once, unless several flowers are desired, when we should allow three or four to grow and rub off the others. If more than this number of buds is desired to a plant, pinch out the end buds in the side shoots when they have made a growth of two or three inches, and allow two shoots to start from each, rubbing off all others.

TRAINING AND TRELLISING.

Arrangements should now be made for supporting the stems. This can be done in various ways (the training to stakes is seen in Fig. 14), but the best method is to run a wire (No. 18) above each of the rows and tie the stems to wire rods (No. 9, galvanized), the upper ends of which are fastened to the wire. Another method

THE CHRYSANTHEMUM. 61

FIG. 15. BED OF CHRYSANTHEMUMS SUPPORTED BY WIRE AND TWINE, NATHAN SMITH & SON, ADRIAN, MICH.

is to run three wires lengthwise of the bed, about a foot apart, the lowest one being one foot above the soil, and tie the stems to them. A third way is to run a No. 18 wire along the surface of the bed and another three or four feet above it, and between these stretch jute or binder twine, to which the plants can be tied (Fig. 15).

The plants for the late crop can be planted at any time from the first to the middle of July, or even as late as the first of August, and will require the same care and will be grown in the same way, except that they do not need more than five or six inches each way, and the tip bud is not removed, but is allowed to grow and form a long, single stem, from which all side buds are removed as they start. The stems are supported as recommended above and the same attention in watering and syringing will be required. The surface of the soil should be stirred occasionally, taking pains not to dig deep enough to injure the roots; and the suckers that start about the base of the plants should be twisted off with the fingers, or carefully cut off below the surface of the soil with a knife.

The growth of the plants should be carefully watched and if, at any time, it seems to slacken, or if the plants take on a yellowish color and the wood hardens, it generally indicates that the plant food in the original soil is about exhausted and that a new supply is needed. Some growers apply it in a mulch of sheep or cow manure, which both supplies food and prevents the evaporation of moisture from the surface. Provided it is not due to the use of an excess of water, the yellow color is often an evidence that the plants are suffering from a lack of potash. At any rate, the use of a peck of unleached wood ashes to each hundred square feet of the bench will be a good thing. Others apply soot, either broadcast upon the surface, or in water. The use of ground bone upon the surface of the bed in

August, and again about the first of October, will be advisable. Liquid manures can also be used to advantage whenever the plants show the need of food, and it will always be well to use them freely once or twice a week, from the time the first flower buds show until hey open enough to show the color of the flowers, when their use should be discontinued.

On the other hand, there is danger from securing too soft and watery a growth, from the use of too much nitrogen in the manure, combined with an excessive amount of water. This should be checked at once by slightly withholding the water, and by decreasing the amount of nitrogen supplied in the manure water. Aside from the thick and watery growth of the stems, the plants also show that they are growing too rapidly, by the appearance of their leaves, which are, in addition to being very large, thick and succulent, likely to become wrinkled and twisted. Until the growth has been checked and become hardened, the plant will not develop first-class flowers. Not only should the general appearance of the flowers be noted, but the needs of each plant should be considered, and it should be given more or less, or, perhaps, none at all, of the manure water.

"TAKING" THE BUDS AND DISBUDDING.

As soon as the flower buds show, the plants should be looked over every day or two, in order that the flower buds may be "taken" at the proper time. This word is given to the choosing or the selection of the bud or buds upon a plant that is to flower, after which the others are removed. The buds may be either of two kinds, which have received the names of "crown" and "terminal." The name "crown" is applied to a single bud at the end of a shoot, upon which all of the other buds are leaf buds, as seen in Fig. 16. Just below the *flower* bud are several *leaf* buds that will be likely to grow up and, as it were, smother the crown bud unless they are removed. As a rule, crown buds appear quite early in the season, and if they are taken then, they will not make good flowers, and even though it is thought best to use a crown bud (if one is formed before August 15), it will be better to remove the crown bud and all but one of the leaf buds below it. A shoot will be developed from

FIG. 16. CROWN BUD.

this, which can be trained up and a "late crown" bud that it may form can be taken. Later in the season it will be likely to produce a terminal bud. As a rule, it will be better not to take any buds until towards the last of August for the early sorts, and from that time until the middle to the last of September for the late kinds. The crown buds are preferred by English growers, but except in special cases are not much used in America, as they are seldom found on plants grown from late struck cuttings, and because, especially in the case of varieties that have very full flowers, they are likely to be imperfect, owing to the increased number of petals that they form. Another point against flowers from crown buds is that the leaves below the flower are

FIG. 17. TERMINAL BUD.

small and scattering. In many cases the flowers from crown buds are larger and the stems are stouter. It can then be seen that they may be preferable in the case of varieties with weak stems, or thin flowers.

The other buds that may be taken are known as "terminals," because they form at the ends of the stems. They can be distinguished from the crown buds by having three or more *flower* buds below them on the stems, as seen in Fig. 17. As soon as these other buds have become large enough to admit of its being done readily, they should be removed. This can be easily done with the fingers, or, as some prefer, with a penknife, forceps, or pointed scissors. If in any way the bud becomes injured, the next best upon the stem should be taken and the others removed. It will be well to begin the disbudding at the end of the stem, so that if a bud is injured there will be one lower down that can be left to form a flower. The flowers from terminal buds will not require more than two-thirds as long a time to develop as crowns, but as crown buds often form from four to six weeks earlier than the terminals, upon some varieties it may sometimes be necessary to take an early crown bud, if needed for exhibition purposes earlier than they can be obtained from terminals; and early crown buds are sometimes taken in the case of early varieties from which early flowers are desired, but except for these reasons, and for those above given, the terminal buds are generally taken. Terminal buds seldom are ready to be taken until the middle of September, but whenever they appear the remaining buds should be removed.

Flowers for exhibitions need about the same care as those for sale, except that it will pay to start them a little earlier and to give them a more liberal space in the beds.

SINGLE STEM PLANTS IN POTS.

A convenient size, whether for exhibition, decoration, or for sale, is a single stem plant, either in a four-inch pot or a five-inch pan. These can be taken from the last batch of cuttings, and it is a common practice to pot off for this purpose any plants that have not been planted or sold. They will need exactly the same care as the single stem plants in the beds. Another method of growing single stem plants in pots is to place from three to six in pots or pans of larger sizes.

These plants being in pots will require greater care than those planted in the beds, to prevent their drying out, and during the hot weather they should be watered at least twice daily, and should be syringed in the morning and again in the afternoon of bright days. The pots can be kept in well-ventilated and partially shaded houses, or out of doors where they will not be likely to be neglected. Plunging them in coal ashes will lessen the danger of injury from the drying out of the soil, but at the same time it will increase the chance of harm coming to them from careless or excessive watering. Especial care should be taken to have the plants free from aphides at this time, and to secure it the houses should be given two or three thorough fumigations just before the buds open. While a light fumigation, if necessary, will not hurt the flowers, it will be better not to be obliged to use tobacco, either as smoke or as a spray, after this time.

Particularly for the late flowers, the ventilators should be kept wide open during the day, but should be closed at night when the outside temperature drops below forty. If the house is damp, so that there is danger of the moisture condensing on the flowers after they have opened, it will be well to have a little heat on the houses, and if necessary leave the upper ventilators a little open. Syringing should be done early enough to give the flowers time to dry off before night.

SPECIMEN POT PLANTS.

Chrysanthemums are often grown in large pots for exhibition or decorative purposes. The cuttings are started about the first of March, and require the same care as those grown for planting in beds, instead of doing which, however, they are shifted until they are in ten- or twelve-inch pots, as may be desired. With each shift the amount of manure in the soil can be increased, until finally it is the same as used for the beds. When the plants are eight or ten inches high, according to the distance between the buds, the tip should be pinched out. This will cause the side shoots to develop, of which eight or ten should be allowed to grow. These should be evenly distributed around and along the center stem. When these are four or five inches long they should, in turn, be pinched back, and from two to four shoots allowed to form on each. While more shoots can be left if desired, a handsome plant will be formed from this number of shoots, and the flowers will be larger and finer than with a larger number. The pinching should be done not later than the first of August, in order to give the plants time to develop their flower shoots and buds. If large flowers are desired, only one flower should be allowed to form on each shoot, all other buds being rubbed off as soon as they form. When the plants are disbudded, all injured and diseased leaves should be taken off, and a number of short stakes of galvanized wire should be set around the plant, to which the flower stems should be tied. In this way they can be trained to form a symmetrical plant.

Plants in six- or eight-inch pots are also very useful, either for decoration or for sale. They will require about the care outlined above, except that they need not be started until April 1st. In order to form compact, shapely plants, the leader should be pinched lower, and not more than five to eight branches allowed to start.

STANDARDS.

As show plants and for exhibition, a few standards and half standards are grown. The former have bushy, or umbrella-shaped, tops at a hight of five or six feet upon a smooth, bare stem, while the stems of the latter are three or four feet high. These plants are grown from cuttings, generally suckers, started in December or January, and receive about the same care as the single stemmed plants. They are not stopped until the desired hight is reached, and the head then formed is trained as desired. While the greatest pains is taken to prevent the development of side shoots on the young plants, the foliage should be preserved, and not removed until the head is formed.

FIELD CULTURE.

When the plants are grown in the field, as is still sometimes practiced by amateurs, the soil should be thoroughly prepared, and enriched either with stable manure or commercial fertilizers. If well hardened in a cold frame, the plants may be put out as soon as danger of severe frost is over, which will be by the middle of May in most localities. The plants, to be well grown, will require about the same care in pinching and training as was described for the pot-grown plants. If side stakes are desired, they should be inserted near the stem of the plant, and incline outward. In this way they can be taken up with the ball of earth, and potted, without being disturbed.

In dry seasons, it will be well to scatter a mulch along the rows, to keep the soil from drying out and, when water is used, to prevent baking. Whenever the soil seems dry, water should be given the plants, evening being the best time to apply it. If the soil has been properly enriched, no liquid manure need be given these plants while in the ground, but if they fail to make a satisfactory growth from a lack of plant food, a forkful of decomposed manure can be used to advantage around each plant. When water is applied, it will be washed out and carried down to the roots, where it will be taken up and used by the plants. The plants should be taken up and potted by the first of August, and will need about the same attention as the plants that have not been planted out.

STAKING THE POT PLANTS.

All pot plants should be provided with a center stake, or wire rod, to which the main stem should be tied, and bush plants will need from three to seven, in order to keep the side shoots in place, and prevent them from breaking down. When perfect plants are desired for exhibition purposes, considerable attention is given to the training of the plants. Commencing at the time of the second pinching, the side shoots should be drawn into place and held there with loops of raffia. When pinched the next time, hoops or rings of wire can be fastened to the stakes, and the laterals can be tied to them. With large plants, a second, and even a third, ring will be found useful.

LIQUID MANURE.

As soon as the plants have become established in the beds, they should receive applications of liquid manure once a week until the flowers open, and the pot-grown plants will need this treatment, commencing the first of July. It is also well, as soon as the weather becomes hot and dry, to mulch the plants in the beds with an inch or so of cow or sheep manure, which will both hold the moisture and supply food for the growth of the plants. As the flower buds develop, there is particular need of liquid manure, and if furnished freely it will increase the size and perfection of the flowers. When the buds open, and during the period of flowering, no manure should be given them, and great care should be taken in watering the plants.

VARIETIES AND THEIR CLASSIFICATION.

The work of crossing the varieties has been carried so far that it is hard to tell where one class ends and another begins. The usual classification takes into account the shape of the florets and the appearance of the blooms, and divides the chrysanthemums into Incurved, Reflexed, Japanese, Anemone, Japanese Anemone, Pompon and Pompon Anemone.

The incurved class is made up largely of Chinese varieties, which have broad, strap-shaped florets that are curved inward, and give the bloom a spherical or globular form. As a rule, the florets are regularly arranged, and make a symmetrical bloom. The reflex class differs from the above in that the florets curve outward, and thus show only their inner face. A perfect flower of this group should have broad florets, a full center, and an even, symmetrical arrangement. As a rule, the florets overlap so closely that the blooms are quite flat. Cullingfordii may be taken as an example of this class.

In the Japanese, the short tubular florets found in the incurved group are replaced by others that may be of almost any shape, length or size, flat, quilled, or fluted, short or long, straight or twisted, thread-like or ribbon-like. The group includes such sorts as Major Bonnaffon and Kioto, classed as Japanese incurved, and Viviand Morel as Japanese reflexed.

The Anemone flowered class have in their disc or center, short quill-like florets, surrounded by rows of broad, flat florets forming a horizontal border. A Japanese section of this class has about the same variation in the character of the ray flowers as is found in the Japanese class itself. The Pompon group contains plants with small and regular, but quite close, blooms, that flower profusely. The florets are all the same, and form a globular bloom from one to two inches in diameter. They are quite hardy, and are among the best for the amateur. The Anemone Pompon class differs in having disc flowers that are quilled like those of the Anemone group.

SELECTION OF VARIETIES.

Among the things to be considered in a variety are the habit and strength of the plants, the character of the foliage and the color, size, shape and substance of the flowers. Very few of the kinds of five years ago are now grown to any extent, so great has been the improve

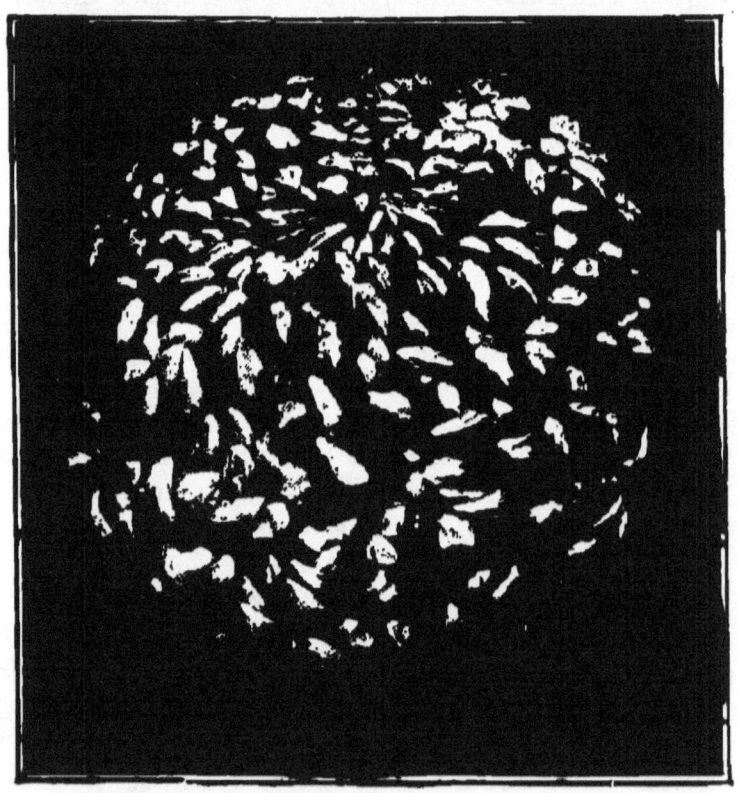

FIG. 18. CHRYSANTHEMUM EUGENE DAILLEDOUZE.

ment with this flower. For the production of cut flowers it is particularly desirable that such kinds be selected as will afford a succession throughout the season. Although they are often in the market before the middle of September, there is but little call before the first of October, but from that time until the close of the season one should be able to show plants in flower.

Among the best of the very early kinds is Lady Fitzwigram, white; following a few days later are Marquis de Montmort, a large early pink sort; Mrs. E. G. Hill, a very handsome, large, pink variety, also Lady

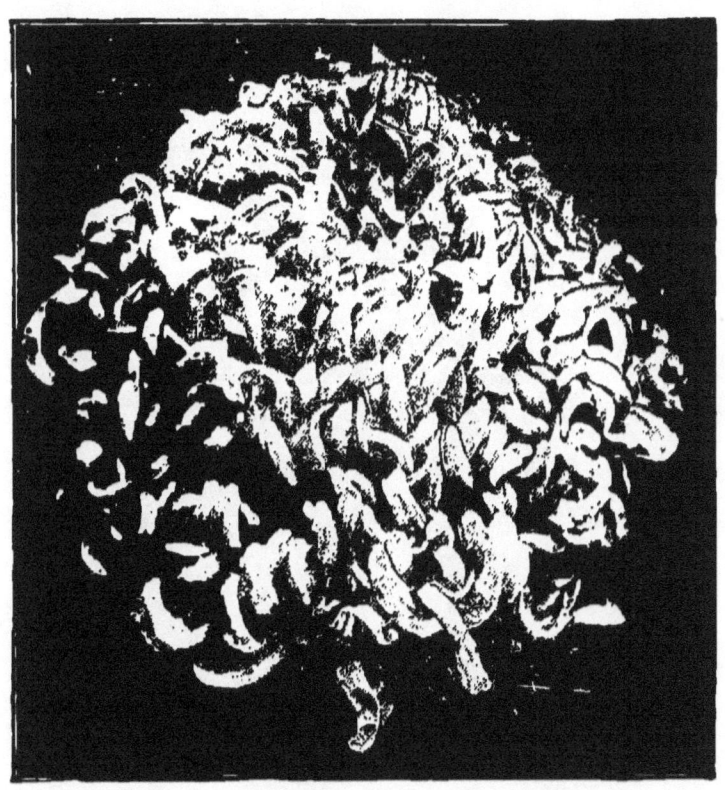

FIG. 19. CHRYSANTHEMUM MAYFLOWER.

Plairfair, another desirable pink variety. Among the early yellow sorts are Marion Henderson, with a handsome flower of good size and color; Miss M. M. Johnson, with a full incurved golden yellow flower; Yellow Queen, Golden Wedding and H. L. Sunderbruch, Gloriosum and Mrs. J. G. Whilldin are still valuable early yellow kinds. Of the new yellow varieties none is more promising than Modesto. It is of a pleasing shade of light yellow, and in form, size and "petallage" is quite satisfactory.

Among the later yellow varieties are W. H. Lincoln, H. W. Rieman, Eugene Dailledouze (Fig. 18), Major

FIG. 20. CHRYSANTHEMUM MRS. PERRIN.

Bonnaffon and Mrs. F. L. Ames. Of the other white sorts, coming after Lady Fitzwigram, Autumn Bride is a very promising pure white variety, as are Mayflower (Fig. 19) and Mme. F. Bergman and Mrs. H. Robinson. Among the other well-known white sorts are Niveus,

FIG. 21. CHRYSANTHEMUM IORA, GROWN BY NATHAN SMITH & SON, ADRIAN, MICH.

which has an excellent stem and foliage and very large flowers, and Queen, a splendid sort with perfect foliage and handsome flowers that keep remarkably well. Ivory, early, Minnie Wannamaker, medium, and Mrs. Jerome Jones, late, of the older kinds, are still valuable. Of the pink kinds, Mrs. Perrin (Fig. 20) is a promising new variety, while Iora (Fig. 21) has made an excellent impression as an exhibition variety. Viviand Morel holds a high place as an early variety, and Harry Balsley, although not good in plant, has a good color. V. H. Hallock, Eda Prass and Mrs. Bayard Cutting are also good.

Among other sorts worthy of a place in a collection are Clinton Chalfant, Jos. H. White, Pres. W. R. Smith, Inter-Ocean, Georgienne Bramhall, Eldorado and Mutual Friend. Cullingfordii still deserves a place as a dark red, as does Hicks Arnold as a bronze. John Shrimpton has been well received as a maroon variety. The flower is of good size, color and form, and the stem is stiff and well clothed. The principal call is for white, pink and yellow flowers and of course the largest number of plants should be of those colors.

Some five or six years ago, Mrs. Alpheus Hardy, a white variety with its ray flowers studded with short hairy growths, and a year later Louis Boehmer, which differed in being of a dirty pink color, were introduced, but have found little favor, except as oddities, with florists. In addition to the above, the class is now represented by Miss Annie Manda, white, Wm. Falconer, pink, and W. A. Manda and Patrick Barry, yellow, which are improvements over the original varieties. Golden Hair and R. M. Gray are still later and better varieties.

INSECTS AND DISEASES.

In addition to the green aphis, chrysanthemums are frequently infested with a black form. These can be destroyed by the same remedies as are used for the others, but they are harder to keep in check. Frequently, when plants are grown in pots, the lower leaves are lost. This may be due to a variety of causes, such as crowding and lack of air, too much water, lack of frequent syringing, exposure to drying winds, etc.; and a remedy can be found by avoiding each and all of these things. We also find that the foliage often takes on an unhealthy color, which may be due from the plant being in too small a pot, lack of food, too much or too little water, crowding, or exposure to the wind. Having found the cause, the remedy will be apparent.

Whatever method of growing the plants is practiced, the best results can only be obtained when strong cuttings are used, and when the plants are kept growing without a check from the time they are potted till they are through blooming. For the "Leaf Spot" and other fungous diseases, the plants should be sprayed with copper sulphate solution.

CHAPTER IV.

THE VIOLET.

Few of our greenhouse plants have so steadily maintained their hold upon public favor as has the modest violet. It is easily grown and is so generally useful that no florist can do without it. For the winter flowering of this plant, a greenhouse in which the night temperature will not be above forty-five degrees is desirable, but they are often wintered in cold frames, and give an abundance of blooms as the warm weather of spring comes on. If a greenhouse is not at one's disposal, the plants may be covered with a narrow frame, around which a wider and deeper one is placed. If the space between the frames is packed with horse manure, and the outer frame banked up with the same material, double sash, mats and shutters will keep out frost, except in very severe weather, and a fair crop can in this way be obtained.

VIOLET HOUSES.

While for the successful growing of violets certain requirements must be observed, the form of the house seems to be of less importance than with many other

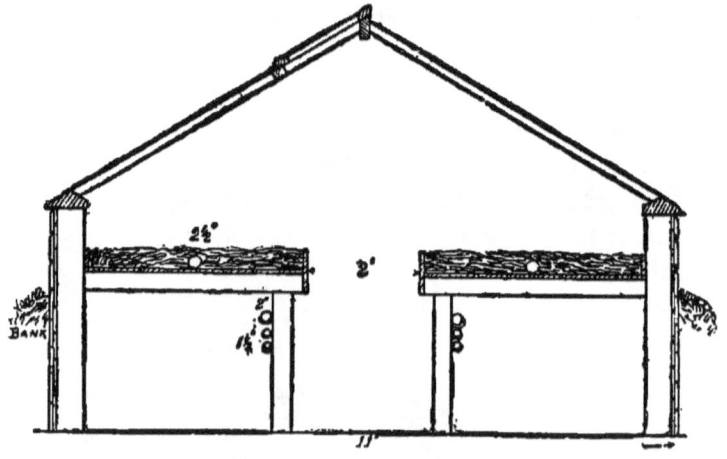

FIG. 22. NARROW VIOLET HOUSE.

plants. Good results can be obtained in lean-to, even-span or three-quarter span houses, but, as a rule, if a house is to be constructed especially for this crop, an even-span house will generally be preferred. The principal objection to the three-quarter span house is the amount of strong sunlight that the plants are subjected to, owing to the exposure to the south. This can to some extent be corrected by good ventilation, and the form of house has the further advantage of being more generally adapted to other crops, in case the culture of the violet should at any time be given up.

THE VIOLET.

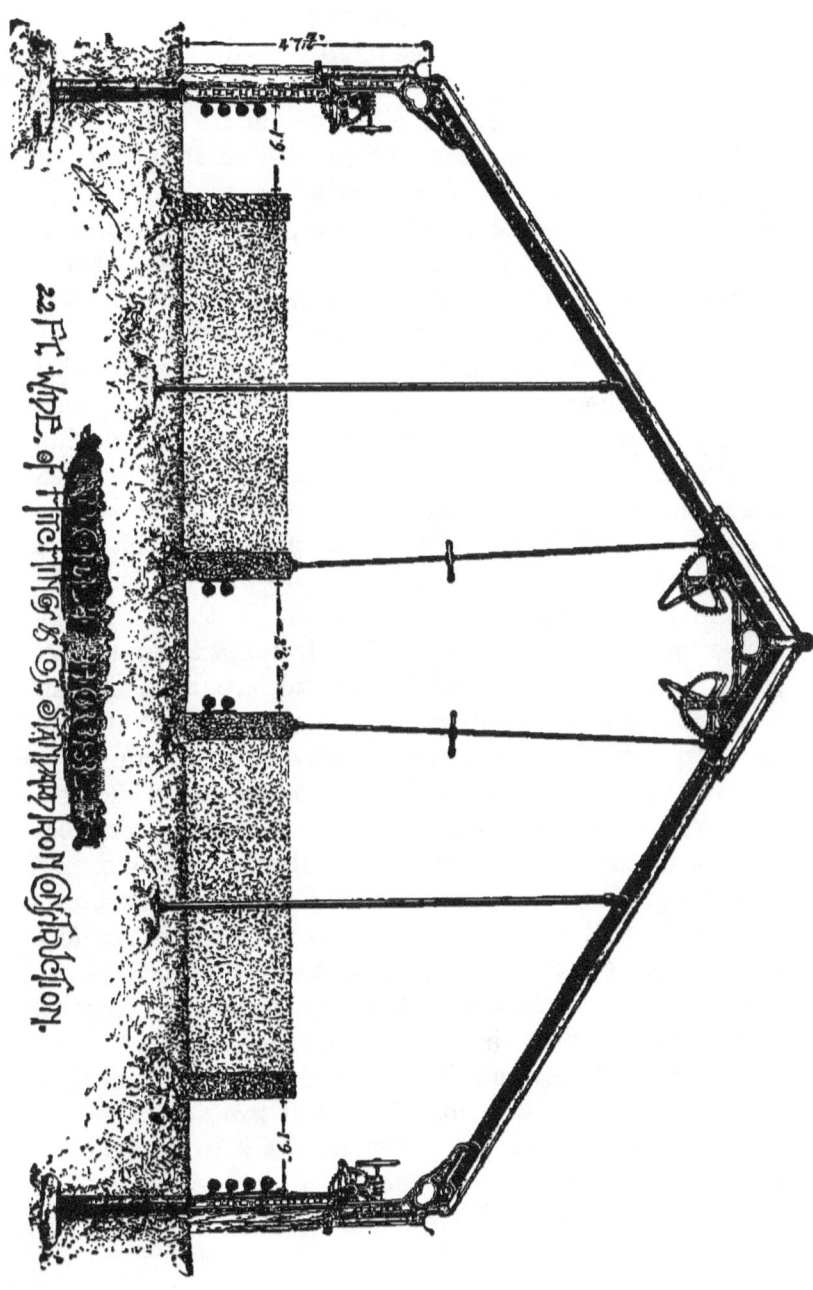

In the past, narrow houses from ten to twelve feet in width (Fig. 22) have been most used, but those of recent construction are twenty feet and even wider. Among the requirements for a violet house are (1) ventilating arrangements that will furnish an abundance of fresh air. On this account, ventilators are necessary in each of the side walls of the house, as well as a row at the ridge. It will be desirable to have the houses stand a little apart to secure this, as well as to prevent the lodging of the snow between the houses. (2) The houses should be so glazed as to avoid drip. For this reason a rather steep roof is desirable; the sash bars should be provided with drip grooves and the glazing should be carefully done. Use 14x14 or 16x16 inch glass, butted without putty, and held in place with a wooden cap. Take pains to lay the panes with the curve up and with the thick edge at the bottom. If carefully laid there will be little drip, although there will be rather more than when the glass is lapped and laid in putty. (3) Use wide, solid beds and have a walk along each wall where it will occupy room of little value to the crop. Thus for a house twenty-two feet wide (Fig. 23) we should have two beds each seven feet wide, and three walks, the center one being two feet and six inches, and the outer ones one foot and nine inches wide. If they are given proper attention in a house of this kind, the plants will do much better, and will be far less likely to be attacked by disease, than when grown in dugouts and other houses with heavy rafters, and covered with hotbed sashes that cause a large amount of drip.

Most of the narrow (ten or twelve foot) houses that have been used for the violet have had two side beds and a center walk, but rather better results will be obtained with a bed in the center of the house seven or seven and one-half feet wide, and a walk along either wall of the house (Fig. 24).

Some have found less trouble from spot and other diseases when the plants are placed in the houses early in the summer, without being planted in the open ground. If this is done, it will be well to take out every third or fourth row of glass. Although sash houses are not desirable on account of the drip, they have the advantage of permitting the removal of the roof, and are very commonly used when the plants are

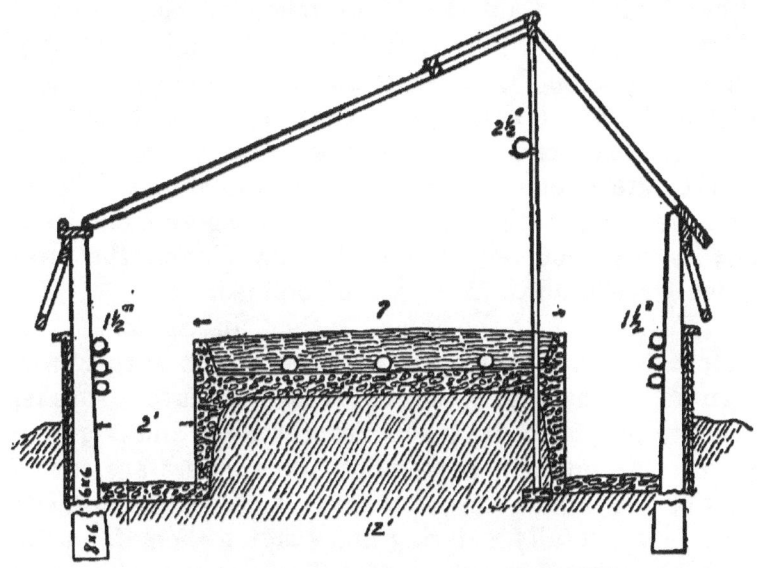

FIG. 24. NARROW VIOLET HOUSE, IMPROVED.

placed at once in the house without being planted out of doors.

The use of hot water for heating the house will be preferable, unless it is a part of a large range, when steam may be used. The piping should be sufficient to secure a temperature of forty degrees during the coldest weather. While a few degrees less than this would do no harm, it will be undesirable to have it go much higher, forty-five degrees being as high as the temperature should be raised at night by fire heat. If it is likely to go above that degree, air should be given.

While it will always be best to buy wrought iron pipe, if one has four-inch cast iron pipe on hand, a violet house will be a better place for it than one requiring a high temperature.

PROPAGATION.

Violets are generally propagated from cuttings of the young shoots, although the old plants are sometimes divided. Care should be taken to select the cuttings from healthy plants, and if only those from strong, vigorous plants, that have given large numbers of large, perfect flowers, are used, the tendency will be to develop an improved strain of the variety. On the other hand, if they are chosen at random, from plants that have been grown at a high temperature during an entire winter, it will not be strange if weak plants, that will quickly succumb to disease, are obtained.

Cuttings may be made either in September or October, or in the spring. If made in the spring from plants that have been forced, they will have a weaker constitution than if taken from strong and vigorous plants. If made in September, the runners are cut off four or five inches long, and set in a bed of light, sandy soil. By carefully watering and shading them for a few days, they will soon take root. These plants, if covered with a cold frame and mulched with leaves, will be in excellent condition for planting out in the spring. In case old plants have been wintered in a cold frame, good cuttings can be obtained in the spring from them, but, lacking these, the plants in the greenhouse can be used as stock plants. The cuttings may be made the last of March or the first of April and placed in a cutting bed; after rooting, they should be boxed or potted off in sandy soil, or, if the ground is moist, or so situated that it can be watered, they may be planted out without previous treatment. As a check at the time they are transplanted from the field to the house has much to do with inviting the development of the violet disease, it is by many thought best to set the young plants at once in the greenhouse beds where they are to flower, and thus avoid the check that is likely to be incurred when they are grown in the field and then transplanted.

SOIL AND PLANTING OUT.

While violets will give good results upon almost any good soil, they will succeed best upon one that is moist, but well drained, and while heavy is not so stiff as to bake or crack. If the soil is naturally rich, the use of from five to ten pounds of ground bone to the square rod will give stronger and healthier plants than if they are grown with stable manure.

The plants, when grown out of doors during the summer, should be set about nine or ten inches apart in the rows, which should be at intervals of twelve or fifteen inches, unless large numbers are grown, when they are better if placed thirty inches, so that they can be worked with the horse. The care required by them is simple, but they should not be neglected. The runners that start should be cut off, to cause the plants to thicken up, and if the summer is a dry one they should be mulched and, as a last resort, watered, a treatment that should suffice to keep down the red spider, which might otherwise trouble them; at any rate, frequent shallow cultivation should not be neglected.

As fall approaches, the plants should be taken up and placed either in a cold frame or upon beds in the greenhouse. While some growers use six- or seven-inch pots, nearly all violet growers place them in beds, in which the soil is from five to eight inches deep, and composed of four parts of rotted sods to one part of cow manure. The beds, whether shallow or solid, should be raised above the level of the floor, so as to bring the plants near the glass, that they may have all of the light possible. The distance at which the plants should be placed in the beds varies from eight to ten inches, according to the strength of the plants.

In case the soil in which the plants have been grown is light or exhausted, the ball may be broken and most of the soil shaken off, but if it is still worth using, the unbroken balls should be set in the bed, with the least possible disturbance. For a few days, the plants should be shaded and syringed frequently, with thorough ventilation, in order that the check from transplanting may be reduced as much as possible. All yellow and diseased leaves should be picked off as soon as the plants have become established. Great care should be taken that the temperature of the house does not get above forty-five degrees at night, although ten degrees more during the day will be desirable. Especially if some or all of the pipes are under the benches, great care should be taken in watering, as the soil at the bottom of the bed is likely to become dry, unless this is properly attended to. When surface watering is given, the water should be applied until the bed drips, and it should then be withheld until the bed begins to dry. Particular attention should also be given to prevent any drip upon the plants or the bed itself. With good care, a house of violets should average twenty to thirty flowers per plant, and there are records of much larger crops.

GROWING THE PLANTS IN THE HOUSE.

If the plants are to be grown in the beds in the house they should be in place by the middle of May, if not before. The soil for this purpose should be even richer than is required for field-grown plants when they are set in the house, and in addition to the rich compost a liberal quantity of ground bone can be used to advantage. If an old solid bed is to be used, the surface should be taken off and three or four inches of compost, composed of three parts of rotten sods and one part of decomposed cow manure, added.

While one strong plant in a place will generally make a good clump, some growers use two or three. About once a week or ten days the surface of the bed should be loosened and all runners should be pinched off. In four or five months after the plants were set, strong plants will be formed and flowers will show. As the weather gets colder, and before severe frosts come, the sash should be placed on the house, but the arrangements for thorough ventilation should be ample, and it should at no time be neglected.

Care should be taken to regulate the time of watering, to permit the plants to dry off before night. If they are syringed, it should be only early in the morning of bright days, and, so far as possible, the water should not be allowed to fall upon the leaves when it is applied to the soil. As sub-irrigation not only admits of applying the water without wetting the surface soil, but aids in keeping the foliage dry, it is especially desirable for this crop.

For several years many growers have experienced considerable loss from what is known as the "violet disease." Really, there are a half dozen diseases that attack the violet, any one of which may practically ruin the crop. The "eel-worms" (*Nematodes*) work havoc, particularly in poorly drained soil, by causing galls upon the roots.

The violet diseases are, doubtless, quite and invited by unfavorable conditions of growth or surroundings. A superabundance of fresh stable manure might cause a soft watery growth; a high temperature and long continued forcing would also weaken their vitality and render them easy victims. The real cause is that the spores (seeds) of the different diseases find conditions favorable to their propagation and growth. Much can be done to hold them in check if the decayed leaves are frequently removed, and the germs destroyed.

With healthy plants to start with, and with proper care in watering and ventilating, the danger of the appearance of the various violet diseases will be greatly reduced, but if any of the plants show traces of any disease, the injured leaves should be pulled off and burned. The surface of the soil should also be occasionally stirred and all litter removed.

The violet is troubled by few insects, the most troublesome being the aphis and red spider; frequent fumigation for the former, and syringing for the latter, should hold them in check.

VARIETIES.

Until recently the Marie Louise was more largely grown than all other varieties put together. It is of a rich, dark blue, with a whitish center. The flowers are large, firm, and quite fragrant. When healthy, it is vigorous and quite floriferous, but for several years many florists have been unable to grow it successfully, owing to its liability to the attack of some of the various diseases of the violet.

Lady Hume Campbell has with many growers superseded the above kind. The plants are strong, compact, and quite free from disease. The flowers are large, double, extremely fragrant, with long stems and of a light blue color.

The Farquhar is a new sort that has been less thoroughly tested, but the very highest claims are made for it so far as health, vigor and freedom of bloom, and the form, color and fragrance of the flowers are concerned.

Swanley White is still the best of its color, but is little grown.

Recently there has been considerable interest in single varieties, as they are generally less subject to disease and are freer in flowering than the double sorts. They have little substance and are less called for than the double flowers. In Paris, however, they are all the rage and they may soon become the fashion in this country.

California is among those most largely grown. It has large, rich green leaves that stand up well from the

FIG. 25. SINGLE VIOLET, PRINCESS DE GALLES.
Grown by Fred. Boulon, Sea Cliff, N. Y.

ground. The flowers are large, of a rich, bluish purple color, and very fragrant. Flower stems long and stout. Thought by some to be identical with Mad. E. Arené.

Luxonne has petals about the same size as those of the California, but they appear larger, as they open out flat. A freer bloomer, flowering from September until April.

Princess of Wales (de Galles) (Fig. 25), is rather smaller than Luxonne, quite free from disease and of a handsome violet color.

Admiral Avellan has dark green leaves, and large reddish-purple flowers that are very fragrant and lasting.

CHAPTER V.

BULBS AND THEIR CULTURE.

During the last ten years this class of plants has come to the front for winter forcing, and bulbs now stand next to the rose and carnation in the attention that is paid to them for this purpose. The kinds that are most commonly used are Roman Hyacinths, Lilies (*Lilium Harrisii* and *candidum*), Narcissus of various kinds, Freesias, Tulips, Lily of the Valley and Callas. Although a few callas and tulips are grown in this country, most of the bulbs are imported during the summer and fall from Holland.

As a rule, we may say that bulbs require a rich loam soil, to which about one-fourth its bulk of sand has been added. The bulbs are imported as they ripen, and will be received at intervals from August to November. They should be at once potted off. Some growers pot about one-half of the bulbs as soon as they are received, and the others are kept from four to eight weeks, that they may be later in coming into flower, and thus give a succession.

HYACINTHS, TULIPS AND NARCISSUS.

The Roman hyacinths, tulips, narcissus and similar bulbs, when grown for cut flowers, are placed in shal-

BULBS AND THEIR CULTURE. 89

FIG. 26. BOX OF ROMAN HYACINTHS GROWN BY J. C. VAUGHN, CHICAGO, ILL.

low boxes (Fig. 26), that are of a convenient size for handling, at a distance apart equal to about twice their diameter, and so that they will just show above the surface. If desired for decoration, rather than for cutting, they can be placed in pots or deep pans, of from four to six inches diameter, with smaller intervals between them. As soon as potted, the soil should be moistened, and they should then be placed where they can be kept cool, in order to give the roots an opportunity to develop. If one has a cold pit they can be placed in that, but any well-drained spot out of doors, where they will be somewhat sheltered from the sun, will answer. The boxes and pots should be so placed that they can be readily covered with from three to four inches of coal ashes or sand. This will hold the moisture and keep them from drying out, but an inch or so of hay over the ashes will aid both in holding the moisture and in keeping them cool. If one does not have a cold pit, an empty cold frame can be used to store the bulbs in, and if this is not available, the boxes and pots should be so arranged that a frame can be placed about them as winter comes on. By covering them with sash, mats and shutters, the frost can be kept out. Hay or straw could be used for the same purpose, and is desirable for the early sorts, as it hastens their development, but they frequently attract mice and the bulbs may, as a consequence, be destroyed, so that it is not safe to use them for the late bulbs. As soon as the roots have filled the pots, the plants may be taken out. It is best to start only a part of them at a time, and these should be placed in a cool greenhouse near the glass, at first, and then removed to one where the temperature is at least sixty degrees.

The Roman hyacinths should be kept in a frame for fully two months, but as a rule six weeks will suffice for narcissus. If either, however, is placed in the forcing house before the roots have made their growth, the flower stalk will be weak, and nothing will be gained, even in earliness. As a rule, the Roman hyacinths, and Early Roman and Paper White narcissus will be in bloom by the 15th to the 20th of December, and by bringing them in at intervals of ten days or two weeks, they can be had in bloom until the first of March, and even later, if desired. Tulips can be brought in before Christmas, and by proper care in selection of varieties and in handling can be had in bloom all winter. Daffodils do not flower, as a rule, before February.

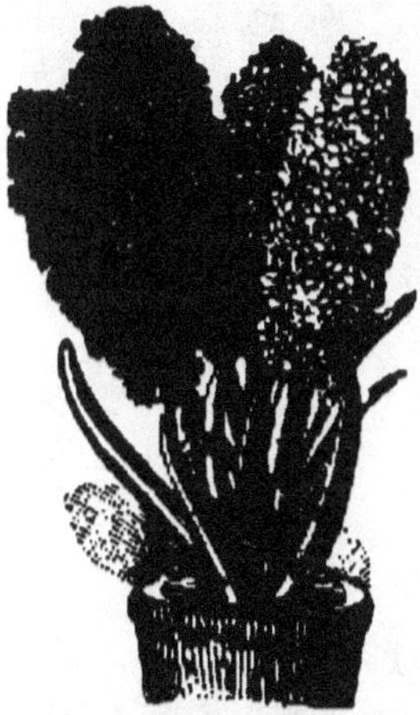

FIG. 27. DOUBLE DUTCH HYACINTHS.

Dutch hyacinths (Fig. 27), which are so commonly grown for bedding purposes and for decoration, are not forced to any extent for their flowers. If desired for sale or to brighten up the houses, they should be grown exactly the same as the Roman hyacinth and tulips. The Roman hyacinth is still the favorite, and although the red and blue varieties are sometimes grown, the number of white ones used exceeds both of the others a hundred fold.

FIG. 28. IMPROVED HYACINTH GLASS.

If good results are desired with Dutch hyacinths, it will pay to buy good bulbs of named sorts, and they will be found profitable if grown for retailing. The bulbs can be placed singly in five-inch pots, but they will be rather more attractive if from three to five are placed in a pan six or seven inches in diameter.

When used as house plants, hyacinths may be flowered in glasses made for the purpose. These consist of a flask to hold water, with an enlargement at the top, in which the bulb is placed so that it will barely touch

FIG. 29. SINGLE EARLY TULIPS.

the water. Roots will soon form and grow downward into the water. The glasses should be kept rather cool and out of the direct sunshine until the roots have formed. An improved form of hyacinth glass is shown in Fig. 28. This has an inner tube in which the roots are confined.

Of narcissus, the Paper White is the favorite with the florists. It is very easily forced and comes at a time when there is a scarcity of white flowers. The Early Roman and Von Sion, Incomparable and Trumpet Major daffodils are most largely grown of the other kinds.

The tulips (Fig. 29) are highly esteemed for their bright colors. They range in color from white and yellow to rose, scarlet and crimson. The single sorts are generally used for forcing; the Duc Van Thol, being one of the best early sorts, is about the only one that can be brought into flower by Christmas. By the first to the middle of January such kinds as La Reine and White Pottebakker, white; La Belle Alliance, scarlet; Brilliant, vermilion; Yellow Prince and Chrysolora, yellow; Rose Grisdelin and Cottage Maid, pink; Keizerkroon and Joost van Vondel, striped, can be brought into flower. Among the later sorts, Murillo, double pink, and Tournesol, red and yellow, will be found desirable varieties for forcing. As a rule, the solid colors in tulips will be found preferable to the striped varieties. By bringing in the Duc Van Thol about the last of November and giving it seventy degrees, it will flower by Christmas. With this and other varieties that show a tendency to have short stems, marked benefits can be obtained if they are shaded with cheese cloth or some similar covering. These varieties are most esteemed for early winter and to follow them there is a long list of named sorts in solid colors or variegated. For other varieties of tulips and narcissus, the reader is referred to any of the bulb catalogues, that are issued each year.

The crocus is also largely grown for purposes of sale or decoration. It requires the same care as the tulip, but is generally used to fill pans, or to border pans of

FIG. 30. FREESIA REFRACTA ALBA.

bulbs of other kinds. The colors are white, yellow or purple, solid or striped.

Freesias (Fig. 30) are generally placed in boxes at intervals during the autumn and kept upon a bench in a cool greenhouse, or in a pit, for five or six weeks, after which they are gradually brought into heat.

LILIES (*Harrisii and candidum*)

The lilies require about the same care as the above mentioned bulbs. They are frequently placed in six-inch pots, or in boxes about five inches deep. The *Lilium Harrisii* or Easter Lily (Fig. 31) is sometimes received from Bermuda, where it is extensively grown, by the middle of July, but the bulbs are immature, and far better and about as early flowers will be obtained if they are given another month in which to develop.

Even after the pots have become filled with roots, several months must pass before the flowers will develop. As soon as the flower stalks start, the lilies should be placed in a cool house for a week or so, before being placed in the room where they are to be forced. A very high temperature is required to bring them in by Christmas, but from the middle of January until April, flowers can be had in abundance, if proper steps were taken to secure a succession. Those for Easter should be brought into the house from the 10th to the 15th of November.

Lilium candidum and *L. longiflorum* require exactly the same care as the Bermuda lily, but they are stronger growers and do not force as readily. The bulbs of all the lilies are graded according to their diameter, the size ranging from twelve to eighteen centimeters (5-7 inches) to thirty or thirty-five centimeters, or about twelve to fourteen inches in diameter. The second size, eight to ten inches, is generally used for forcing.

96   GREENHOUSE MANAGEMENT.

LILY OF THE VALLEY.

Lily of the valley pips are generally imported from Hamburg, Germany, about the middle of October.

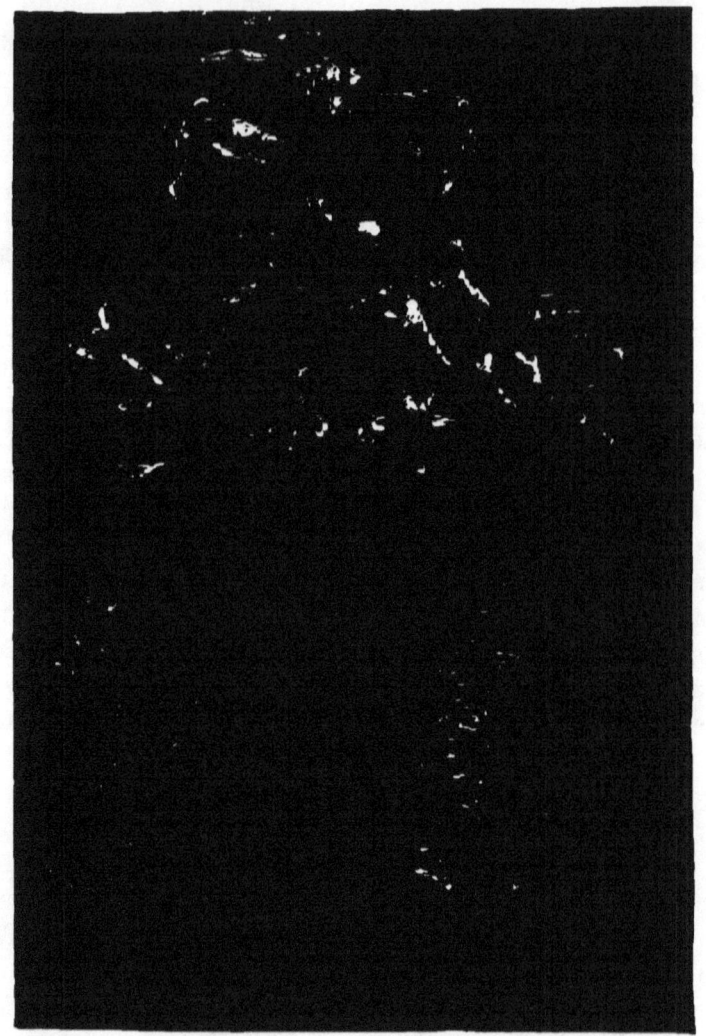

FIG. 31. LILIUM HARRISII.

When received, they should be packed away in the original bundles, in boxes of soil, and placed in some cool place to complete their period of rest until about a month before they are to be flowered, when they should be placed about an inch apart in boxes of sand or sandy loam, with the pips about half their length in the soil. They should be placed in partial shade (Fig. 32), where

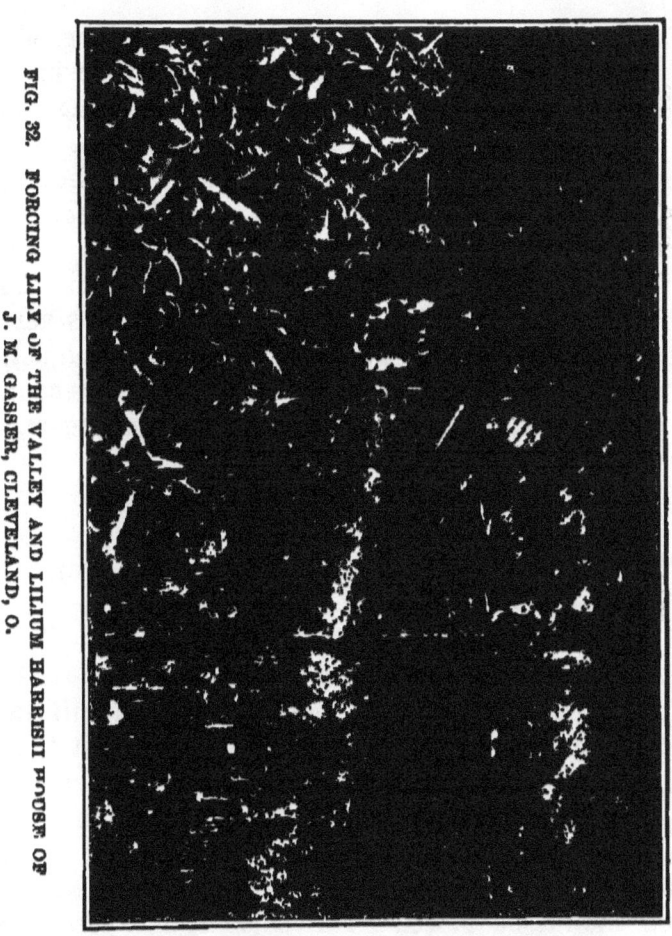

FIG. 32. FORCING LILY OF THE VALLEY AND LILIUM HARRISII HOUSE OF J. M. GASSER, CLEVELAND, O.

they can have a strong, bottom heat of nearly one hundred degrees. If the pips can be kept in a cool pit, where the temperature is about thirty-five degrees, until ready for forcing, flowers can be obtained in three weeks,

7

or even less. When placed in a cold storage house, they can be kept for a year. Unlike other bulbs that are forced, they do not require to form roots before being brought into heat.

THE TUBEROSE.

The tuberose, some ten years ago, was extensively forced, but it receives little attention to-day for winter blooming. For spring flowering, the first lot may be placed in four-inch pots soon after Christmas, and plunged in damp sphagnum or sand, in a forcing house, where they will have a bottom heat of eighty degrees. A succession can be secured by starting others at intervals of three weeks. If designed for flowering in the fall, the bulbs should be kept in a cool place, where they will be moist enough not to dry out, until August, when the first batch can be started, and with a second a few weeks later, flowers can be obtained from November until January.

CALLA.

The calla is one of the easiest flowers to force, and it can generally be used to good advantage. The bulbs should be potted in August, having first rubbed off all suckers, and after receiving a good watering should be kept for a month in some cool place, where they will not be allowed to dry out. It requires a richer soil than most bulbs and delights in an abundance of water. A seven-inch pot will answer for a large bulb, and if a larger pot or tub is used, there should be several bulbs placed in it. As soon as the season of growth is over, the pots should be placed on their sides, and kept in a cool, airy place, without water, for several months. Unlike the hyacinths and narcissus, the calla can be grown for several years without renewing the stock, although many florists prefer to purchase each year bulbs grown in California. The Little Gem is a miniature calla that has many uses.

Of the other bulbs, the lilies are the only ones that can be forced for a second year, after having had good cultivation in the open ground for two years. While the others are worthless for forcing, or even for bedding, if good results are expected, the tulips, in particular, can be used to good advantage by planting them about the shrubbery, and under the edges of evergreens.

OXALIS.

Although not a florists' bulb exactly, the oxalis should be more commonly grown. The Boweii, red; Lutea, yellow; and Versicolor, red and white, are among the most desirable sorts as pot plants, or for hanging baskets, vases, etc. They have a decorative effect and find a ready sale. The bulbs should be planted in a rich, sandy compost in October, in small pots, and will require no care, except an occasional watering, until they have filled the pots, when they should be shifted into the four-inch size.

The oxalis is well adapted for use in hanging baskets, window boxes and as a border for beds, as well as for use as a pot plant. The bulbs should be started at intervals during the fall, if a succession of bloom is desired. They may be planted where they are to flower, or the bulbs may be placed in three-inch pots and shifted to the beds or pots. A good bulb will fill a five-inch pot, or several may be placed in a large pot or pan. The oxalis does well at quite a range of temperature, but about sixty degrees will give the best results. When through flowering, and the leaves begin to turn yellow, water should be gradually withheld. During the resting period the bulbs may be left in the pots, which should be turned on their sides in some place where they cannot become wet, or they may be taken out and kept in boxes.

CYCLAMEN.

The cyclamen (Fig. 33) was formerly sown in the spring, but better results are obtained if the seed is planted in September. The plants are kept in two-inch pots until March, when they should be placed in four-inch. About the middle of May, they should be re-

FIG. 33. CYCLAMEN.

moved to a frame and, if well cared for, will be large enough for six-inch pots by July. They should be covered with cloth sash during the summer, but it should be raised to give thorough ventilation.

During the summer the plants should be syringed

if the weather is hot and dry, and they should have plenty of fresh air. Liquid manure should be given when the roots have filled the flowering pots. As cooler weather approaches keep a little closer and if the plants have been kept in a cold frame remove to a house where they can have some heat, if necessary to secure a warm, dry atmosphere. During the winter they should be kept at 55 or 60 degrees until through flowering. When the leaves begin to turn yellow induce rest by moving the plants to a cooler house and gradually withholding water. They should not be allowed to become dust dry so that the bulbs will shrivel. After a short rest the new leaf-stalks will begin to start and the bulbs should be repotted into four- or five-inch pots, using a light and open but rich compost, and giving thorough drainage. Repot when necessary up to six- or seven-inch pots and give the same care as the first year.

FORCING THE GLADIOLUS.

The gladiolus is coming into favor as a bulb for spring forcing. It can be grown with but little care, and the flowers will be even finer than those grown out of doors. The bulbs need to complete their period of rest before they are started into growth, and nothing will be gained by planting them before the last of December, unless bulbs are used that have been forced the previous year. They can be grown either in beds, boxes or pots, but one of the latter will generally be found preferable, as it admits of keeping them in a cool place until the roots have formed, which is desirable. They also do well planted out in the beds with carnanations and even in rose houses, but it will be best to start them in pots and transplant them to the beds after the pots have become filled with the roots.

They can be grown in the boxes about the same as Holland bulbs, using rather heavier and richer soil.

102   GREENHOUSE MANAGEMENT.

The bulb should be barely covered with the soil, and as there is danger of the damping off of the shoots if overwatered, it is a good plan to have the surface half-inch

FIG. 34. GLADIOLUS MAY, ORIGINATED AND GROWN BY THE CUSHMAN GLADIOLUS CO.

of sand. Water thoroughly and place under the benches, where the temperature will be fifty degrees, until the roots have filled the soil and the leaves have started. Gradually increase the heat to sixty and to seventy-five degrees. When the buds begin to form, give liquid manure once a week. If properly handled, the flowers will be ready to cut by Easter.

Among the best varieties for forcing are May (Fig 34), Buchanan and Shakespeare.

CHAPTER VI.

TUBEROUS BEGONIAS.

During the past ten years, few plants have increased in public favor more than the tuberous begonia (Fig. 35). The plants are rapidly propagated from seed, and can be grown as readily as geraniums, while for six months of the year they are resting and require no care. For pot or out-of-door culture they have few superiors. The "tubers" can be purchased at reasonable rates, or they can be grown from seed.

PROPAGATION.

The seeds should be planted about February 1, in shallow flats or seed pans. The boxes or pans should be half filled with broken crocks or other drainage, upon which there should be about an inch of fine compost, composed of rotten sods, leaf mold and sharp sand. Moisten the soil and scatter the seeds quite thickly, cover with a thin layer of sifted sphagnum and fine sand, using just enough to hold the seeds in place.

To prevent the soil from drying out, cover the box with glass, paper, or, better yet, long fibers of sphagnum. Place out of the direct sunlight, in a moderate bottom heat, with a night temperature of sixty degrees. If glass is used, it is well to cover it with paper and to

FIG. 35. HOUSE OF TUBEROUS BEGONIAS.

keep it slightly raised, to afford ventilation. When the seeds have germinated, the sphagnum and paper should be removed, and a close and warm atmosphere should be avoided. As soon as the second leaves appear, they

FIG. 36. SINGLE TUBEROUS BEGONIA.

should be pricked out in flats or pans, and from this time on they should never be allowed to stop in their growth.

A good potting soil for the begonias is made of well-rotted fibrous sods, to which the same amount of a mixture of well-decomposed leaf mold, cow manure and sharp sand in equal parts is added. A little ground

FIG. 37. DOUBLE TUBEROUS BEGONIA.

bone will also be of value. As soon as the plants begin to crowd, they should be placed in pots, and should be repotted whenever the pots are filled with roots. If desired, they may be grown in flats or in a cold frame during the summer. For the first few weeks, they should be kept in a narrow, low house, where they can be near the glass and with a temperature of sixty to sixty-five degrees. They should be shaded from the sun, and will be benefited by frequent applications of liquid manure. As the season for rest approaches, they should be gradually dried off, and stored where they will be dry, in a temperature of forty-five to fifty degrees. They can be kept in any frost-proof cellar. If the air is very dry, they should be placed in a box and covered with dry soil or sphagnum, to prevent shriveling. The tubers should be started into growth in March or April. They may be placed in small pots at once, or they may be started in shallow boxes filled with sphagnum. The first pots should be but little larger than the tubers, but the plants should be shifted as soon as the roots show the necessity. Good results can be obtained when the final shift is into seven-inch pots, but the best plants and largest blooms cannot be secured in less than ten-inch pots, and some go still larger. As a rule, it may be said that, for specimen plants (Figs. 36 and 37), the repotting should be kept up as often and as long as the roots fill the pots fairly well, and the larger the pots that can be filled with roots, the better the results.

Throughout the season, frequent applications of liquid cow manure should be made, and if it is desired to grow them in small pots, they should be top-dressed with cow manure as soon as the roots fill the pot after the last shift. During the summer, when grown in a greenhouse, they require an abundance of light and air, but the best success cannot be obtained unless draughts of air and direct sunshine are avoided. The optimum temperature for growth is about sixty-five degrees, and during the summer the air should be cooled and kept moist, by frequently wetting down the walks.

For out-of-door culture, the plants should be hardened in a cold frame, and should be planted out, either from flats or four-inch pots, as soon as danger from frost is over. They are particularly valuable for bedding, as they have no insect enemies, and are not injured by heavy rains. When they begin to ripen off, they should be taken up, dried so that the soil will shake off, and stored in a dry cellar.

Of the named varieties, the following are recommended for growing in pots, by F. J. Meech & Sons, the well-known tuberous begonia specialists of Charlevoix, Mich. "Double: Glow, bright scarlet; Incendie, flaming scarlet; Triomphe de Nancy, creamy yellow; Mrs. Windsor, shell pink; Marquis of Stafford, crimson; Mrs. Hall, white; G. Bryceson, deep salmon; Lafayette, cinnabar scarlet (the only one of its color); Mrs. Cornwallis West, very free, yellow; A. F. Barron, deep pink; Terre de Feu, deep rose, flowers very large and heavy; Blanche Duval, creamy white, tipped blush." As the best single named sorts for bedding, Mr. Meech names: "Prince of Wales, crimson scarlet; Norma, reddish magenta; Queen Victoria, rose; and Mrs. F. A. Willard, cream center, blush outside." There are very few sorts that succeed better as bedders than selected seedlings of good strains.

THE CANNA.

Although most used for out-of-door bedding purposes, the canna is quite largely grown by florists in the greenhouse for purposes of propagation, and as a decorative plant. For the former, the plants may be started in midwinter, after they have had a short rest, first dividing them so that there will be a strong bud upon each piece, by placing them in shallow beds of very rich, sandy compost, where they can be given sixty-five to seventy degrees with a good bottom heat. After the first thorough watering, they will require little more until they have begun to grow, after which it should be applied liberally. As soon as the new shoots that form have developed roots, they should be carefully taken off, and either placed in other beds to still further multiply, or they may be potted off. The same thing may be done with growing plants at any time, but the most common method is to plant in the open ground in the spring, and continue to divide the plants, as above, until the last of August, when those desired for winter propagation are taken up and planted in the greenhouse beds. This method of propagation is, of course, used only with new and high-priced kinds. Ordinarily the "roots" are stored on racks, or in trays, in some place where it is neither very moist nor so dry that they will shrivel, and where a moderate temperature can be maintained. If well dried when stored for the winter, a warm potting shed, warm and dry cellar, or the space under the benches of a warm greenhouse, if out of the drip, will answer for them.

For flowering in the greenhouse, dormant plants, or those at almost any period of growth, provided they have not been long in flower, may be placed in pots, tubs, or beds, and after forming roots will soon develop a number of strong shoots and supply an abundance of bloom. Among the best varieties for this purpose are the well-known Madame Crozy, Florence Vaughan, Chas. Henderson, Explorateur Crampbel, Alphonse Bouvier, Egandale, and Queen Charlotte, as well as the newer Italia, Austria and Burbank.

THE GLOXINIA. (*Sinningia speciosa*.)

Gloxinias are in nearly all colors, from light rose to dark purple, and in the better strains many of them are beautifully shaded and striped. As a house plant for summer blooming (Fig. 38), or for greenhouse decoration (Fig. 39), the gloxinias have few if any superiors. They require little care, except in watering, and during the winter they are dried off and packed away. They are readily grown from seed or by means of leaf cuttings, but when only a few plants are required, it will be as well, even for the florist, to buy one-year "dried roots." These should be potted in February or March, in three-

FIG. 38. GLOXINIA.

or four-inch pots, according to their size, the top of the bulb being just level with the surface, and placed near the glass in a temperature of sixty degrees, where they will have a little bottom heat. Until the leaves start, very little water will be required, but from that time it should be gradually increased, giving the plants all they can use, as, if at any time they are allowed to wilt, the flowers will be much injured. Gloxinias do well in a compost of two parts of rotten pasture sod and one part of well-rotted cow manure, to which enough sand is added to open up the soil. Instead of the rotten sods, equal parts of garden loam and leaf mold may be used.

Thorough drainage should be given by filling the pots two-thirds full of charcoal, or broken crocks, covered with a layer of sphagnum. As soon as the leaves extend beyond the edges of the pots, the plants should be shifted to the five- or six-inch size, in which they can be flowered, or sold as house plants. If designed for use as cut flowers, they can be planted out from the small pots, or the boxes, in which they may be started, either on benches in the greenhouse or in frames outside, where much less care will be required. When thus grown, they should be mulched with sphagnum.

During the season of growth, every precaution should be taken that they do not receive a check.

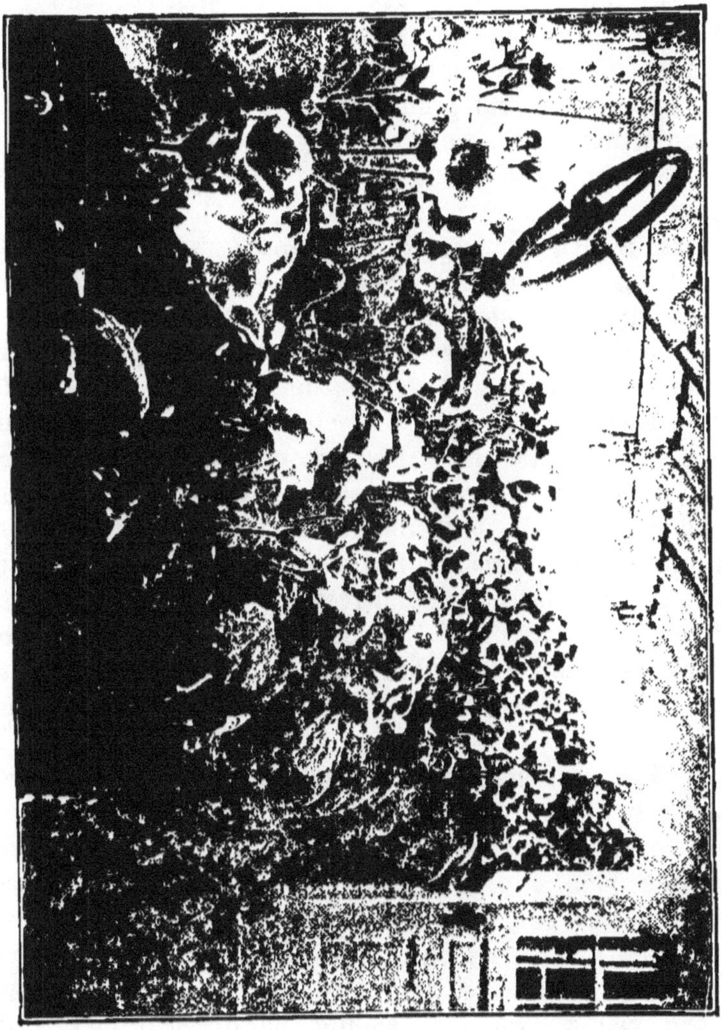

THE GLOXINIA. 111

FIG. 39. HOUSE OF GLOXINIAS.

While the atmosphere should be kept moist by syringing the walks and benches, overhead watering or syringing of the plants should be avoided, as, if drops of water remain on the leaves they will be spotted, and their beauty will be marred, if they are not entirely destroyed. On warm, bright mornings a fine spray upon the leaves will soon evaporate, and, while being beneficial to the plants, will do no harm. They should, at all times, be shaded from the direct sunlight, and during the hottest part of the summer, in addition to the wash upon the glass, a lath screen, or cloth shade will be desirable. Ventilation should be given in good weather, but strong draughts of air should be avoided.

When kept near the glass, and with proper attention to watering and ventilating, the gloxinia has few insect enemies, but if neglected, the thrip and spider will be troublesome. The use of tobacco stems about the plants, and frequent light fumigations, will destroy the thrips, while the spiders can best be fought by regulating the moisture of the air. If only a few plants are grown, the infested leaves can be sponged. Should "rust" appear upon the leaves, the diseased portions must be cut off and burned. In case it shows on the same plants a second year, it will be best to throw them away.

Plants started in February should be in bloom from June or July until August and September, and a succession of plants will give flowers until the chrysanthemums come in November. After the flowers appear, their season can be prolonged if kept in a slightly lower temperature. As soon as the flowering period is over, watering should be gradually lessened until the leaves turn yellow, when it should be discontinued. The leaves should then be cut off, and the plants in the pots laid on their sides under the benches in a warm room, or they may be shaken out and placed close together in single layers in boxes, or on shelves, where they should be barely covered with sand, and kept in a cellar, or room, where the temperature will be about fifty-five or sixty degrees. In case anyone desires to raise the "bulbs" from seed, the following brief directions may be of value: Sow the seeds in February in pans or in pots drained as above; the soil should be the same as for the bulbs, except that no manure should be used; cover lightly, and after syringing, shade and place in a room with a temperature of sixty-five or seventy degrees. The seeds will germinate in about two weeks, and the plants will then need careful attention to prevent damping off. When large enough, they should be pricked out in flats, placed in a brisk bottom heat, and later on transferred to pots. Re-pot finally to the three-inch size, and give the same care as large plants; by the end of July they should come into flower. When growth is over, they should be dried off and stored for winter.

From a good strain of seed, one should be able to obtain a good collection of plants, but if it is desirable to propagate any particular variety, cuttings of the leaves should be taken soon after the plants finish flowering. If the petiole of a leaf, with the lower half of the blade attached, is set in the sand where it will have bottom heat, a bud will soon develop from which a bulb will form.

FANCY CALADIUMS.

The so-called fancy caladiums (Fig. 40), occupy about the same place among the summer foliage plants as the gloxinias do among the flowering ones, and much the same reasons can be given for their popularity. Most of the varieties in cultivation are from *Caladium bicolor*, a native of Brazil, and they naturally require a high temperature for their perfect development.

They are readily propagated, by removing the

suckers that start out from the old tubers soon after they are brought into growth, or by cutting the tubers into pieces, on each of which there is, at least, one bud. The cuttings can be left on until they have formed roots, but will start most readily if placed, with the cuttings made from the old tubers, in sand in a propagat-

FIG. 40. FANCY CALADIUM.

ing case, until roots have formed, when they can be potted off.

When the period of growth begins, which is about the first of March, the old bulbs can be potted off, using equal parts of rotten sods, leaf mold or peat, sand and cow manure. There will be less risk, however, if, before they are potted, the bulbs are placed in sand, with bottom heat, until the roots have started. After the bulbs are potted, they should be kept at a temperature of sixty-five degrees, with a little bottom heat. At first, little more than frequent syringing will be necessary, but after the leaves start the amount of water required will rapidly increase.

They need partial shade, but if it is too dense, the color of the foliage will not come out well. Throughout the entire period of growth, they should not be allowed to suffer for lack of water, and the air should be kept moist by syringing. If given a mild bottom heat, growth will be hastened, and they will soon be ready for a shift. As a rule, a five- or six-inch pot will carry them through the season of growth, if free use is made of liquid manure, but some of the stronger bulbs may be grown to large specimens by potting them up to six- or seven-inch pots. If an early effect is desired, five or six of the bulbs may be placed in one large pot.

Caladiums need ventilation and plenty of room. If properly hardened, they can be used in the conservatory or the sitting room, but they will not thrive with the temperature below fifty-five degrees. As the temperature drops and autumn comes on, and the leaves begin to droop and die, the water should be gradually lessened, until they are ready to be packed away for winter. This should be in some place where the temperature will not fall below fifty-five degrees. Even during the winter the water should not be entirely withheld, as, if kept too dry, rot at the center may ensue. Among the twelve best varieties are, Candidum, Chantinii, Clio, Leplay, Mad. A. Bleu, Mad. Marjolin Scheffer, Meyerbeer, Mons. A. Hardy, Princess of Teck, Reine Marie de Portugal, Reine Victoria and Triomphe de l' Exposition. Owing to the fact that new forms are being constantly brought from Brazil and others obtained by crossing, any list is, at best, a temporary one.

CHAPTER VII.

ORCHID CULTURE.

As the requirements for the successful growing of orchids become better understood, the extent to which they are grown will rapidly increase; even now, they form a part of all large collections, and have quite an extensive sale as cut flowers.

The orchids may be divided into two classes, the terrestrial and the epiphytal. To the first section belong such species as live upon, and draw their nourishment from, the ground. Others grow upon the trunks and branches of trees, or upon rocks. They thrive under varied conditions, some being on the branches of trees overhanging streams or pools of water, where the atmosphere is quite damp, while others cling to rocks on the mountain side. Many kinds are found only in the tops of lofty trees, and some are generally on the trunks near the ground. Orchids have also been found at altitudes as high as 14,000 feet, but the jungle seems preferred by them, although many forms grow at an altitude of 2000 to 8000 feet. They are widely distributed through the tropics, being found in great quantities upon both hemispheres, and many handsome forms are found in the temperate zones.

The tropical orchids abound in Venezuela, New Grenada, Peru, Central America and as far north as Mexico. In the Eastern Hemisphere, they are found in the East Indies, Australia, Ceylon and India, and they are grouped according to habitat into East Indian forms, which flourish in a night temperature of seventy to seventy-five degrees in summer, and sixty to sixty-five degrees in winter, with about ten degrees higher during the day; Brazilian and Mexican forms, with a night temperature of sixty-five to seventy degrees in summer, and sixty in winter, and the Peruvian orchids, that do not need over fifty-five to sixty degrees at night in summer, and forty-five to fifty degrees in winter; in each case they may be ten degrees warmer during sunny days.

In our treatment of orchids, we should endeavor to provide them with surroundings similar to those that they are accustomed to, in a wild state. Many of the East Indian orchids are supplied with an abundance of moisture for a part of the year, during which they make their growth, and rest during the dry season. As they grow upon tree tops and on the sides of mountains, they are fully exposed to all movements of the air, and from this their need of an abundance of fresh air can be readily seen. The Peruvian orchids, on the other hand, are found at high altitudes, where the climate is cool and moist, and the supply of water throughout the year is abundant. For such species, it will be seen, it would be improper to provide any extended period of drouth. While some of these plants grow in the full sunlight, others are found in the dense jungles, and will not stand the full sunshine, even of our climate. The conditions under glass are, moreover, quite different from those in the open air just above, and for most plants, it is desirable to provide some way of shading them, during the summer months. For this purpose, permanent shading, using some wash for the glass, rolling blinds, canvas or netting, may be used.

Orchids are collected and shipped to this country and Europe in large quantities, and can be purchased, while yet dormant, at comparatively low prices. Most of the importers are large growers of orchids, and, if desired, can furnish established plants, at prices rang-

118   GREENHOUSE MANAGEMENT.

FIG. 41. PHALÆNOPIS AMABILIS. CŒLOGYNE CRISTATA. CATTLEYA TRIANÆ. DENDROBIUM.

ing from less than one dollar for small plants of common varieties, to hundreds of dollars for rare ones.

If dormant plants are obtained, the dead and decaying portions should be cut off, and the healthy growths sponged with some insecticidal solution, to destroy the scale and other insects that may be upon them. They may then either be placed upon sphagnum in a shaded portion of the house, where they should be kept comparatively dry until signs of growth appear, or in pots or baskets nearly filled with broken crocks, charcoal and other drainage. By the latter method, they can be watered more freely, and stronger growths can be obtained. As soon as the roots appear, the drainage should be covered with a mixture of fibrous peat, sphagnum, and finely broken crocks and charcoal.

With many orchids, the plan of hanging them in the house with the roots up, for two or three weeks, is an excellent one, particularly with Phalænopsis. Vanda, Aerides and similar genera, as it lessens the chance from decay, on account of water collecting between the leaves. Nearly all orchids should be kept in the shade until they have become established.

ORCHIDS FOR BEGINNERS.

In making a selection of orchids, care should be taken to choose species that are easy of culture, that are quite sure to flower, and that are ornamental. If kinds can be selected that are low priced, all the better. The appended list contains sorts that fulfill these requirements.

STOVE ORCHIDS

Night, summer 75°, winter 65°. Day, summer 85°, winter 75°.

Calanthe Veitchii.
Cypripedium Boxallii.
" caudatum.
" Harrisianum.
" Lawrencianum.
" Spicerianum. (Fig. 42.)
Cypripedium villosum.
Dendrobium nobile.
" Wardianum.
Oncidium papilio.
Phalænopsis amabilis.
Stanhopea insignis.

FIG. 42. CYPRIPEDIUM SPICERIANUM.
(Grown by Pitcher & Manda, Short Hills, N. J.)

INTERMEDIATE ORCHIDS.

Night, summer 65° to 70°, winter 55° to 60°.   **Day,** summer 75° to 80°, winter 65° to 70°.

Aërides odoratum.
Cattleya Gaskelliana.
" Mossiæ.
" Percivaliana.
" Trianæ. (Fig. 43.)
Cœlogyne ocellata.

Lælia anceps.
" purpurata.
Lycaste Skinneri.
Phaius grandifolius.
Trichopilia suavis.

COOL HOUSE ORCHIDS.

Night, summer 55° to 60°, winter 50°.   **Day,** summer 65° to 70°, winter 55° to 60°.

Cypripedium insigne.
Epidendrum vitellinum majus.
Masdevallia Lindeni (Harryana).
Odontoglossum grande.
" Pescatorei.

Odontoglossum Rossii majus.
Oncidium tigrinum.
" unguiculatum.
Zygopetalum Mackayi.

While a room is desirable for each group of orchids, it is not necessary, and good results can be obtained with all in one room, if the East Indian and other stove forms are placed at one end, which is kept quite warm, while the Mexican and Peruvian forms are grown at the other. Moreover, the classification is at best a provisional one, as some of the stove plants would thrive in an intermediate house, as would several of the cool house orchids.

THE POTTING OF ORCHIDS.

Orchids may be grown, according to their nature, upon pieces of bark or cork, or in baskets, pans or pots. The baskets are generally made of cypress or cherry, in a square or octagonal form, or as cylinders, boats, or rafts, as shown in Fig. 44. The material is cut into strips about three-quarters of an inch square and from four inches to a foot or more in length, according to the size of the plants. Holes are bored about half an inch from the end of each stick, and galvanized or copper No. 18

wire is run through them, binding them firmly together. Loops are made at the upper end of these wires, to which the handles are fastened.

For growing in pots, Cypripediums (Fig. 42), Cat-

FIG. 43. CATTLEYA TRIANÆ.

tleyas (Fig. 41), Aerides (Fig. 45), Lycaste, Oncidiums, Masdevallias, Epidendrums, Lælias, Phalænopsis, Vandas, Calanthes, Dendrobiums (Fig. 41), Trichopilias, Odontoglossums, Phaius, Cœlogynes and

Zygopetalums, may be selected. Many of them do fully as well, however, in orchid pans, and, with the exception of Cypripediums, Phaius, Lycaste, Cœlogynes, Calanthes, Masdevallias and Zygopetalums, which are terrestrial orchids, baskets will generally be found better for them. Stanhopeas need an open pan or basket, while Cattleyas, Lælias, Phalænopsis (Fig. 46), Vandas, Den-

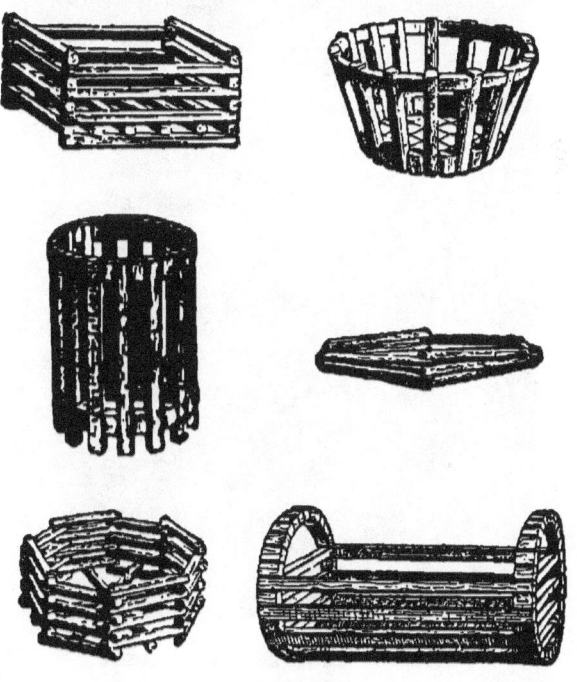

FIG. 44. ORCHID BASKETS.

drobiums, Odontoglossoms, Epidendrums, and a few others may be grown in sphagnum, on rafts, or upon blocks of wood or cork, but they will require more attention than if grown in baskets. The terrestrial forms, as enumerated above, should be grown in pots about one-third filled with broken crocks, over which a layer of sphagnum is spread; upon this the plants are placed in a mixture of equal parts of good loam, fibrous peat, chopped sphagnum, broken crocks and charcoal. Lycaste and Cœlogyne are benefited by an admixture of sand, and Calanthe by chopped, sandy loam sods, while a little decomposed manure will be desirable for the others.

FIG. 45. AERIDES SAVAGEANUM.

The top of the soil should be a little below the edge of the pot to aid in watering (Fig. 47, E).

When epiphytal orchids, such as Lælias, Cattleyas, Phalænopsis, Vandas, Dendrobiums, Odontoglossums and Aerides, are grown in pots, they should be nearly filled with potsherds and covered with a layer of peat and sphagnum; the plants placed upon this, with their roots covered with coarse peat and chopped sphagnum, should be held in place by pegs and stakes. If a small pot is inverted in the bottom of the large one, before the potsherds are put in, the drainage will be improved and will be less likely to become sour.

For Vandas, Phalænopsis and other true epiphytes, peat is not necessary. It will generally be advisable to raise the plant two or three inches above the top of the pot (Fig. 47, A, B and D), but in covering the roots, care should be taken not to raise the sphagnum much above the base of the pseudo-bulbs, as it might both cause decay and prevent development of the flower scapes. When orchids have been freshly potted, great care is necessary in watering until roots have been developed. When orchids need repotting, as much of the old material as possible should be shaken off, without breaking the roots, and the plants then placed in pots as before.

If plants are to be grown in baskets, the size selected should be as small as can well be used, and the basketing should be done in the same way as the potting, using coarse potsherds and sphagnum at the bottom, and filling up with fine potsherds and chopped sphagnum. The plants should be placed upon this and the roots covered with sphagnum. For Cattleyas, Lælias, Dendrobiums and Odontoglossums, coarse chopped peat should be added to the compost, while for Aerides, Phalænopsis and Vandas it is not used.

Many of the true epiphytal orchids, such as Vandas, Aerides and Phalænopsis, as well as Cattleyas, Lælias, Dendrobiums, Odontoglossums and Epidendrums, may also be grown upon blocks of wood, rafts, cylinders and pieces of cork and bark, upon which they are bound with copper wire, the roots being covered with sphagnum, with which peat is mixed for the last five named.

While there is much less danger from over-watering when these plants are upon blocks than when in baskets, it is also true that watering becomes necessary much more frequently, in order to prevent their drying out. For this reason, unless careful oversight is given the plants, the basket will be better than blocks and rafts, except, perhaps, for certain species of Epidenlrum, Odontoglossum and Dendrobium.

FIG. 46. PHALÆNOPSIS GRANDIFLORA.

The repotting of orchids is generally done just before growth commences. It should be performed annually in the case of Calanthe and Phaius, but a top-dressing will be all that most species require, until they outgrow their basket or pot.

ORCHID CULTURE. 127

WATERING ORCHIDS.

When the plants are starting into growth, if the moss is kept saturated with frequent waterings, the new growths are liable to rot off, hence the moss should be

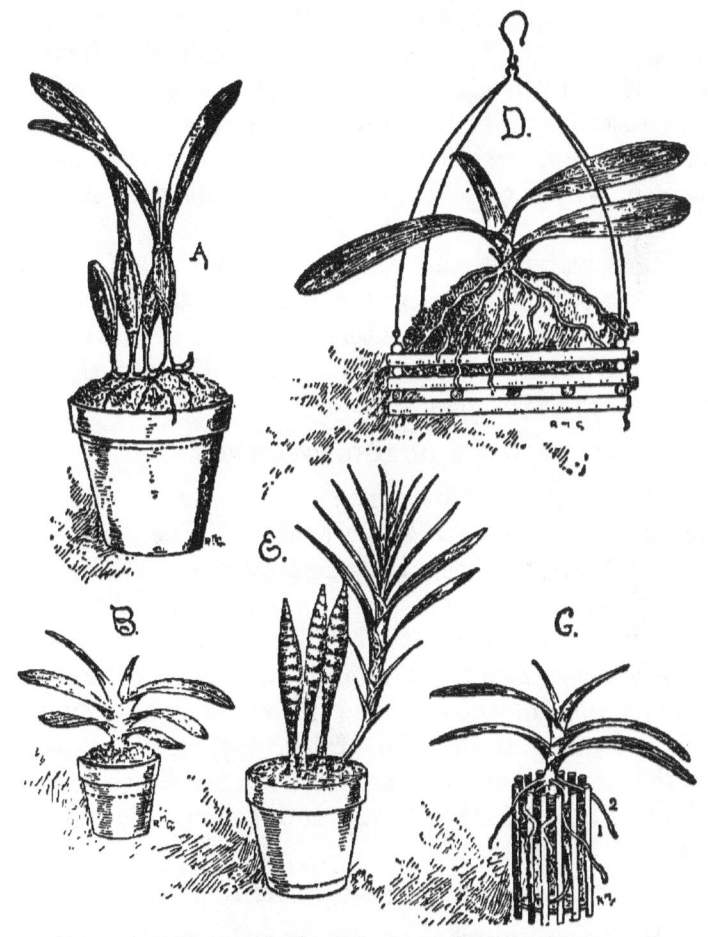

FIG. 47. POTTING AND CRIBBING ORCHIDS (After R. M. Grey)
The dotted line upon the pots shows the amount of drainage used in each case.

kept only barely moist. As the growths develop, more water can be given, and towards the last of the season there need be no limit, provided the pots and baskets are properly drained. If the plants are upon rafts or blocks, they should be syringed two or three times a day during the summer, and should be occasionally soaked by being dipped in water. Plants in baskets should receive similar treatment, and whenever they are dry in the morning they should be dipped. It is an excellent plan, during the bright days of summer, to close the house by the middle of the afternoon and syringe the plants with a fine rose. By wetting down the walks once or twice a day, in hot weather, a moist atmosphere can be obtained, which will be favorable to the growth of the plants.

Hard water should not be used for orchids, and a cistern in which rain water can be caught is quite desirable. For use in winter, it is well to have a tank inside the house, so that the water will be of the same temperature as the plants.

CARE DURING GROWTH.

As a rule, orchids make their growth during the summer, and rest during the winter. When the season for growth approaches, the temperature should be raised ten degrees, and the air kept moist. Since the epiphytal orchids obtain most of their food from the air, through their roots, an abundant supply of moisture should be maintained in the air so long as growth is made. During the middle of the day, it is well to dry out the atmosphere and admit fresh air by ventilation, when it can be done without unduly lowering the temperature.

TREATMENT DURING RESTING STAGE.

As winter approaches, the growths will harden, and the plants enter on their period of rest, during which time the temperature should be lowered about ten degrees, and maintained at the following temperature for winter: Stove orchids, night, 65°; day, 75° to 80°. Intermediate house orchids, night, 55° to 60°; day, 65° to 70°. Cool house orchids ten degrees lower.

During the resting stage, the Cattleyas, Lælias, Dendrobiums and similar forms, should be kept as dry as possible and not shrivel. On the other hand, several genera, such as Aerides, Vanda, Phalænopsis and Zygopetalum, keep up more or less growth during the winter, and should be given more water than the others and never allowed to become dry at the roots.

The Dendrobiums and Calanthes of some species drop their leaves as soon as growth is over, and, in order to ripen the growth, should be placed near the glass, and kept quite dry. Although the moisture should be withheld, during the winter, the atmosphere should not be allowed to become hot and dry, and on bright days the walks and tables should be wet down.

MANAGEMENT DURING BLOOM.

There is quite a variety in the habit of bloom in orchids, as some forms like *Lælia anceps, Cattleya Trianæ, Calanthe, Cœlogyne, Phaius* and *Cypripedium insigne* bloom in December, during the resting period, while many bloom during the summer. When the blossoms open, it is a good plan to remove the plants to a cooler house, as, in an atmosphere that is cool and dry, they will last much longer than in one that is hot and moist. If the drop is not more than ten degrees, no harm will be done to the plants, especially if the change is made gradually. If the blossoms are wet, in syringing, they soon become spotted and fade, hence no water should be allowed to fall on the flowers.

From the fact that most orchids can be grown in baskets, and hang from the sash bars, where they take but little room, many florists are taking up orchid growing for the sale of cut flowers, and find it very remunerative.

DISEASES, INSECTS AND OTHER ENEMIES.

The "rot" and "spot" are among the worst diseases of the orchid. The former is caused by a superabundance of water at the roots, and the method of prevention is plain. If rot appears, the diseased portion should be cut away. Spot is most troublesome when rotting manure, or similar material, is placed at the roots, although a sour compost, or overwatering, brings it on, especially if the house is kept closed.

Slugs are among the worst enemies that the orchid grower has to contend with, as they sometimes eat off the soft flower stalks, and destroy the points of the new roots. They can be trapped by placing sliced potatoes on the benches, and the same thing will attract snails, wood lice, and roaches, although molasses and some form of poison is used for the last two. It is always safe to place a little cotton batting around the base of the flower stalk, to protect it from its enemies.

Various scale insects are also frequently troublesome, and for these, as well as for mealy bugs, thrips, red spiders and similar insects, some insecticidal wash, as whale-oil soap, should be used. Strong tobacco water will also be quite effectual, as will fir tree oil. Kerosene emulsion will also destroy the insects, and, if properly prepared, will not injure the plants, although after a few hours it is well to wash it off. The other insects that attack orchids are the same as are troublesome to a great variety of plants, and similar remedies should be used.

CHAPTER VIII.

AZALEAS. (*Azalea Indica.*)

As a rule, the azaleas used by the florist are imported from Europe. They are obtained in the fall, and should be potted at once and placed in a cool room, where they can be shaded for the first few days. While they should be watered sparingly at first, the frequent syringing of the plants should not be neglected. During the winter the plants should be kept in a cool house, and will need careful attention in watering, ventilating and fumigating. The amount of heat they will require will depend upon their condition, and the time the flowers are needed; as a rule, 40 to 45 degrees at night, and ten degrees higher during the day, will be satisfactory. As the principal call for these plants is at Easter, most of them should be brought into flower at that time, but by taking a little pains to accelerate some plants and retard others, their development will be so distributed that they can be had in bloom for several months. While in flower, if in a cool house they will last longer. After flowering, they should not be neglected, as, if they are not given proper attention at this time, they will not make a satisfactory growth, and flower buds will not be formed. They should be kept in a partially shaded house until the middle or last of May, when, if settled weather has come, they should be plunged in some partially protected, but unshaded, place in light, well-drained soil. Marsh hay, or some similar material, will be desirable as a mulch to keep the roots cool and, unless they have been repotted, a thin covering of rotted manure will be of advantage. Frequent watering and syringing will be necessary, but while they should not be allowed to get dry at the roots, care should be taken not to give them an excess of water, since, plunged as they are, it might be fatal to them. Good results can also be obtained in a well-ventilated and partially shaded greenhouse.

For the use of the florist, at least one-half of the plants should be white and the others mostly pink or

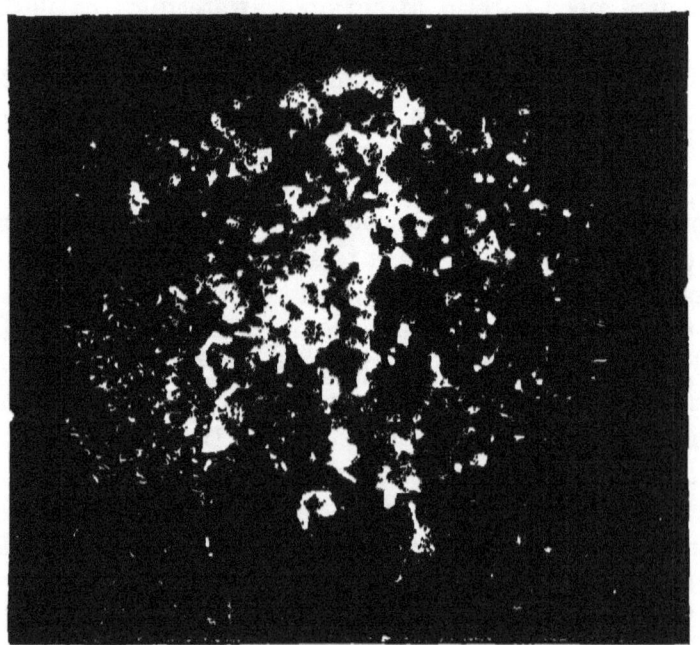

FIG. 48. AZALEA IN COMPACT FORM.

salmon, although a few scarlet and variegated ones will be valuable in the collection. Deutsche Perle is one of the best early whites, and Bernhard Andrea alba will also be satisfactory. Vervæneana, Imperatrice des Indes and Simon Mardner are among the best pink and rose sorts, while Cocarde Orange, scarlet, and Mme. Camille Van Langhenhove, variegated, have shown up well. Azaleas succeed well in a soil composed of one part each of fibrous peat, rotten peat and garden loam, with the addition of sand in proportion to the character of the soil. In Fig. 48 is shown a well-grown azalea, with a compact head, while Fig. 49 shows a more open form, which would be preferred by many. The principal enemies of the azalea are the red spider and thrip, for which remedies are given elsewhere, together with descriptions of the insects themselves.

HYDRANGEAS.

As a house plant, or for the florist, to be used for purposes of decoration, the hydrangea is always desirable. Coming as it does at Easter, it can be used to good advantage for decoration, or in baskets or designs of cut flowers, and the sale of plants in five-, six-, or seven-inch pots is generally large, and at remunerative prices. As a rule, there will be a demand for the plants as late as May or June, which will enable the florist to clean out the plants that were late in coming into bloom. It is well to have the plants out of the way as early as possible, in order to make room for other plants.

Hydrangeas are readily propagated from half-hard cuttings, struck at any time from February to June; for Easter sales they should be in the cutting bed as early as March. After being potted off they can be handled in various ways, that requiring least care being to plant them out as soon as the weather permits, in the open ground, where they should be mulched and watered if the season is dry. To secure bushy plants, they should be headed back, and the branches pinched once; late pinching will destroy the flower buds which should form the first season. As autumn approaches, they should be taken up and potted, using pots of generous size. To ripen the wood, they should be placed in cold frames, where they should have abundant ventilation, the glass being removed on bright days. Thorough ripening is necessary, if the best results are desired.

When the weather gets cold, they should be placed in a cool greenhouse, or should be packed away in a cool pit, where they should be kept in a dormant condition until January. About twelve weeks will be required to bring them into flower, and the time of starting them will depend upon the date at which Easter, or any other

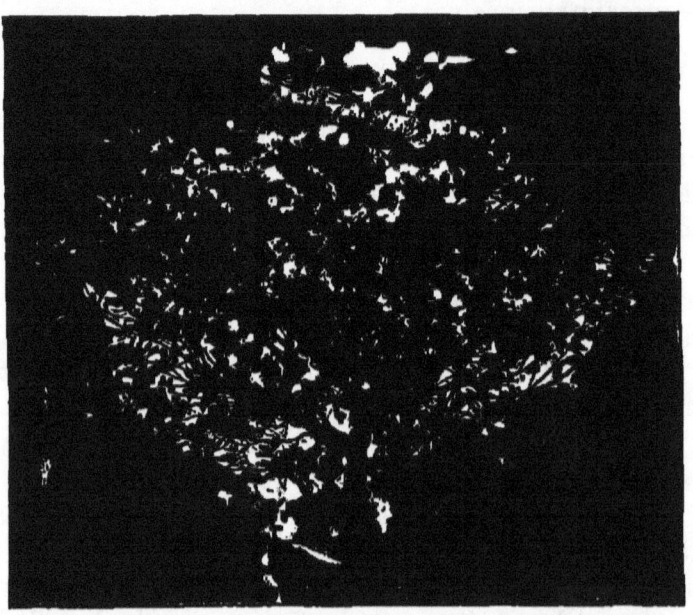

FIG. 49. AZALEA WITH AN OPEN HEAD.

occasion for which they are desired, comes. At first, they should be given 50 to 55 degrees at night; this may soon be raised to 60 or 65 degrees, and even 70 degrees may be given, if necessary, in order to bring them into bloom in time. After they are thoroughly started, the plants will use a large amount of water and should not be stinted. When they have filled the pots with roots, they should receive liquid manure two or three times a week and a top-dressing of half an inch of well-rotted manure will be of advantage to the plants. At no time during their growth should they be crowded as, for the best development, they need an abundance of room. In order to form a symmetrical plant, the branches should be staked, and if the shoots are too thick the weaker ones should be removed. In order to harden the plants, as soon as the flowers have expanded, they

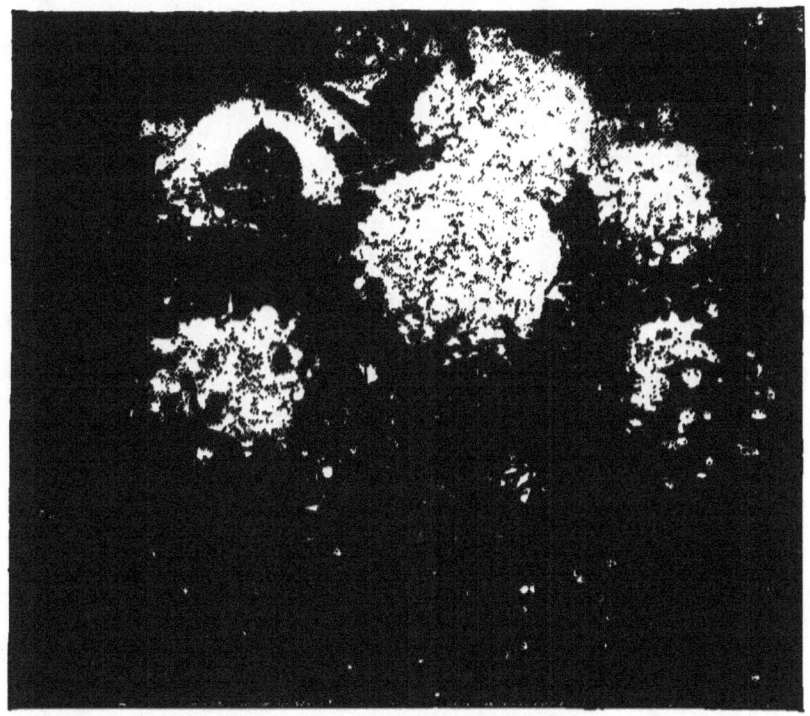

FIG. 50. HYDRANGEA OTAKSA.

should be given a lower temperature and an abundance of air.

Another method is to grow the plants in pots, plunged in the ground out of doors. Here they will require the same care as when planted in the ground, except that more attention to watering them should be given. By July they should be large enough to be shifted to six-inch pots, and should then be headed back, their final pinching being given in August. The cuttings made as late as June are best grown in a cool house, during the summer, either in pots or planted in the beds. If large specimen plants are desired, they can be obtained by cutting back the old plants after flowering, and growing them another year.

The best varieties are Hydrangea rosea, Otaksa (Fig. 50), and Thos. Hogg. A red-branched variety is also quite popular as a house plant, but it does not force as well as the others. The Rosea is the earliest to flower, and is generally of a clear pink, although, like all of the others, its color is variable. Otaksa, with flesh colored flowers, is, perhaps, most grown by florists, as it is most in demand as a house plant. The Thos. Hogg is a white variety, and is especially desirable for Easter decorations. By the use of iron filings in the soil, or by applying alum water, the flowers of this variety, and of Otaksa, take on a light blue color. Peat or soil containing iron, will have the same effect.

If hydrangeas are kept dormant until March or April, they will come into flower in May or June, and will make excellent plants for the porch or veranda, and in tubs or vases can be used with good effect upon the lawn.

CYTISUS (*Genista*).

Although this may be classed among the old-fashioned flowers, it is one of the most useful to the florist and is one of the best spring-blooming house plants. *Cytisus* (*Genista*) *Canariensis* has, in the past, been most commonly grown by florists, but *C. racemosus* is now taking its place; by some it is regarded as a distinct species, but it is quite likely only a garden variety. It differs from *C. Canariensis* in having longer and pointed leaflets and a longer raceme of larger flowers.

Either form is readily propagated from cuttings

taken off in February or March. They need only ordinary care, but should be kept in growth during the summer. They may be planted in the open ground in May and left there until September, when they should be taken up and potted, or they may be placed in four-inch

FIG. 51. CYTISUS.

pots and plunged. They may also be grown in a cool, well-ventilated greenhouse and should in any case be large enough to go into five- or six-inch pots by September. They naturally branch, but they can be thickened up by pinching them in once or twice. Some florists even use sheep shears in cutting them back and thus produce a dense head. If desired in a standard form, they can be so grown by selecting a strong plant, and training it to a single stem to the hight desired and rubbing off all side shoots. It is then topped and a head formed.

During the winter the plants are allowed to rest at a temperature of 45 or 50 degrees, until within seven or eight weeks of the time the flowers are desired, after which they will need 60 or 65 degrees. With proper handling, a plant can be kept in flower for two to four weeks, and a succession of bloom can be secured for six weeks or two months. After flowering, they should be given a partial rest for two or three months, when they should be repotted, and plunged out of doors. The after-treatment is the same as for small plants. An average sized potted plant is shown in Fig. 51.

ARDISIA (*Ardisia crenulata*).

This plant adds to an attractiveness in leaf and flower, that of showy red berries, which often hang on for a twelve-month. While it can be grown from half-hard cuttings during the summer, the use of seed is more simple and gives better plants. These should be sown in an open, sandy soil, and if placed in a stove temperature with a strong bottom heat, should germinate in two weeks. Although the seeds germinate thus readily, the seedlings are somewhat difficult to start into growth. The stronger ones should be potted off and kept rather close until they have become established. They should be kept growing until in four- or five-inch pots, and, as soon as these are filled, liquid manure should be given until the blossoms form. To aid them in setting their fruit, they should be kept in a rather dry atmosphere and near the glass. If, after the fruits have set, they are kept at 45 or 50 degrees, they will last much longer. During their growth, they do best if kept at a stove temperature during the summer, after which they will be best at 50 to 55 degrees until the period of growth begins in February, when the temperature should be raised.

When the plants lose their lower leaves, if rested and then cut back and repotted, a new head can be formed. Young plants are, however, most satisfactory. The thick, waxy leaves of the Ardisia render it little subject to insect attacks, although the scale and mealy bug are sometimes troublesome; they readily yield, however, to the usual remedies.

THE GARDENIA (*Gardenia florida*).

When grown in a warm, moist atmosphere, and kept free from scale, mealy bugs and other insects, this plant, with its profusion of white, waxy flowers, with their unequalled fragrance, and shining, green leaves, is certainly worthy of admiration. It is readily propagated from half-hard cuttings under a hand glass, or in a propagating case, with strong bottom heat. The rooted cuttings should be potted in fibrous, sandy soil, and should be gradually hardened, but to avoid a check they should be kept at a stove temperature with bottom heat. They like a peaty, fibrous soil with an admixture of sand, and, with proper attention in the way of watering and repotting, cuttings struck in the early winter will make strong plants in one season. During their growth, the water supply should not be stinted, and frequent sprayings should be given. When the growth is completed, they should be allowed to ripen their wood, and then receive a partial rest by restricting their heat and moisture. Young plants, at most two years old, should be used, and it will not pay to attempt to recuperate a stunted plant. Gardenias are quite subject to the attack of some of the more common greenhouse insects, such as the red spider and scale, but with proper care they will

140   GREENHOUSE MANAGEMENT.

not be troublesome. If they make their appearance the ordinary remedies can be used.

THE FORCING OF HARDY PLANTS.

Although this is a comparatively new industry, it is worthy the attention of every retail florist, as the flowers

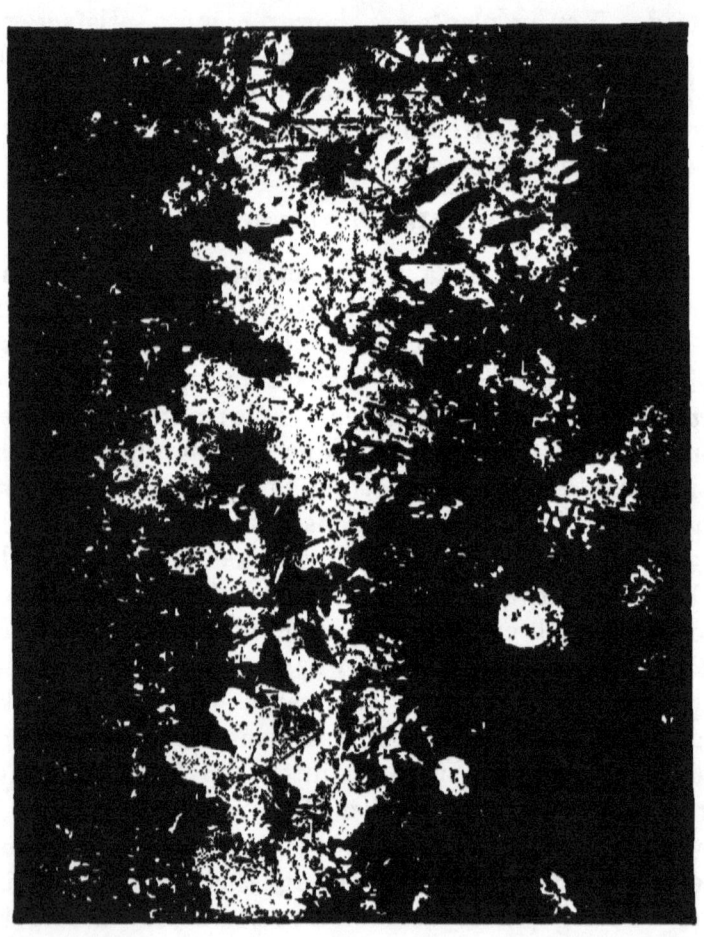

FIG. 52. BENCH OF LILACS.

from many of the hardy plants have much merit for cutting, in themselves, and, what is of fully as much importance, they are a new thing and out of season, and are likely to be much sought after, if properly brought to the attention of the public.

A considerable number of the hardy shrubs are well adapted for forcing, but the best results will be obtained from those that naturally flower outside previous to the first of June. We should also select well-grown plants, that have been prepared for the purpose, and be sure that they have a resting period of at least two or three months, before they are brought into heat. *Deutzia gracilis* and *D. scabra* were among the first to be forced, and are well adapted for it. The various kinds of lilac, (*Syringa vulgaris* and its varieties, also *S. Persica*) Fig. 52, force readily. The many varieties of mock orange (*Philadelphus coronarius*) are also easily forced, as are the snowball (*Viburnum Opulus sterilis*) and *V. plicatum*. *Spiræa Van Houttii* and *Exochorda grandiflora* give good results, but they should be kept cool and forced slowly. Among the other plants adapted for forcing are *Azalea mollis, Kalmia glauca* and *K. latifolia* (Fig. 53), *Daphne Cneorum* and *Andromeda speciosa* and *A. floribunda.*

The plants may be cheaply imported from Europe, all prepared for forcing, or they may be grown by the florists. Whether the small plants are propagated, or purchased from some nurseryman, they should be planted out in nursery rows and grown for two or three years. In order to secure a mass of fibrous roots that will favor their growth in pots, they should be transplanted each year. When strong enough for forcing, they should be dug as soon as the leaves drop in the fall, and potted off, using a light, but rich compost. Wet down thoroughly and set in some sheltered place until there is danger of the cracking of the pots by frost, when they should be removed to a deep, cold pit. Here they will require no care, except an occasional watering if they become dry, and airing on warm, or bright, days.

About Christmas, the first batch can be started, and others may follow at intervals. Place at first in a cool greenhouse and gradually increase the temperature until it is 60 degrees, at which time the growth should be started. The development of the buds can be aided if

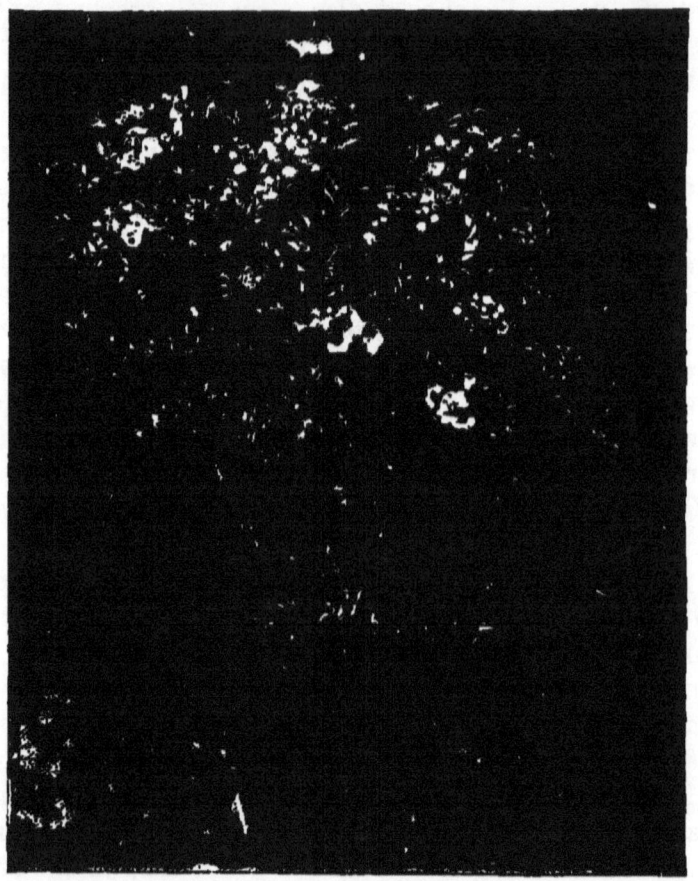

FIG. 53. KALMIA LATIFOLIA.

the shrubs are frequently sprinkled. The care needed by these plants is about the same as that required for other plants under similar conditions.

While most of the herbaceous plants will have little value for forcing after the first season, many of the deciduous shrubs can be used more than once. After flowering, they should be removed to a cool room and from there to a cold pit, from which they should be planted again in nursery rows, and in two years can again be used for forcing.

CHAPTER IX.

CALCEOLARIAS.

The public is beginning to appreciate the value of calceolarias as spring-blooming pot plants. They are very interesting in their structure and striking in their general appearance (Fig. 54). For early planting, the seeds, which should be of some choice strain, are sown as early as the middle of June, but for April flowering, during which month they should be in their prime, reliance should be had on July-sown seed, while to secure a later succession another batch should be put in some time in August.

The seed should be sown in shallow pans upon a light compost, with a slight covering of sifted soil, and placed in a cool house, or, better, a frame, which should be well ventilated and shaded. If the frame is in a sheltered spot, faced to the North, and a lath screen is used in addition to a shaded sash, which is raised a few inches above the frame, we have given the seeds and future plants as nearly perfect surroundings, during a hot, dry summer, as can be secured. As soon as large enough, the seedlings should be pricked out into flats, and later into two- and three-inch pots, using a rich, fibrous compost composed of equal parts of rotted sods, loam, decayed manure and sand. Leaf mold can be added to advantage for the small plants. The plants should be returned to the frame and kept there until November; they will need copious watering, on which account perfect drainage is necessary. The leaves should be kept as

FIG. 54. SPECIMEN CALCEOLARIA.

dry as possible, except that they should have a gentle syringing on warm, sunny mornings.

The green fly must be kept down at all hazards, as, if it gets the start, it will be hard to control; to aid in this, chopped tobacco stems may be scattered between the pots, both in the frame and in the house. As soon as the plants begin to be pot-bound, shift into four-inch pots and later into five- and six-inch. They should be removed into a cool greenhouse, where they can be kept at about 40 degrees, as soon as there is danger of frost working into the frame, which should be covered upon cold nights with mats, during the last month. Keep the

FIG. 55. CINERARIA HYBRIDA.

plants near the glass, but shade from the direct sunlight.

The early started plants should be established in their flowering pots by the first of December, and should be in flower soon after New Year's. During the winter, give ventilation even on cold days, and give attention to the watering, so that the plants can by no chance become dry. Keep the moisture off the leaves as much as possible. As soon as the roots fill the pots after the final shift, supply manure water liberally, but discontinue its use when the flowers begin to open.

In addition to the plentiful use of tobacco stems upon the greenhouse benches, to keep the aphis in check, frequent light fumigations should be given. To avoid disease, keep the leaves dry, and at once remove and destroy all diseased and decaying leaves. With careful management, the greenhouse can be kept in a blaze of color from January until the middle of May, and florists will find a growing demand for calceolarias as house plants.

CINERARIAS.

The greenhouse cineraria occupies about the same place, both in the conservatory and the house, as the calceolaria, and it flowers at about the same time. The single forms are of little value for cut flowers, but some of the double kinds may become useful. The cineraria is even more injured than the calceolaria by a hot, dry air, and a slight frost that might not affect the calceolaria would prove very injurious, if not fatal, to it. Like that plant, its greatest enemy is the green fly, but the principal reliance must be placed on the chopped tobacco stems, or the vapor from tobacco tea, or extract, as tobacco smoke, unless in a mild form, affects the foliage. Unlike the calceolaria, the cineraria delights in water upon its leaves and on every bright morning, even in winter, the plants should be syringed.

In a general way, its care is the same as given for the calceolaria, and may be briefly stated as follows: Sow the seeds in shallow pans, from June to August; prick out the young plants in flats or pots, and later transfer to three-inch pots, repotting, before growth is checked, into five- or six-inch pots. Sometimes they can

CINERARIAS. 147

be made to fill even larger sizes. The soil should be of a rich, light compost, with an increased amount of manure for the older plants. Cinerarias should be kept in a well-shaded frame or cool house from the time the seed is sown until October, when they should be placed where they can be kept at 45 degrees at night. The plants, when in large pots, should have liquid manure

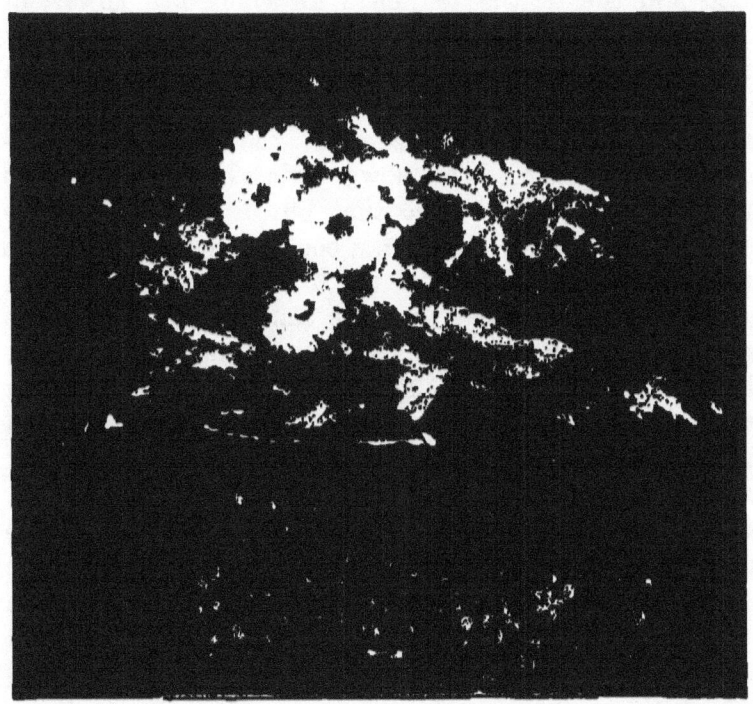

FIG. 56. SINGLE CHINESE PRIMROSE.

once or twice a week. By careful attention to the time of sowing the seed and to the forwarding of the plants, constant bloom can be secured through the winter and spring. While the method will not be much used in practice, a promising plant can be perpetuated by taking off and rooting the suckers that form after the flowers fade. A well-grown specimen plant is seen in Fig. 55.

PRIMULAS.

Although more modest in their appearance than the showy calceolaria and cineraria, the primula (Fig. 56) has been and still is a more general favorite. The sorts that are most commonly grown are the single and double forms of the Chinese primrose (*Primula Sinensis*). The single primulas may be divided into two classes, the fimbriated and the fern-leaved, each of which has flowers in two colors, white and rose. They are grown from seed from May to July, in well-drained seed pans. The soil should be light and fibrous, and the covering should be light and evenly distributed. If the soil is well moistened before the seeds are sown, a glass laid over the pans will hold the moisture so that but little more need be applied, if they are placed in a cool, shaded frame. The seedlings should be pricked out into pans or flats, which should be well drained, and the transfer to pots and the repotting should be the same as for cinerarias; as a rule, however, the plants can flower in five-inch pots. After they get to growing, they should be well watered and the foliage should be wet down occasionally on bright mornings during the summer; after winter comes on, the leaves should be kept rather dry. After the middle of September, the plants should be grown in the house at an average temperature at night of 50 degrees. As with the other plants of this kind, liquid manure should be applied as soon as they have filled the pots, after the last shift.

Primulas should be kept near the glass, and, although they like a certain amount of sunlight, they require partial shade, during the heat of the day in summer, from its full intensity. It is well to pinch the flower buds from young plants, as it checks the growth of the plants if they are allowed to develop. In potting the primulas, care should be taken not to press the soil too firmly, as it would obstruct the free passage of the water. In repotting, while it is advisable to keep the lower leaves well down upon the soil, the crown should not be covered.

The double primulas are increased by division. After flowering, the leaves are removed from the lower portion of the stems and moist sphagnum is packed around them. If placed in a frame, and kept rather cool and moist for a couple of weeks, roots will form and the branches can be taken off and repotted. For a few days, until they become established, they should be kept rather close, after which they should be gradually hardened. The plants require about the same care as the single sorts, except that as they are forced for their flowers, a somewhat higher temperature should be given them.

Another species of primula, *P. obconica*, has for several years been considerably grown, but has now nearly gone out of use, from the fact that it is poisonous to many persons; but for this, it is a desirable plant, as it is multiplied readily, either by division, or seeds, and furnishes its delicate pinkish-white flowers in profusion.

Although it is easier to keep the aphis in check upon primulas than on either cinerarias or calceolarias, as they admit of fumigation, it is always well to keep the benches strewn with tobacco stems as a precaution.

MIGNONETTE.

Few plants can be grown with as little care and attention, and yet the number of florists who reach the highest success with mignonette is comparatively small. A narrow, span-roof house, with a solid bench on either side of the walk, seems best adapted to this crop. Thorough drainage should be secured, and in no way can it be obtained more readily than by placing drain tile across the beds, about fifteen inches below the surface. They will have a marked effect if placed twelve to twenty-four, or even as much as thirty-six, inches apart, but a closer arrangement will be better.

The soil for the plants should be not less than fifteen inches deep and many of the best growers prefer eighteen or twenty. Its composition may vary considerably, but a preparation of four parts well-rotted sods, four parts of garden loam and one part of decomposed manure is desirable. In filling the beds with this amount of soil, more than usual care is necessary that it be well pressed down and compacted. If the compost is coarse, a fine seed bed can be obtained by spreading sifted soil over the bed to the depth of an inch. The bed should be sown before it has time to dry out, the usual date being about the first of August, or a little earlier in some cases, in drills fifteen inches apart, covering with sifted soil to the depth of three-eighths of an inch. It is a good plan to scatter sand in the drills in which the seeds are to be sown, and to use the same material for covering them. The bed should now be thoroughly watered, and from this time it should not be allowed to become dry. The use of cloth or lath screens, until the plants have appeared, is desirable, after which they should be removed. The ventilation should be ample, preferably from the ridge, and air should be given at all times, as the plants, at this period of their growth, should be kept cool. Good results can also be obtained in shallow beds, by placing an inch of cow manure in the bottom and filling up with three or four inches of rich but light compost.

When the true leaves appear, the plants should be thinned so that they will stand at least twelve inches apart in the rows. In about two months the flowers will form, and if large spikes are desired the laterals that form on the leading shoots should be removed. This should also be done with the shoots that appear later on, as fine spikes can only be secured when disbudding is

FIG. 57. MACHET MIGNONETTE.

carefully done. A night temperature of 45 degrees is generally considered a maximum for the mignonette and 40 degrees is preferred by many; during the day the ventilation should be such as will keep the temperature as near 58 degrees as possible. In caring for this crop, the well-known grower, Mr. J. N. May, of Summit, N. J., uses fine brush stuck into the soil around the plants to support the spikes, and this seems as good as any other way of trellising, although a desirable method is shown in Fig. 57.

Where the caterpillars are troublesome, the method used by Mr. May to keep out the moths will be desirable; it consists in covering all openings with mosquito netting. The use of hellebore, slug shot, or of Paris green, either in water or plaster, in a very dilute form, will also be a sure remedy. The most destructive disease of this crop is described and figured in Chapter XXV.

The seed ordinarily sold is very uneven and much of it will give worthless plants. It is always desirable, after securing a good strain of mignonette, to select seed for future use from the plants that are nearest to perfection. In this way the type will be fixed and an improved strain for forcing will be secured. The variety known as Machet (Fig. 57) is one of the best for forcing; it has a strong stem, dark green, healthy foliage, and the spike is large and fragrant. Miles Spiral is preferred by some.

Some growers have had good success with pot culture. The seeds are sown in flats or beds, and the seedlings pricked out into two-inch pots. When large enough to repot, they are transferred to four-inch pots, using very rich soil. They, of course, will need to be staked and tied and should receive the same care as when grown in beds.

CHAPTER X.

FERNS.

For greenhouse or house decoration, or for supplying florists with "green," ferns, and Adiantums in particular, are very useful. While many species are easiest propagated by the division of the plants, others are commonly grown from spores, which should be sown at once, although the spores from some species can be kept for some time. They should be sown either in pans or pots, or on beds, using garden loam, over which half an inch of fine sphagnum should be placed. Moisten this thoroughly and scatter the spores evenly over it, and after sprinkling cover with glass. Water only when they show they are dry. Keep covered until the seedlings have started. It will be best to prick out the young seedlings into flats, from which they should later be transferred to pots. Pot them in soil one-half leaf mold and the remainder of loam and sand. For propagating on a large scale, a box covered with a glass sash, of suitable size, will answer. The seed bed can be prepared upon the bench itself. Ferns for dwellings should be grown at 55 to 60 degrees, as they will then be firm and well hardened, and will thrive far better than soft, spindling plants, in the dry atmosphere of the living room. For small fern pans, two or three plants will be enough. Fern pans can be filled to advantage by using some erect growing kind in the center, with fine Adiantums, Selaginellas or similar kinds, around it.

Many varieties are readily increased by dividing the crowns. To increase them rapidly, they should be bedded out where they can be kept well moistened at a temperature of 60 to 65 degrees. In dividing and transferring to pots, it is hardly desirable to make a very fine division, as, although more plants can be obtained, they will be slower in starting and less satisfactory. During the spring and early summer, the young plants should be kept in a cool house or in a frame, where they can be properly shaded and watered.

If to be used for cutting, the best results can be obtained if the plants are bedded out. This should be done early in August, in order that the plants may have time to develop and harden off. The beds should contain from four to five inches of compost, consisting of two parts pasture sods and one part each of sand and rotten manure. For most ferns a temperature of 60 to 65 degrees is desirable, and the stove ferns are benefited if it is slightly higher, although some of the greenhouse species do well if it is considerably lower.

For the florist's use, in addition to the well-known *Adiantum cuneatum* and *gracillimum*, such others as *A. elegans, A. Capillus-Veneris, A. concinnum* and *A. c. latum, A. St. Catherina* and *A. decorum* will be useful. *Adiantum Farleyense* (Fig. 58) is among the best of the Adiantums for decorative purposes, but except for very elaborate cut-flower work, it will be less useful than some of the more delicate sorts. The *Pteris serrulata* and *P. s. cristata*, and other forms that are readily grown, are also desirable for planting out, either on or under the benches, while *Pteris tremula*, and its variegated form, *P. argyrea*, and *P. cretica alba lineata* should not be neglected.

When ferns are shifted, or planted out, they should be shaded from the bright sun for several days, and the foliage should be frequently syringed. If to be used for cutting, after they have made their growth, the shading should be taken off, and abundant ventilation should be given, in order that the fronds may harden off, and thus

FERNS. 155

stand up longer when used. The florist will find specimen plants, and baskets and pans of ferns useful in decorating his house, as well as for outside work. If well-

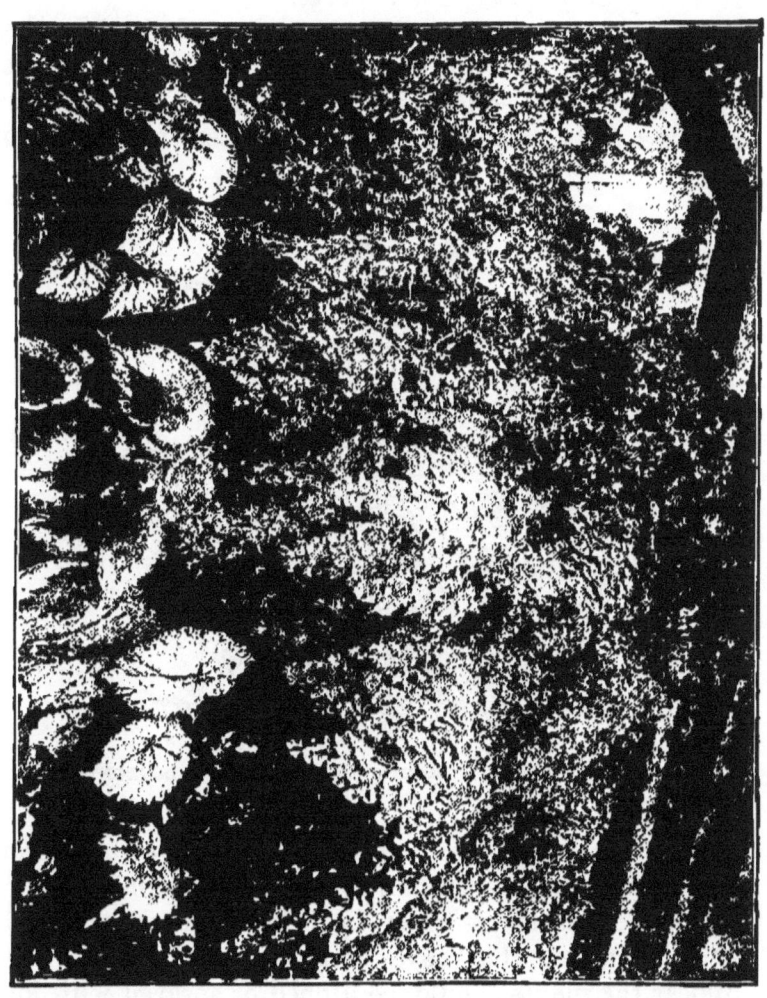

FIG. 58. ADIANTUM FARLEYENSE.

grown and of well selected kinds, the visitor will be attracted to them, and they will have a ready sale.

For large conservatories the large tree ferns are quite desirable. While the *Dicksonia*, *Cyathea*, and other similar forms, grow very slowly, and, as a result, are imported in a dormant condition, at a large expense, the *Alsophila Australis* is quite rapid in its growth and is readily propagated from spores.

Ferns thrive in a moist atmosphere, but while they need a steady supply of moisture at their roots, an excess is sure to bring serious consequences. The thrip and scale are among the worst insect enemies of ferns. For

FIG. 59. BOSTON FERN (NEPHROLEPIS EXALTATA BOSTONIENSIS).

the former, the frequent spraying of the plants with tobacco decoction will be found useful, or moderate fumigation may be employed upon the stronger kinds. The scale insects are most likely to make their appearance on plants that have been neglected, and if they appear the plants should be dipped or sprayed with kerosene emulsion, or fir tree oil, and receive better attention in the future.

Ferns, as a rule, do not thrive as house plants, but for this purpose, the sword fern (*Nephrolepis exaltata*) is one of the best, as it can stand a dry room better than most of them. A variety of the sword fern to which the name of *N. exaltata Bostoniensis* (Fig. 59) has been given, has been recently introduced. It has a graceful drooping habit and seems well adapted to house culture. Of the more delicate and yet easily grown kinds are *Davallia Fijiensis, Onychium Japonicum, Microlepia hirta cristata* and the *Gymnogrammes* (gold and silver ferns).

SMILAX.

This for many years has been, and, in fact, it is yet, one of the most commonly grown and the most useful of the plants used by the florist as "green." It is readily grown from seed, which should be sown any time from January to March, after soaking it for twenty-fours in warm water. The seedlings should be potted off, and as soon as they fill the thumb pot they should be shifted to the three-inch size. With proper care, they should be ready to plant out by June or July. While deep, raised beds are often used for growing smilax, less constant attention to watering will be required if it is grown in solid beds. In the first case, five or six inches of rich compost will be required, while for the latter it should be at least eight inches deep. It is desirable that there should be ten or twelve inches between the rows, and six or seven between the plants. For the training of the smilax, No. 14 galvanized wire should be stretched in two lines above each row, one line being near the bed and the other from six to ten feet higher. The green twine, thread, silkalene, or other material, used for training the smilax, should be fastened to these wires above and below. As the shoots start into growth, they should be trained up the proper strings, and they will need frequent attention that none of them get astray. Watering should, of course, not be neglected, and on bright days syringing will be helpful. After the first crop is off, an application of manure may be made to the surface of the bed, or reliance may be had on liquid manure.

While the principal call for smilax is at Christmas and Easter, it is needed at all times during the year, and a supply should always be kept on hand. Many growers throw out their smilax beds at the end of each year, but unless they have been unduly forced, good results can be obtained from them for several years. If to be retained, they should be dried off and kept dormant for two or three months in the summer, and before they are brought into growth again the surface soil should be removed and replaced with a rich compost. If dried off in the early spring, a bench can be erected over the bed for bedding or other plants.

Smilax, to be well grown, should have a night temperature of 60 degrees, with the usual increase during the day. As with ferns, after the growth has been made, if it is hardened by gradually increasing the amount of ventilation, smilax will keep longer after it is cut. Under the best conditions, a crop can be secured by November, and two others can be taken off during the season, but, as a rule, two crops are all that can be cut.

ASPARAGUS.

This valuable climber was slow in coming into favor with the public, partly because it was by many associated with the vegetable of the same name, but it now seems to have come to stay. In a general way, its cultivation is about the same as has been given for smilax, from which it differs principally in its method of propagation. Asparagus is best propagated from cuttings of the young stems. If made in May and rooted under a hand glass, or in a propagating case, they will be strong

FIG. 60. ASPARAGUS SPRENGERI.

enough to give a fair crop the second year. A more common method is by the division of the old plants, and, after potting them off in light soil, plunging in a mild bottom heat.

Strong plants should be set preferably in solid, although they will do fairly well in deep, raised beds, about ten or twelve inches apart; if planted closer than this, every other plant should be removed after the second year. If well grown, from three to five strong shoots should be obtained from each plant. Asparagus is forced for several seasons, being best from the second to the fourth year. During the summer, it should be dried off, from June until August, and treated the same as smilax.

The species most commonly grown is *Asparagus plumosus*; although a dwarf form, *A. plumosus nanus*, is preferable for many purposes. The latter is more nearly like a fern, as a rule being only eighteen or twenty inches high, and as it has shorter joints, it is much more plume-like in appearance. A new form, *Asparagus Sprengeri* (Fig. 60), is claimed to be a strong grower, but of graceful habit, and of a bright green color. It will remain fresh for a considerable time even in a heated atmosphere. When grown rapidly, *Asparagus plumosus*, and to some extent, its dwarf variety, has the habit of sending up stems with the lower part devoid of foliage, and as this is worthless, some growers, among them W. H. Elliott, Brighton, Mass., have erected houses with high roofs (Fig. 61), thus enabling them to cut a good "string" above the bare portion of the plant. Aside from their delicacy, and their rich, green color, all the greenhouse species of asparagus are found more valuable than smilax for decorations, or for cut-flower work, where permanency is desirable, as they will remain fresh for a number of days, if the ends are in water.

The temperature required is slightly lower than is needed by smilax, but with the exception of this, and

ASPARAGUS. 161

FIG. 61. ASPARAGUS HOUSE OF W. H. ELLIOTT.

the points noted above, the care required **is not unlike** that needed by that well-known plant.

CHAPTER XI.

PALMS, PANDANUS AND ARAUCARIAS.

Few families of plants contain more cultivated species than does the one to which the common name of palm has been given. Although they have for long years been grown quite generally in greenhouses, they are coming more and more into favor for purposes of decoration. The well-known Fan palm (commonly known as Latania), and the Corypha, with its broad leaves, were formerly used for this purpose, but they were often badly torn, even with the most careful handling, and they did not grow in favor; although desirable in the conservatory, other kinds are now regarded as more useful. The present favorites are some of the pinnate leaved Arecas and Kentias, and they seem admirably adapted for it, as they are not injured by rough usage, and as they succeed better than most palms in a dry atmosphere, they are much used as house plants.

Nearly all palms grow readily from seed, and although thousands are imported annually, hundreds of thousands are each year grown in this country from imported seed. The seed should be obtained as fresh as possible and planted immediately, in sandy loam soil, in a good bottom heat. Although they can be sown on the beds, it is best to use pans, pots, or boxes, in order to be sure of proper drainage. While 70 degrees can be taken as an average temperature for germination, some stove plants need more, and a few greenhouse forms will start as well at a lower temperature. If the seeds are

PALMS, PANDANUS AND ARAUCARIAS. 163

large, with thick, bony coverings, germination can be aided by filing through the shell and soaking for twenty-four hours in hot water.

As soon as properly germinated, the plants should be potted off in three parts rotten sods (or two parts of leaf mold and two of rotten sods), one part of rotten manure and one part of sand; if the soil is stiff, a little peat or leaf mold can be added to advantage. During the sum-

FIG. 62. FAN PALM LIVISTONA (*Latania Chinensis*).

mer, the young plants should be kept in the growing house at about 70 degrees.

Some of the plants with small leaves grow quite well in comparatively small pots, but as soon as they fill them with roots, liquid manure should be added. As a rule, there is more harm done from over-potting them than from under-potting. In case a plant needs a change of soil, when a shift is not desirable, the loose soil can be removed and the roots cut away, and the plant can go back into the old size without crowding. Whenever palms are repotted, they should be shaded and carefully syringed for a few days. As the season of growth approaches, unless the plant is repotted, liquid manure should be applied. Oftentimes it will be of advantage to

FIG. 63. DWARF RATTAN PALM (*Rhapis humilis*).

remove the surface soil from around a plant and replace it with rich compost.

During the summer, it is well to remove the large plants from the house and plunge them, under a partial shade, out of doors, where they will be somewhat sheltered from strong winds. A lath screen makes an excellent covering for palms and similar plants. Many of the palms can be kept in the full light, but should be plunged in the ground to lessen the danger of their drying out. If properly supplied with water, palms are better off out of doors than in the house; although the leaves may become slightly yellow, they will recover their green color on being returned to the house.

As noted above, while the Latania (Fig. 62) (properly *Livistona Chinensis*) and Corypha (*Livistona Australis*) are much used, both for the greenhouse and house, the forms commonly known as Kentias (*Howea Belmoreana, H. Fosteriana* and *Rhopalostylis Baueri*), the Arecas (*Areca lutescens, A. rubra* and *Hyophorbe Verschaffeltii*), Seaforthias (*Archontophœnix Alexandræ* and *A. Cunninghamiana*), Date Palms (*Phœnix dactylifera, P. rupicola* and *P. reclinata*), and Rhapis (*Rhapis flabelliformis* and *R. humilis*) (Fig. 63), are generally useful and are much more grown.

PANDANUS.

These plants, commonly known as Screw Pines, from the spiral arrangement of their leaves, are both interesting and, particularly in the variegated forms, attractive. *Pandanus utilis*, the best known species, is easily grown from seeds, which start readily in a strong heat, and should be potted off in a rich, sandy compost containing leaf mold or rotten sods. During the summer, they need a partial shade and a high temperature. In well-drained pots, they can use large quantities of water during the growing period. The air should be kept moist at that time by frequent syringings, but in the winter water should be used sparingly, both in the pots and on the leaves.

The other forms that are commonly grown are *P. candelabrum* (*Javanicus*) *variegatus* and *P. Veitchii*, the latter being more useful than either of the others. They are propagated by taking off and rooting the suckers which form about the base of the plants. If these are placed in sand in a propagating case, they will take root readily, and can then be potted off. These species require the same care as has been outlined for the *P. utilis*.

THE ARALIA.

Of the other decorative plants, none are better than the Aralia (including *Panax* and *Fatsia*). While the common hardy and half-hardy species grow readily from cuttings of the roots, only a few of the stove species of the Aralia, such as *A. Guilfoylii*, propagate with ease from cuttings of the stems, and other forms, such as *A. leptophylla* and *A. Veitchii*, are generally grafted. The above mentioned forms are among the best of the Aralias proper. *Aralia V. gracillima* has long, narrow, undulated leaflets (with white midribs), and is an improvement on the species.

Panax plumosum and *P. Victoria*, both probably varieties of *P. fruticosum*, are delicate plants, with plume-like leaves, which are variegated in the latter. They are propagated by means of either stem or root cuttings, or by suckers. The more showy stove Aralias are now placed with Fatsias. Of these *Fatsia papyrifera*, *F. Japonica* (syn. *A. Sieboldii*), and the white and yellow variegated forms of the latter, are especially valuable. They are propagated from seeds, from suckers, or from cuttings of the stems.

The plants of all these genera need a rich compost, of equal parts of rotten sods, manure and sand.

ARAUCARIA.

This is one of the few conifers grown in greenhouses. The more common species are *Araucaria excelsa*, the Norfolk Island Pine, and *A. imbricata*, the Chilian Pine. Propagation is by seeds or cuttings. The seeds are a long time in germinating, and generally have a low vitality. They should be sown in a mild heat. If cuttings are used, they are taken from the tops of plants in the autumn and placed in sand, where they should be kept at a cool house temperature until they begin to callus, after which they should have a gentle

FIG. 64. THE VARIEGATED ASPIDISTRA.

heat. Then place in four-inch pots, using rich loam and sand, and keep rather close until they have become established, when they need more air and water. After this, they need ordinary care and should be repotted each summer before growth begins, until they are in eight-inch pots; after that, once in two or three years will answer.

ASPIDISTRA.

This genus, of which *Aspidistra lurida*, with its variegated form (Fig. 64), is the best known species, is of value as a house plant, and to the florist, to be used in decorations, on account of its hardiness and its ability to stand rough treatment. It is propagated by division, and with an abundance of moisture and a moderate temperature, it makes a rapid growth. A compost of rotten sods, sand and manure in equal parts seems adapted to it.

CHAPTER XII.

DRACÆNAS AND CORDYLINES.

The value of these plants is each year more and more recognized by florists, as their use for decorations is better understood; their increased popularity is also undoubtedly due to the many distinct and beautiful varieties that have been brought out in recent years. In these two genera are found a large number of plants, most of which are commonly known as Dracænas, but which are properly termed Cordylines. It is not strange that the nomenclature should be confused, as the genera contain many plants that can only be distinguished by their flowers and fruits, both of which are small and inconspicuous. The Dracænas, as a rule, have but a single ovule in each cell of the ovary, while the Cordylines have many; the flowers of the Cordyline are also much smaller than those of the Dracæna.

In the genus Dracæna, we find only a few species in cultivation, *D. concinna*, *D. Draco*, *D. elliptica*, *D. fragrans* and its varieties, *D. Goldiana* and *D. marginata* being best known. Among the Cordylines are the following species and varieties: *C. amabilis*, *Aus-*

tralis, Baptistii, cannæfolia, excelsa, gloriosa, imperialis, indivisa and its varieties, *magnifica, splendens, stricta, stricta congesta, terminalis* and *Youngii*. Several of the above, which are often put down as species, are merely varieties of the well-known *Cordyline (Dracæna) terminalis*.

Many of the Cordylines produce seed abundantly, and these can be used for propagation; they are sown in light, sandy soil, at a temperature of 60 degrees, and are potted off and treated the same as cuttings. Cuttings of the stems are commonly used for the propagation of the less common species, as well as Dracænas. The tips can be top-layered, or can be cut off and rooted; the lower portions of the stems are then cut into pieces two or three inches in length, and these are placed on the sand of a cutting bench and covered with sphagnum; they may be covered with sand or light soil, but there is more danger of decay. The fleshy roots of some species may be treated in the same way. In a strong bottom heat and with proper watering, sprouts will soon be sent out from both the stem and root cuttings, and as soon as these are of suitable size they should be cut off and rooted the same as any other cutting. In a propagating case, there will be but little risk, but it is still surer to root them in water, or by the saucer system. In the case, of choice species, the cuttings are sometimes set singly in small pots, filled with sandy soil, which are then plunged. In this way, all danger of breaking the roots in potting, thus checking the growth, is obviated. A light, rich soil, with perfect drainage, seems to suit these plants. If properly handled, they can be kept in quite small pots, and overpotting should be carefully avoided.

While some of the species belong in the stove, others will thrive with greenhouse treatment. During the summer they can be kept outside in a frame, or in a house where thorough ventilation and frequent syringings can be given; as with the Croton, the red spider and thrip are the worst enemies of these plants, and similar remedies should be given.

Dracæna marginata and *D. fragrans* are about the only plants of that genus that are of value to the florist; *D. Draco* is a magnificent plant for a large conservatory, while, although *D. Goldiana* is a very pretty little plant, it is of small value commercially. Of the Cordylines, *C. indivisa, Australis, grandis,* and *terminalis,* with their many varieties, are most useful. Some of the varieties with large, bright-colored leaves, such as *C. Alsace-Lorraine, Baptistii, imperialis* and *gloriosa* (syn. *Shepherdi*), present a more striking appearance in the conservatory, and if carefully handled will do well for decoration.

CROTONS (CODIÆUMS).

Few stove plants are more striking in their appearance than well-grown Crotons (or Codiæums, as they are more properly called), and none are easier to propagate and care for. Although it is supposed that all have come from not over three species, the variations in shape and color of leaf, and the habits of the plant, have been so great that there are hundreds of well-marked varieties in cultivation.

While Codiæums will grow at temperatures as low as 50 or 55 degrees, it is better to give them 60 degrees as a minimum night temperature in winter. They are readily propagated by top-layering the main stem or side branches, or, as is much easier and a more common method, by terminal cuttings of the half-hard wood. They may be made at any time, but generally the best plants are produced when started in the winter or early spring. The cuttings root readily when placed in sand in a propagating case or hotbed, but as they are likely to be checked if the roots are broken in potting, it is better to place them singly in small pots filled with light, sandy soil, and plunge in strong bottom heat under a hand glass, or other propagating case. As soon as rooted, they should be gradually hardened, until the pots fill with roots, when they should be repotted in a fibrous, sandy compost and returned for a few days to the propagating case, or a hotbed, to avoid a check; after being hardened and established they may be taken out. They require at all times a moist atmosphere to keep them free from the red spider, and hence frequent syringing is necessary. While they should never be allowed to become dry, care should be taken against over-watering, and as a safeguard they should be kept in as small pots as possible, helping them out in their growth with liquid manure. The use of water from which the chill has been taken will be of great value. If branching plants are desired, they can be secured by heading back the main stem to the proper point and, later, pinching in the branches. In this way, large specimen plants can be grown. In order to have them take on a good color, they should be given as much light as possible, by keeping them near the glass and out of the shade of other plants.

Codiæums can be used to advantage in brightening up a conservatory, or cool house, but the change from the stove room should be gradual, lest the plants receive a check and the leaves drop. While they have been used for bedding with success in the southern part of the country, it is only in warm and protected situations that they thrive north of latitude 41°. When thus used out of doors they should receive daily syringings.

Among the best varieties are *Codiæum Disrælii, C. Evansianum, C. gloriosum, C. illustris, C. interruptum, C. pictum, C. Queen Victoria, C. recurvifolium, C. Rothschildianum, C. variegatum, C. Veitchii* and *C. volutum.*

With the exception of the red spider, as mentioned above, the only other really troublesome insect enemy is the thrip, but with a proper amount of moisture, air and light, neither of them is particularly to be feared.

RUBBER TREES.

For decorating purposes, or as a house plant, the rubber tree has few equals, owing to its ability to withstand rough usage and neglect. The plants are generally propagated from single eye cuttings, and in this way they are multiplied quite rapidly. The plants are topped about the first of January and the tips are placed in the cutting bed. To succeed well in growing plants by this method, large, plump buds are desirable and the wood should be quite firm. If the plants are started into growth as they should be, the buds upon the stem towards the upper end will swell, and the stems can now be cut up and a cutting made from every portion that contains a bud. If the wood is hard, they will strike quicker if every cutting has a portion of bark removed from one side at the base of the bud, or cuttings can be made by splitting off from the stem the buds with bits of wood two inches long and one-fourth inch thick. The cuttings need a strong bottom heat, and if they can be in a propagating case, all the better. Some growers place the cuttings in pots filled with leaf mold and sand and plunge them into the cutting bed. When grown in this way, the lower leaves are generally quite small and, as they are inclined to drop from the stems, the cuttings are likely to make spindling plants.

A better, but a slower and more expensive, method of propagating the plants is by top-layering. For this, a plant from six to twelve months old, with short-jointed, thick stems, should be selected, and one that has lost its lower leaves is as good as any. To induce them to throw out roots, the stem should be cut or pierced, the best way being to bend the stem and make a sloping cut, upwards and towards the center of the stem, from an inch and one-quarter to an inch and one-half in length, according to the size of the plant. The plant is then wrapped with wet sphagnum, or moss of some kind, and staked securely. If kept properly moistened, roots will soon be emitted and the cutting can be potted off within four or five weeks. The buds left on the stem of the old plant will soon break and a branching plant will be formed. When propagated in this way, the young plants will be strong and vigorous and will be clothed with large, well-colored leaves from the pot up, and the time required will be comparatively short. The common rubber tree and its variegated form are both propagated in this way.

Rubber trees should be kept at about 60 degrees, and during growth need an abundance of liquid manure and frequent shifting. *Ficus Parcelli*, a beautifully variegated stove plant, is readily grown from cuttings or eyes, and requires the same care as *Ficus elastica*, except that as it is deciduous, more care should be taken to give it a period of rest during the winter.

CYANOPHYLLUM AND SPHÆROGYNE.

When well-grown, these are the most attractive of our stove foliage plants. They have a general resemblance, although the former has a nearly smooth stem and leaves, while those of the latter are quite hairy and fuzzy. They can be grown either from crown or eye cuttings, or from seed, if it can be secured. The eye cuttings are made by cutting the stems into pieces about two inches long, with a node at the center, and then splitting them, so that one of the opposite buds will be in each half. The cuttings may be placed on a layer of sphagnum in a propagating case and covered with sand, or, as is better if only a few are to be grown, by filling a small pot half full of fibrous peat, or sphagnum, and after the cuttings have been placed upon it, filling the pots with sand and plunging in a hotbed or propagating case. As soon as rooted, they should be repotted in a mixture of fibrous peat, rotten sods and sand. Thorough drainage is desirable, but the atmosphere can hardly be kept too moist, as the leaves expand; if the air is allowed to become dry, the leaves will be shrivelled and imperfect.

During the resting period, in winter, the temperature may drop to 60 or 65 degrees, but while making their growth they like a temperature of 75 or 80 degrees. When properly grown, they will be but little trouble, but they should be carefully watched that the mealy bug does not gain a foothold.

The most desirable species of these plants are *Sphærogyne latifolia* and *Cyanophyllum magnificum*. The foliage of the former has a particularly unique appearance, owing to a well-marked network that extends over the leaves.

MARANTAS AND CALATHEAS.

The genus Maranta formerly contained a large number of desirable stove plants, but most of them have now been placed in the genus Calathea. However, as they require about the same care, they can be treated together. The plants have tuberous or creeping rhizomes, and one species yields the arrow root of commerce. Although most of the species can be readily propagated by dividing the plants, the long rhizomes can also be made into cuttings. If cut up into pieces two inches in length, and these are placed in moist sphagnum in a hotbed or propagating case, the dormant eyes will each throw out shoots. These can be separated, rooted and potted off the same as any cutting.

The Maranta thrives in a loose, rich, moist soil, composed of rotten sods or leaf mold, peat and sandy loam, with perfect drainage. If propagated by division, the best time is in the spring before growth starts; the plants should be shaken and the rhizomes separated, leaving at least one eye upon each piece. After being potted, they should be watered and placed in a hotbed or propagating case until they become established. After being gradually hardened, they can be taken out.

During the summer, they like an abundance of moisture, particularly in the air, which can be secured by frequent syringings. During the summer they should have partial shade, with partial rest in the winter, and repotting will be desirable in the spring. Among the best varieties are *Maranta bicolor*, *M. Chimboracensis*, *M. Porteana*, and *M. smaragdina*. Of the Calatheas, we have *Calathea Kerchoviana*, *C. Legrelliana*, *C. Leitzi*, *C. Makoyana*, *C. Massangeana*, *C. roseapicta*, *C. Van der Heckei*, *C. Veitchii*, *C. Warscewiczii* and *C. zebrina*.

NEPENTHES.

This interesting genus of plants is not difficult of cultivation, if a proper amount of moisture in the air is provided. They are propagated from tip cuttings, or by cutting the ripened stem into pieces one or two inches long and placing them in moist sphagnum and fibrous peat in a brisk bottom heat, in the same way as the Dracæna is increased. Nepenthes thrive best in orchid baskets in fibrous peat and sphagnum, and as soon as the shoots have thrown out roots, they should be so arranged. The plants should never be allowed to become dry, and during their period of growth frequent syringings should be given them. The temperature for Nepenthes should not be allowed to drop below 60 degrees. When well grown, each leaf should bear at its extremity a pitcher from two to six inches in length, according to the variety. Among those of easy culture

176   GREENHOUSE MANAGEMENT.

FIG. 65. GROUP OF ANTHURIUMS AND ALOCASIAS.

are such well-known sorts as *Nepenthes Dominiana, N. Hookeriana, N. Mastersiana* and *N. Rafflesiana.*

DIEFFENBACHIAS.

The plants of this genus are very attractive and are readily grown. They are generally propagated by cutting the stems into single eye pieces, and if these are dipped in land plaster and slightly dried, it will lessen the liability of their decaying in the cutting bed. They can be started in the same way as explained for Cordylines, or pots can be half filled with sandy soil, on which the cuttings are placed, and the pots filled with sand and plunged in a brisk bottom heat.

As soon as the roots form, the cuttings should be potted in a rich, sandy compost, containing either peat, or rotten sods. Spring is the best time to propagate Dieffenbachias, as they require a high temperature. They should be kept near the glass, and repotted as is necessary. If desired, bushy plants can be secured by heading them in, and by a liberal use of manure water they can be grown to a large size. They need a moist atmosphere, and during the summer, syringing should not be neglected, as otherwise the red spider will gain the ascendency.

Among the best kinds are the *Dieffenbachia Bausei, D. Bowmanni, D. Leopoldii, D. magnifica, D. regina,* and *D. rex.* Resembling the above are several desirable species of Schismatoglottis, which are grown in about the same way as Dieffenbachias.

ANTHURIUMS.

In every collection of stove plants there should be at least a half dozen species of this showy and interesting aroid. The two classes, flowering and foliage, give us, on the one hand, a variety of large, velvety, distinctly veined leaves, and, on the other, flowers that are very durable, always present, and striking in form

178   GREENHOUSE MANAGEMENT.

FIG. 66. ALOCASIA METALLICA IN A STOVE HOUSE.

ANTHURIUMS. 179

and coloring. By hybridizing, many new and promising varieties have been recently brought out.

They are readily grown from seeds, when they can be obtained, but the usual method is by means of suckers and cuttings of the rootlike stem. The cuttings root readily in most species, but they should not be taken off until roots have been formed. Anthuriums

FIG. 67. AGLAONEMA PICTUM.

need a temperature of at least 55 degrees except when in flower, when they may be kept slightly lower, although some of the foliage sorts are benefited by 60 or 65 degrees at night. A slight shade from the bright sun is beneficial to them, and like all plants of the kind, they need an abundance of water while growing and should never be allowed to become dry. In the summer a daily syringing should be given them, with **slight** ventilation. Thorough drainage is necessary for them, and in potting the pots should be half filled with broken crocks on which the plants should be placed in a compost made of fibrous peat, sphagnum, fine crocks and sand, formed into a mound from one to three inches above the top of the pot. The plant should be held in place, if necessary, by means of small stakes. As the plants grow they should be repotted, using the same compost with the addition of a little rotten sods and manure, for the flowering sorts in particular.

Of the more desirable and common, hence lower priced, sorts are *Anthurium Andreanum*, with its large, dark red, leathery and corrugated recurved spathe; it is easily grown and a perpetual bloomer. *A. Scherzerianum*, with long leaves and scarlet spathe on red stems; the spadix is spotted with the salmon flowers. *A. S. maximum* is a form having much larger spathes; other forms of *A. Scherzerianum* vary in the color of their spathes. *A. Ferrieriense* (at upper part of Fig. 65), is a strong grower resembling *A. Andreanum*, except that the spathe is reddish pink with a white spadix. The spathe is not recurved as in that species. There are also many varieties and species of each of the above. Among the foliage anthuriums the better kinds are *A. crystallinum*, (at right of Fig. 65), with large, cordate, white veined, dark green velvety leaves; *A. Waroqueanum* (center of Fig. 65), deep green, velvety, lanceolate leaves often thirty inches long and eight or ten wide; and *A. regale*, having large cordate leaves with white veins. *Anthurium ornatum* and *A. splendens* are also valuable. One thing that makes this genus of plants particularly desirable is that, if reasonably well cared for, none of the insect pests of the greenhouse trouble them.

ALOCASIAS.

Allied to Anthurium is this genus of foliage plants, which, when well grown, present a striking appearance, with their distinctly marked and often oddly shaped leaves. Like the Anthuriums, the plants are propagated from suckers, seeds or cuttings of the rhizomes. The soil suited to them is not unlike that for Anthuriums, except that a larger proportion of lime can be used. They prefer a temperature of 60 to 65 degrees at night during the winter, and 75 or 80 degrees in the summer, with a moist atmosphere. An exception to this rule regarding the soil is *Alocasia macrorhiza*, and its variegated form, which delight in a rich compost of fibrous loam, sand and rotten manure in equal parts, in which, with an abundance of water and plenty of heat, they will grow to a large size. One of the most interesting species is *Alocasia Thibautiana* (at the left in Fig. 65), which has curiously lobed, greenish-black leaves, with broad, white veins. *A. metallica* (Fig. 66), (properly *A. cuprea*) has glossy, metallic, dark green leaves, with a purple luster beneath.

Aglaonema (Fig. 67) is an Arum closely allied to Alocasia and requires the same care.

CHAPTER XIII.

LETTUCE FORCING.

Within the last ten or fifteen years, the growing of crops of winter lettuce, in houses especially erected for the purpose, has become quite an important industry in many localities. Owing to improper methods of handling the crop, it was for a long time thought that hotbeds were preferable to forcing houses for lettuce growing, when large perfect heads were desired, but except for late fall and early spring, they are but little used to-day.

While every large city has one or more persons engaged in lettuce forcing, the industry seems to have reached its largest dimensions in the vicinity of Arlington, Mass., and Grand Rapids, Mich. Owing to the perfection of their methods, the lettuce growers of Arlington and Belmont have been able to compete with local growers, in the New York market. The industry is a comparatively new one in Grand Rapids, as it is but little more than ten years since Eugene Davis engaged in the business upon a small scale. So successful has he been that hundreds have gone into it, and the glass area used for the purpose has doubled each year since 1888, until in 1891 several hundred thousand square feet of glass were used in the erection of houses for lettuce forcing. The markets of Detroit, Cleveland, Columbus, Cincinnati, Chicago, Milwaukee and, in fact nearly all of the large cities within a radius of from 300 to 500 miles, are supplied with Grand Rapids lettuce, and it has been sent nearly one thousand miles to New

LETTUCE FORCING. 183

FIG. 68. EVEN-SPAN LETTUCE HOUSE, TENNESSEE EXPERIMENT STATION.

York city, and there competed successfully with the Long Island and Arlington product.

Much of the success obtained by these growers is due to the fact that they have varieties well adapted for forcing, and yet the kinds grown at Arlington and Grand Rapids are quite unlike. At the former place, and in fact throughout the lettuce-growing section of New York, New England and New Jersey, the cabbage or head lettuce is grown, the favorite sorts being selected strains of White Tennis Ball. Those that seem best adapted for the purpose are Hot House, selected and largely grown by W. W. Rawson of Arlington, Mass., and Belmont or Big Boston, which is the favorite sort with Hittinger Bros. of Belmont. At Grand Rapids, the only kind grown is one obtained by Mr. Davis by selection from Simpson, and which is known as Grand Rapids. Although in many markets it has been claimed that only head lettuce would sell, the dealers have seldom been able to supply the demand for Grand Rapids lettuce since it was introduced.

Among the strong points of this variety may be noted (1) its early maturity, as it develops about one week sooner than any other variety; (2) the closeness of planting that it will admit of, owing to its erect habit of growth. This permits the growing of as large heads when planted six inches each way as can be obtained from the spreading Tennis Ball sorts, at eight inches. (3). It seems to require less care, and to be less injured by neglect than most other varieties. Improper ventilation or watering frequently leads to the appearance of mildew, rot or burning of the leaves, but it is far less noticeable in the Grand Rapids than in any other variety.

LETTUCE HOUSES.

The even-span house (Fig. 68) is still commonly used for lettuce growing, but is being supplanted by the three-quarter span house, and by the lean-to

LETTUCE HOUSES. 185

lettuce house (Fig. 69). Unless of the low ridge and furrow plan, lettuce houses should not be less

FIG. 69. LEAN-TO LETTUCE HOUSE, MASSACHUSETTS AGRICULTURAL COLLEGE.

than twenty feet wide, and preferably should be as wide as thirty to thirty-three feet. Houses forty and fifty feet wide are not uncommon and prove satisfactory. The lean-to lettuce house described in Greenhouse Construction is cheaply constructed and gives excellent results, particularly if built upon a side hill, but the three-quarter span house is supplanting it in some localities, and will be found preferable for houses upon level ground that are more than thirty feet wide. The benches may be either raised or solid, a common plan when three beds are used in houses twenty feet wide being to have one solid bed in the center and raised benches at the sides, or the arrangement may be reversed. In some of the large houses, even if as wide as thirty-three feet, one solid bed is made in the center, leaving only space for narrow walks next to the walls, but a center walk in addition is desirable. Solid beds raised one or two feet above the walks, and not more than fifteen feet wide, are generally preferred to raised benches.

In many sections where fuel is cheap, the old-fashioned flue is still used with good results, and in fact a large per cent of Grand Rapids lettuce is grown in flue-heated houses. Steam is also largely used, and the heating plant is cheaper than hot water to put in, but, even in large houses, hot water in small pipes is preferred by many who have made a careful test of the two methods.

COMMERCIAL LETTUCE GROWING.

With good management, three or four crops of lettuce can be harvested, and the houses can then be used for the growing of vegetable plants, cucumbers, or tomatoes. It is desirable to have the first crop come on by Thanksgiving, or before, and for this purpose the seed should be sown in an old cold frame, or in a seed bed outside, especially prepared for the purpose, about the last of July or first of August. The bed should be marked off into rows six inches apart, and the seeds scattered thinly in the drills, or they may be sown broadcast. They should be covered with about one-half inch of soil, and the surface of the bed rolled, or pressed down with a board. After giving the bed a thorough watering, it should be covered with lath screens, and watered whenever it shows signs of becoming dry. When the plants have formed their first true leaves they should be transplanted to about two by six inches, or, if in drills,

FIG. 70. POT PLANT READY FOR PLACING IN PERMANENT BED. TENN. EXPERIMENT STATION.

thinned to two inches in the row. These plants will be ready to transplant to the beds about the 15th to the 20th of September, and all designed for the Thanksgiving trade should be in the beds by the first week in October. If the Christmas market is preferred to Thanksgiving, the seeds need not be sown until the middle of August, or a portion of the crop can be put in early and the balance held for a succession.

About the first of October, a second sowing should be made, and another for the third crop about the first of December, in beds or flats in the forcing house. That there may be no delay, it is a good plan to make a small sowing every week or two. When one inch high the plants should be pricked out into beds or flats, three or four inches apart each way, and as soon as they crowd should be placed in the beds at a distance of six inches for the Grand Rapids and seven and a half or eight inches for the large Tennis Ball sorts.

Another method, which is more economical of room, is to prick out the plants in flats or beds one and one-half or two inches each way, and when they begin to crowd transplant to the permanent beds, at distances varying from three to four inches, according to the variety. They are grown in this way until the leaves touch, when the extra plants are taken out, leaving the permanent plants from six to eight inches apart.

POT CULTURE OF LETTUCE.

A method of growing lettuce in which the plants are placed in flower pots has been tested by Prof. S. A. Beach of the Geneva, N. Y., Experiment Station, and Prof. R. L. Watts of the Tennessee Station. The seedling plants are pricked out in two and one-half or three-inch pots, and are grown there until the plants crowd, when the pots are placed close together (Fig. 70). They are then transferred to the permanent beds, where they are plunged at the usual distance, so that the tops of the pots will be covered one-half inch. They will require the same care as when planted in the bed and when marketed the plants may be slipped out of the pots, or not, according to circumstances.

It is claimed for this method that there is no check from transplanting, that the beds will only be occupied for four weeks, while if the plants are placed at once in the permanent beds it will be at least eight weeks before the crop can be taken off, and that there will be less loss in marketing, as, whether in the pots or not, the balls of earth (Fig. 71) will prevent the wilting of the leaves, and with proper care the heads can be kept over a week.

Our experience in lettuce growing in pots does not warrant our recommending it for general use, although the above claims have for the most part been substantiated. We find, however, that the check from transplanting is more than counterbalanced by the reduced size of the plants grown in pots, while by the use of the

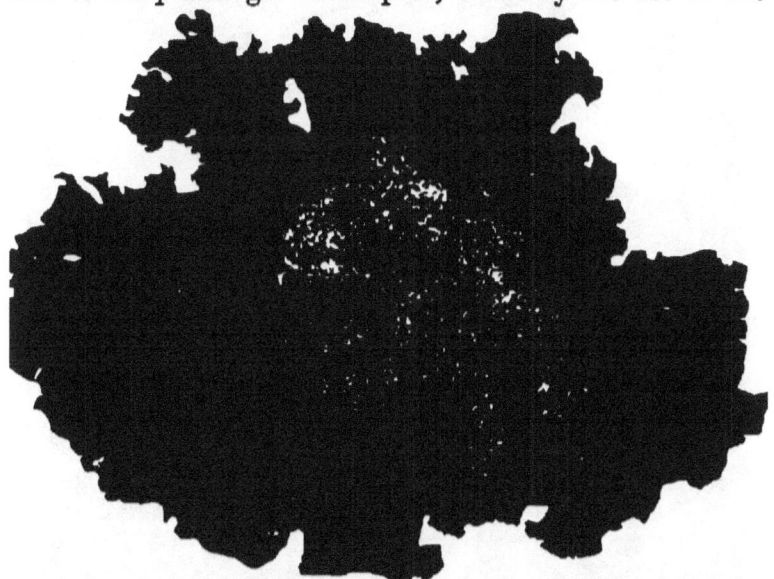

FIG. 71. POT PLANT READY FOR MARKET. TENN. EXP. STATION.

system of transplanting recommended above there is little if any saving in room, while the labor of transplanting is less than will be required in handling the pots and in plunging. There will undoubtedly be less loss when the plants are marketed with balls of earth attached, and this may make it a desirable method of growing lettuce for supplying small dealers.

PREPARATION AND CARE OF THE BEDS.

When shallow beds are used, the soil will all need to be replaced each year, but in solid beds it will suffice

FIG. 72. INTERIOR OF LEAN-TO LETTUCE HOUSE, HITTINGER BROS., BELMONT, MASS.

if three or four inches of the surface soil are removed, and the benches filled up with fresh manure, which should be thoroughly worked into the soil. The best compost for lettuce growing is made by mixing one part of fresh horse manure with two parts of rich, sandy loam. If this can be prepared in June, and worked over in August, it will be in good condition to use by the time it is wanted in September. The raised beds will need about five or six inches of soil, and after each crop has been taken off, it will be well to add about an inch of thoroughly decomposed horse manure. The soil in the solid beds should be ten inches deep, and should also be top-dressed as above.

After setting the plants, the beds should be thoroughly wet down, but while the plants are small care should be taken not to saturate the beds, particularly during dull weather in the winter. On sunny days the plants may be syringed in the morning, but if they are syringed in dull weather, or at the edge of evening, it is likely to invite the development of mildew and rot. As soon as growth starts, the bed should be worked over with a hand weeder, and this should be repeated once in two weeks, until the plants cover the bed (Fig. 72).

The temperature of lettuce houses should be kept below 50 degrees at night and in dull weather, while 45 degrees is high enough for the cabbage sorts at night. The houses should be kept well ventilated, using the sash that opens opposite to the direction of the prevailing wind, whenever this is possible. Keep coolest just after planting and when they begin to form heads.

The most troublesome insect pest in lettuce growing is the green fly or aphis, but this can be kept in check, if taken in time, by the use of tobacco stems. It is well to cut them up by passing them through a hay-cutter or coarse sieve, and then scatter the pieces over the beds. The stems themselves can be used in the same way and will tend to keep the fly in check. As soon as the presence of green fly can be detected, the house should be filled with tobacco smoke. This should be repeated at the end of two or three days, and, if properly done, the aphides will be destroyed.

As the insects develop, the tobacco smoke does not seem powerful enough to destroy them, and if for any reason fumigation has been neglected too long to be effective, resort must be had to some other insecticide. A strong decoction of tobacco stems and tobacco extract will destroy them, while pyrethrum or buhach seems quite effectual as a remedy against adult aphides, and may be put on as a dry powder with a bellows, or in water with a syringe, using at the rate of a tablespoonful to a gallon. When the houses are large, a small spraying pump will be convenient for applying these and similar insecticides.

When given proper conditions, the beds planted the first of October can be cut for Thanksgiving purposes, and can be cleaned out ready to be reset by the first of December. The next crop will develop by the first of February, and the third crop will be off by the first of April. Under especially favorable conditions, two or three weeks can be gained upon this, which will allow a fourth crop to be taken off by the middle of April.

About two months should be allowed for growing the plants after sowing the seed, and seven or eight weeks more for the growth of the heads after planting out. This will be none too much during the cloudy and short days of November and December, but as the sun gets higher in February and March, six weeks will generally suffice.

In marketing lettuce, the heads are placed vertically in baskets or boxes (Fig. 73) when supplied to the local trade, or in barrels for distant shipment. It is best to pack the cabbage sorts with the stems up, while

FIG. 73. LETTUCE PACKED FOR LOCAL MARKET. TENN. EXPERIMENT STATION.

the Grand Rapids and similar sorts are laid on their sides with the butts overlapping. Ventilate in warm weather, and line the barrels with newspapers in winter. Cover the top of the barrel with burlap.

As indicated on a previous page, the Grand Rapids is one of the best varieties for forcing purposes, while Boston Market, Hot House and Belmont are the best of the cabbage varieties.

ELECTRO CULTURE OF LETTUCE.

Some eight or ten years ago Mr. W. W. Rawson of Arlington, Mass., noticed that lettuce seemed to be benefited by the light from the electric street lamps, and to test its efficacy he placed a 2000 candle power arc lamp over one house, and ten 30 candle power lamps inside another house, with the effect of hastening the maturity of the crop fully five days, which would make a saving of fifteen days for three crops. Mr. Rawson is so convinced of the value of the electric light that he now has three 2000 candle power lights over one of his houses, and finds himself repaid three-fold by the effect on the crop.

These results induced Prof. Bailey to make various tests at the Cornell Experiment Station of the efficacy of the electric light upon the growth of different plants. After several years' trial, he finds decidedly beneficial effects from the electric light upon large lettuce plants, and that the maturity of the crop may be hastened at least one week. The lights were not run more than five hours a night. The results obtained by Prof. Bailey agree quite closely with the conclusions of various French investigators. It was found that naked lights inside the house injured most plants, but when opal globes were used the effect was quite beneficial in the case of lettuce. When the light enclosed in an opal globe was hung outside, about six feet above the glass, the best results were obtained. Even when forty feet away, the plants were noticeably benefited, except those newly transplanted, which were injured. Radishes, beets and spinach were also benefited when the lights were placed outside the houses, although the naked light inside the house was detrimental to their growth.

It has not been determined whether the effect of the light is in increasing the hours of growth, or in hastening the rapidity at which they grow during the customary period. The effect upon tomatoes and cucumbers is, if anything, injurious, and Mr. E. A. Lorentz of Orange County, New York, reports that with a street light 325 feet from the house, and running every night, all night, radishes were induced to run to seed, and the same effect would have been produced upon the spinach had it been given time. Upon lettuce, however, the effect was beneficial, and the crop was marketed two weeks earlier than that grown in another house, not exposed to the light.

LETTUCE IN HOTBEDS.

When one has a forcing house, or can afford to build one, it does not pay to grow lettuce in hotbeds in the Northern States earlier than the fifteenth of February or the first of March. If one has no forcing house, or other place for starting the plants, a small hotbed can be made for growing them as early as the middle of January, and they will be large enough to transplant by the middle of February. If they are put in thickly at first, and again thinned out, as recommended for growing them in forcing houses, a large number of plants can be started in a small bed, and besides saving labor in caring for the large beds, it will admit of giving the plants a fresh bed when finally transplanted.

Hotbeds can be used to good advantage in connection with a greenhouse, as seeds planted about the first of February will form plants large enough to place in the hotbeds by the fifteenth to the twenty-fifth of February, and will be ready for market as soon as the third crop has been cut from the house. By sowing seed at intervals of three or four weeks, a succession can be obtained from hotbeds and cold frames until field-grown crops mature. When there is a demand for lettuce during November, it can be grown in cold frames at a low cost, and if they are deep and are well covered on cold nights, it can be carried until Thanksgiving.

For hotbed and cold frame uses, the forcing house sorts answer very well, and such varieties as Chicago Market, Denver Market, and Black Seeded Simpson, will also be found desirable.

CONDITIONS FOR SUCCESS.

The principal reason why the lettuce specialists have such remarkable success is that every detail of handling the crop is properly attended to.

As of prime importance we consider (1), the character of the soil. This should be of a sandy nature, with less than five per cent of clay. If the clay is present in much larger quantities the surface of the soil, on becoming dry, will bake and form clods, and as it will remain wet and cold after watering, it is likely to induce the appearance of the rot. A good lettuce soil, properly supplied with drainage, will allow the surplus water to pass through it, and the roots will penetrate to a much greater depth than in a cold, heavier soil.

(2.) They not only have suitable varieties, but the best growers take pains to have selected plants from selected seeds of selected strains of those varieties. Having found a variety adapted to the wants of a particular market, each grower should raise his own seed, selecting it from plants that come nearest his ideal, carefully pulling up all others before they have blossoms. Care should be taken to reject all of the small, light seeds, as they will develop much weaker plants than will be obtained from large, plump seed. When transplanting, the weak plants should be rejected, and in this way an even stand of plants will be secured that will be ready for cutting at the same time, thus both securing a better crop and a saving in time.

(3.) Careful attention to regulating the temperature at night and to ventilation during the day. The burning of the edges of the leaves, which is so troublesome with head lettuce, is undoubtedly due to some neglect in these particulars. Sixty degrees answers well as a day temperature, but even at this, air should be given, and if it rises higher the ventilators should be opened wide.

(4.) Securing a steady growth of the plants and guarding against a check. Aside from the top-dressing that is desirable after each crop is taken off, the application of a little ground bone, wood ashes and nitrate of soda to the surface, will both increase the size of the plants and hasten their maturity.

(5.) So handling the houses that insects and fungous diseases cannot gain a foothold.

CHAPTER XIV.

CUCUMBERS, TOMATOES AND MELONS AS WINTER CROPS.

For many years, the forcing of tomatoes and cucumbers for winter marketing has been quite profitable near some of the large eastern cities, but at the present time there are fewer inducements to engage in the business than formerly, owing in part to the low price at which the southern-grown crops can be placed on the northern market, and the competition from the large number of persons who are now engaged in the business.

During the spring and early summer, after the time when lettuce can no longer be grown with success in the houses, there is still an opportunity of growing both of these crops with profit, as the houses can be used for nothing else at this time, and there will be but a small expenditure for fuel. In the winter, however, the expense of keeping up the necessary high temperature in the houses will be very large, and the prices sometimes run very low, but with good care fairly profitable returns will be secured.

When these crops are grown in beds, a crop of beans or lettuce can be taken off before the entire space will be needed by the vines. If either cucumbers or tomatoes are grown in solid benches, to follow a lettuce crop, the growth of the plants can be hastened, and fuel can be saved, by digging trenches under where the rows of plants are to be set, one foot wide and deep, and filling with fresh horse manure. This will gradually decompose and will furnish bottom heat to accelerate the growth of the plants and, later on, supply food for the development of the crop of fruit.

CUCUMBERS UNDER GLASS.

Many growers have found the cucumber a profitable crop, particularly to follow the second or third crop of lettuce, to be sold during the early summer. While cucumbers thrive in lean-to or span-roof houses, the three-quarter span forcing house seems particularly adapted to their growth. The house should be arranged so as to provide for thorough ventilation, but as cold air is injurious to the tender plants, the ventilators should be so situated as to admit fresh air without producing a draft. Ridge ventilators, hinged at the lower side, seem best of all for this purpose.

The heating apparatus should be arranged to furnish a night temperature of 65 degrees, and the pipes should be, at least in part, overhead. Perhaps the best arrangement will be to have the flow pipes overhead, and one or two returns on each side brought back on the plates, with the remainder under the benches, where they will provide the necessary bottom heat, when raised benches are used, or in the walks in houses with solid beds. This arrangement will prevent any downward currents of cold air upon the plants. The tables or beds may be arranged as in a rose house, or they may consist of a wide bench in the center and a narrow one at each side (Fig. 74). A house eighteen feet wide will be adapted for growing cucumbers, but any width up to thirty feet may be used, and the wider houses will generally be preferable.

When used as a succession crop, the cucumbers are not started until about December or January, but with a good market they will be found profitable if started in the fall, and fruited during the winter. The seeds should be sown either in four-inch pots, or in trans-

200 GREENHOUSE MANAGEMENT.

planting boxes, using light, sandy compost. Only one or two plants should be allowed to grow, but it is well to use one or two extra seeds. When the seeds are sown, the pots or boxes should not be filled more than one-half full of soil, but as the plants develop they should be filled up with rich compost. The seeds will germinate best at 70 or 80 degrees, and if started in a lettuce house, they should be placed in the warmest portion, upon about six inches of fresh horse manure, over which three inches of soil should be placed, and covered with hotbed sash, to hold the heat. Another method is to sow the seeds in flats filled with sand, and transplant to pots. The beds should be ten to twelve inches deep, with an inch or so of drainage at the bottom. Upon the clinkers, or similar material that is used for this purpose, a layer of rich pasture sods should be placed, and on this about six inches of rich compost, prepared about the same as for roses, except that more manure is desirable, and the soil used should be of a rather more sandy nature. While in the pots, the plants should not be checked by lack of water or of plant food, and under no conditions should they become pot-bound; they can be easiest cared for if plunged in a brisk bottom heat.

PLANTING AND TRAINING.

When about to run, they should be planted out, giving each plant at least four square feet of space. In houses with wide beds, it will be well to have the rows at least three feet apart, while five or six will be preferable, and to grow the plants with two in a box or pot, setting them three feet apart in the rows, and training the plants in opposite directions. Between the rows the trellises are placed. These consist of wires one foot apart upon either side of an A-shaped framework, extending nearly to the glass. The vine will be trained up on either side and it will form a series of galleries.

within which the cucumbers can be gathered and the vines tended. Still another way, in lean-to, or three-quarter span houses, is to plant them in rows two feet apart, with five or six feet between the rows, training them towards the south upon wire trellises inclined at an angle of about 45 or 50 degrees. The rows should be about five feet from the south side of the beds. For use in ordinary even-span houses, with a wide bed in the center, and narrow ones on the sides, a good method is to plant two rows in each of the side beds and four in the center, at intervals of two feet each way, but so that the plants in one row will stand halfway between those in the adjoining row. The wires, each of which is to support one of the vines, are placed one foot apart and run from the walls to a point below the ridge, at a distance of from ten to twelve inches below the glass. Stakes or strings are used to support the vines until they have reached the wires upon which they are to run. When the vines in the outer row have reached a point over the edge of the center bed, they should be pinched off, as should those in the center bed when they reach the ridge. This will cause side shoots to be sent out upon which the fruits will be formed.

When grown in solid beds, the necessary bottom heat can be provided by making a hotbed under each row. When the rows are close together, it will be necessary to place the heating material under the entire bed, but if three feet or more apart, it will only be necessary to make a bed of fresh horse manure, about one foot wide and deep, which is tramped down and covered with eight inches of soil. When upon raised beds, the required bottom heat can be secured from steam or hot water pipes, as can also be done in solid beds.

To supply a crop during the early winter, the seed should be sown about the first of August, and can be transplanted to the bed in about one month. In less than two months after being placed in the beds the cucumbers should be ready for market. If to follow the second crop of lettuce that will be taken off in January, the seed should be sown the first of December, and after being transplanted into four- or five-inch pots, will be ready to be placed in the beds as soon as they are filled with roots.

For a few days after the plants are set in the beds, the temperature at night should not be above 60 degrees, but as soon as the plants are established it should be gradually raised to 65 degrees at night, and it may reach 80 or 85 degrees during the day if the sun is shining, but it will be desirable not to have it above 70 degrees in cloudy weather. With this high temperature, there is great danger of red spider, and the walks should be wet down morning and evening, and the plants should be occasionally syringed on bright mornings, with water from which the chill has been taken.

Unless the soil is deep and rich, liquid manure can be used to advantage once a week after the roots have penetrated all parts of it, especially if the plants are close together, and mulching is also advisable.

POLLINATION.

In order to secure the development of fruit upon most of the common varieties of cucumbers, artificial fertilization of the flowers must be resorted to, when they are grown in forcing houses during the winter, unless a hive of bees is placed in the house for the purpose of carrying the pollen from the staminate flowers to the pistils. It can be done by taking the pollen upon a small brush and dusting it over the pistils, and will be necessary unless some of the English forcing varieties are grown. They will develop without pollen, and it is thought by some growers that they should not be pollinated, as it is likely to cause an enlargement at the ends of the fruit. Of course, the seeds will not fill out unless

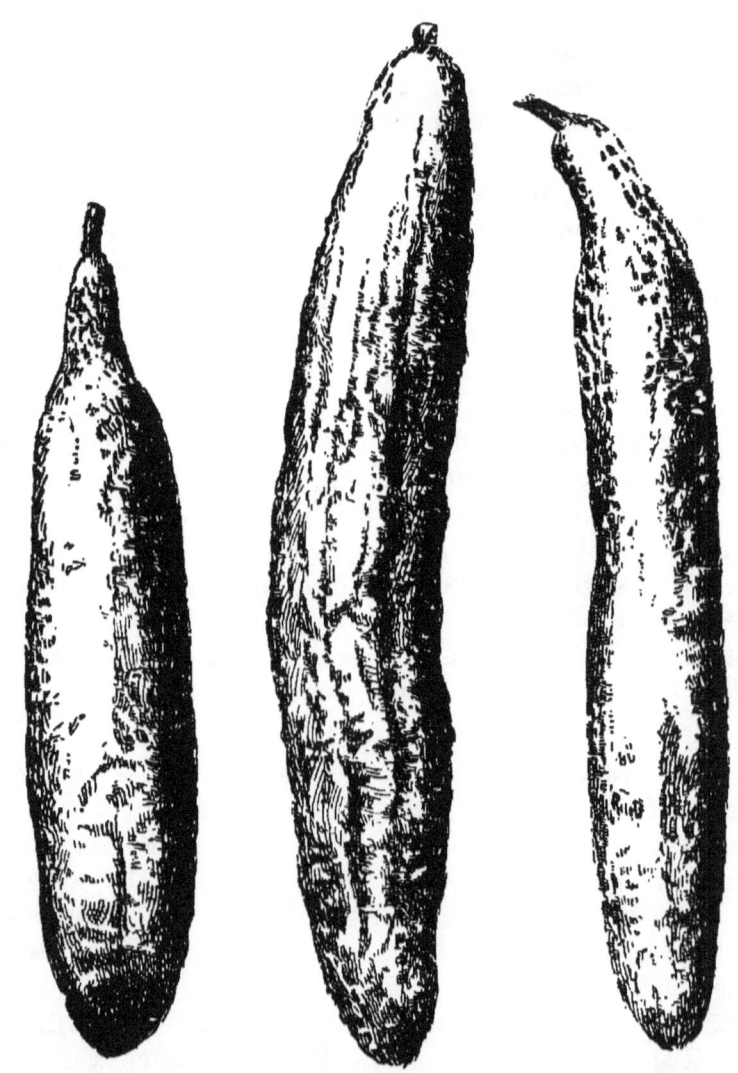

SION HOUSE.   DUKE OF EDINBURGH.   TELEGRAPH.
FIG. 75. ENGLISH FORCING CUCUMBERS. TYPICAL FORMS GROWN AT CORNELL EXPERIMENT STATION.

the flowers are fertilized, and this will be an improvement, in addition to what is gained in the improved form of the fruits, and in labor.

As the fruits develop, the larger ones should be supported by slings of raffia, to relieve the vines of their weight and prevent their being torn from their supports, but if the vines are carefully tied to the trellis, with raffia, the ordinary varieties can be grown without tying up the fruits. The crop should be ready for market in from sixty to eighty days from the date of sowing the seed.

VARIETIES.

For most markets the common garden varieties are the only ones that are profitable, the White Spine and a strain known as Arlington White Spine being most commonly grown. The English forcing cucumbers have a flavor distinctly their own, and retain their green color much longer than the ordinary sorts. They often reach a length of two feet, and are edible after they attain their full development. Of the forcing sorts, Sion House (Fig. 75) is most commonly grown. It is smooth, regular in shape, and something over a foot in length; Telegraph is long, smooth and slender, with a length of from sixteen to twenty inches; Marquis of Lorne is still larger, and is an excellent variety for one of its size. Duke of Edinburgh is another very long variety. In growing cucumbers under glass, the black plant louse and the spotted mite are quite troublesome, but they can readily be kept in check by syringing the plants with fir tree oil, or tobacco water.

The plants are also subject to the attack of various fungous diseases, one of the most injurious of which is the powdery mildew. For diseases of this kind, evaporated sulphur will be found an excellent remedy.

THE FORCING OF TOMATOES.

The tomato flourishes under about the same conditions as the cucumber, and may be grown in the same house, with good results. If it is desired, two crops can be grown, one ripening in December and the other in April. For the first crop, the seed should be sown in July, and the seedlings transplanted into shallow boxes in August; about the first of September they may be placed in four-inch pots, or again in flats, and by the first of October may receive their final transplanting. This can be into ten-inch pots, into beds similar to those used for cucumbers, or into deep boxes. If grown in pots or beds, the soil should be prepared in the same way as for cucumbers; if boxes are used, they should be one foot deep and from ten to eighteen inches square, according to the number of plants grown in them. The large size with four plants will, perhaps, give best results. Unless a large crack has been left in the bottom of the box, several holes should be made, in order to provide thorough drainage. For commercial growing, the use of beds is preferable, with two rows of plants on side benches three to three and one-half feet wide; from eighteen to twenty inches each way will be right for wider beds.

If a succession is desired, seeds may be sown at intervals of four weeks, and for the second main crop the sowing should be made about the first of December. When the plants are desired to follow the crop of lettuce taken off in February, the seeds may also be sown at that date. The same care will be required as for the seeds sown in August.

The best temperature for the tomato for the first few weeks after planting is about 55 degrees, but when established it should be raised to about 65 degrees, and should not be allowed to fall below 60 degrees at night. During the day the temperature may run up to 75 or 80 degrees, but ventilation should be given when it can be done without creating a draft or dropping the temperature below 65 or 70 degrees. If only a cool

THE FORCING OF TOMATOES. 207

FIG. 76. INTERIOR OF TOMATO FORCING HOUSE, MAINE AGRICULTURAL COLLEGE.

house is available for starting the plants, a hotbed should be made for them, the same as for the cucumber.

As recommended for the cucumber, it is well to fill the pots or boxes only about half full at first, thus allowing of the application of a liberal amount of rich compost, when needed

TRAINING AND PRUNING.

As soon as the plants start into growth after being finally transplanted, some arrangement should be made for supporting them. They may be tied to stakes (Fig. 76) with raffia, or, which is perhaps a better method, to vertical supports of linen twine. If a stout wire is run along the rafters over each row of plants, the twine can be fastened to it as a support, while the lower end can be held in place by a stake, inserted near the plants, or it can be tied to the plant near the ground. Others use trellises similar to those described for the cucumber. If early fruits are desired, the vines should be trained to simple shoots, and all suckers that form in the axils should be rubbed out as soon as they show themselves. At the hight of six feet, the growth of the main shoot should be stopped. If the growth is so rank as to shade the plants, some of the larger leaves should be pinched off, but if they have plenty of light and air, the leaves should all be allowed to develop, unless they become diseased, when they should be removed and burned.

When the crop is not particularly needed as an early one, two or three shoots may be trained from each plant, if desired. In either case, the method of pruning and training is the same, and the shoots should be tied at frequent intervals, to hold them in place. If the plants have been set about twenty inches apart each way (from eighteen to twenty-four according to the variety), the pruning recommended above will be ample.

For the winter and early spring crops, artificial fertilization of the blossoms is very desirable. At the time the pollen is shed, the house should be kept quite warm and the atmosphere dry. By gently shaking or tapping the blossom shoots, the pollen will be scattered to some extent, but larger and more regular fruits will be obtained if the flowers are artificially cross-fertilized. Perhaps the easiest way of doing this is to take pollen, obtained from flowers collected the previous summer and dried, upon a small paddle and touch it to the stigmas of the flowers. Bees may also be used for fertilizing this crop. As the fruits develop, if large varieties are grown, it will pay to support the clusters by means of slings of raffia. From the plants started about the first of August, fruit should be obtained in November, and from three to four months will be required by the spring crop after the seed is sown.

VARIETIES.

In selecting varieties for forcing, the very early angular sorts should not be chosen, as, when forced, they are very small and irregular; neither should the very large, rough sorts be used, as they will be more irregular than when grown in the open air. The Beauty is one of the best of the purple sorts, and Ignotum and Volunteer, of the red kinds, answer well for the spring crop, but as an early winter variety, the Advance, or Lorillard, should be used. Nicholson is also well adapted to winter forcing. From two to five pounds per plant, according to the season, would be a fair crop, and the wholesale price will vary from ten cents per pound in May, to forty or fifty in January, and at this rate will be quite remunerative.

GENERAL RULES.

To obtain the best results in forcing tomatoes during the winter months: (1.) The house must be built so as to afford the plants as much sunlight as possible; it should have a space of at least six feet above the tables.

and the heating apparatus should be ample to keep the house at 60 degrees during the coldest weather. (2.) The plants should be of forcing varieties and should never be subjected to a check for want of food, water, air, or warmth, or from an excess of any of these. (3.) In watering, use enough water to moisten the entire soil, and then withhold until the plant shows signs of needing more. When the plants are small, and at other times when the fruit is not setting, syringe the plants on

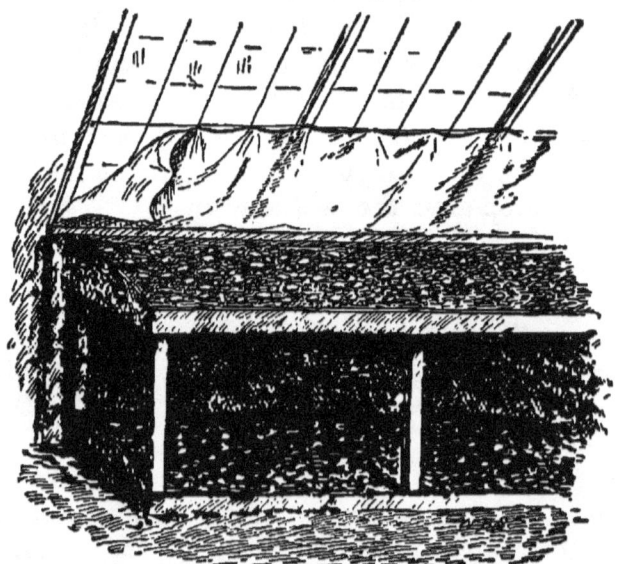

FIG. 77. GROWING MUSHROOMS ON GREENHOUSE BENCHES.

bright days and keep the walks wet down. Whenever fruit is setting, the house should be kept warm and dry. The atmosphere can be deprived of much of its moisture by ventilating during the warm part of the day.

The red spider is one of the worst enemies in the tomato forcing-house, but the above treatment will keep it in check. If the soil is kept too wet, the development of nematodes or eel worms upon the roots is invited and they frequently rot off. The stems and foliage are also attacked by various bacterial and fungous diseases. They are induced by overwatering, or ventilating, and by syringing the plants upon dull days and late in the day, when the moisture remains a long time upon the foliage. When fungi of any kind appear, the diseased portion should be burned and the plants syringed with ammoniated copper carbonate, or copper sulphate solution.

MELONS.

During the early summer, vegetable houses can often be used for forcing melons, with profit. They should be started in March, and grown in four-inch pots until the lettuce or other crop is taken off in April. The care is the same as for the cucumber. Hackensack is one of the best sorts for the purpose.

CHAPTER XV.

MUSHROOM CULTURE.

It often happens that in greenhouses there is no occasion for using the space beneath the benches for ordinary greenhouse crops, and many florists have found in the mushroom a crop that can be grown at a slight extra expense of labor and material, and if a good yield is obtained the proceeds may more than equal those from the plants grown on the bench itself. If any of the tables are not to be used until spring, a mushroom bed can also be made upon them, and the crop can be harvested before the bench is needed.

The best results are obtained at temperatures of from 55 to 60 degrees, and this is secured in the average greenhouse. When houses are run at a slightly lower temperature, a larger amount of heating material can be

212   GREENHOUSE MANAGEMENT.

used, and if the sides of the table are closed in, the temperature can be kept at the desired point. The great trouble in growing mushrooms under the benches is in

FIG. 78. GROWING MUSHROOMS UNDER THE BENCHES.

the soaking of the bed by the drip, but when the plants on the benches are planted out, there will be less drip than when grown in pots, and with care in watering, no harm need be done. If drip cannot be prevented in any other manner, it can be kept from the mushroom bed by placing spare shutters or glass sash over the bed, at an angle so that the water will be carried away. Fig. 77 illustrates the use of spare benches in the greenhouse, for mushroom growing, while Fig. 78 shows the results that may be obtained under the benches.

In growing the mushroom, quite a quantity of manure is required, and it is considerable labor to prepare it and to make the bed, but as the manure, after being used to grow the mushroom, is worth as much as before for many greenhouse crops, the labor of preparation only can be charged to the mushrooms. Mushrooms are usually grown in cellars, where the heat and moisture can be controlled, but they can even be grown successfully in open sheds during the fall, and in England they are very largely grown in the open air. When grown in hothouses, the thing to avoid is an excess of heat, which would destroy the bed, but in the ordinary rose houses, or those of a still lower temperature, they can be grown without difficulty.

PREPARATION OF THE MATERIAL.

For the growing of mushrooms, fresh horse manure is necessary, and if this is carefully prepared, if the spawn is good and if the proper conditions are given, mushrooms are quite a sure crop. For this purpose, the horses should be fed on hay and grain and not on roots, as they injure the manure for mushroom beds. It has been recommended by some, that all straw be shaken out and only the clean droppings used, but while it is not desirable to use the clean straw from the bedding, if it is urine-soaked it may be used to advantage to the extent of at least one-half. Manure that has been made for several weeks, if it has not become "fire-fanged," can be used, and, in fact, it is better to use manure that has been well packed down in a pile for a month, even, than to take manure as made in small quantities, placed in a pile and forked over every day until a supply is obtained for the bed, as is recommended by some authors. When fresh manure is used, the crop comes on quickly, and although it may last only a short time, it will be fully as large as one from old manure, which will last twice as long, and occupy the space for that much longer time.

Having obtained a sufficient quantity of manure, it should be prepared for use in the bed. This can best be done under a shed, as the rain will then be kept off, and the manure will be less subjected to the drying action of the sun and wind, although during the summer and early autumn months, the manure may be prepared in the open air, if the pile is kept covered with straw and mats, or shutters, to keep off the rain. If a sufficient amount cannot be obtained at one time, care should be taken that what is first obtained does not burn or fire-fang. It should be placed in a pile, and after being leveled off should be well tramped. If it shows signs of heating, it is well to spread it out, and after it has become cool, replace as before. As soon as a sufficient supply has been secured, it should be worked over and broken up, thoroughly mixing it together, rejecting all portions that are "burnt," as well as the coarse, dry straw and all foreign matters.

It is then placed in beds about three feet high, and five or six wide, leveling off the pile and packing it down with the fork. If the manure is at all dry, it is well to moisten each layer, using tepid water, if convenient, particularly in the winter. As soon as fermentation begins and the pile has warmed through, the mass should be turned over and made into a rectangular bed, as before. As it is being worked over, it should be well shaken out, and the outside portions worked into the center. If any of the manure seems dry, it may again be watered, using a watering pot with a fine rose, and, if the pile was well warmed through, it will be well to tread the bed lightly, as it is made up, thus lessening the liability of burning in the center. In perhaps three or four days, the mass will again warm up, and before it has had time to burn, it should be again turned over; the turning should be repeated generally from three to five times.

The working over is for the purpose of securing a regular, even heat throughout the pile, and of preventing "fire-fanging." As the mass warms up, the rapidity of fermentation can be checked by firmly tramping the pile, as it is worked over. The turning should be kept up until the violent heat is over, and the strong offensive odor has been dissipated. When properly purified and sweetened, the bed should be a homogeneous mass of a warm brown color, and with a "sweet," agreeable and slightly pungent odor. If properly prepared, the material should have a greasy appearance, but should not be so moist as to allow even a drop of water to be squeezed out. Most growers add to the manure about one-fourth its bulk of loam, the amount varying with the freshness of the manure, more being used when it is fresh than if decomposed. The addition of the loam is thought to benefit by hindering decomposition and thus extending the productiveness of the bed; it also serves to retain the ammonia and in this way may be of value, although its use is not regarded as necessary, and it is entirely dispensed with by some growers.

The loam is generally obtained from land that has not been pastured for two years at least, as it otherwise might contain worthless fungi that would prove troublesome, although by some of the most successful growers this precaution is considered unnecessary. The manure may be mixed with the loam, at the time it is first piled up, at any time during its preparation, or when ready to be placed in the mushroom bed, but an excellent plan is to use it to cover the pile, after it has been worked over once or twice, and then as it receives its next working it can be thoroughly mixed with it. By incorporating it with the manure at this time, it will serve to lessen the danger of burning, and the pile need not be turned as frequently. Ordinary field loam will answer, but Mr. Falconer recommends the use of sod loam, if the material in the spent bed is to be used for potting plants which would certainly make it more valuable for that purpose.

MAKING THE BED.

The depth of the bed should depend upon the freshness of the material and the location of the bed, so far as the temperature of the surrounding air is concerned. With fresh manure alone, in a warm place, nine inches will answer, but if loam has been added it should be from ten to twelve inches deep. Decomposed manure would need to be made about three inches deeper than that in a fresh state, but should not be used in a cool place, without the addition of fresh droppings. In making the beds in a greenhouse, the top should be level, or with a slight slope toward the walk. Perhaps the best plan is to have the bed at the front about nine inches deep, and at the rear twelve inches.

Whether made under the benches or upon them, it is well to have a board of the proper width along the front. If the space allows, it is an excellent plan to place a hotbed frame under or upon the bed, or at least to place boards about six feet apart, to form the edges of the mushroom bed, which should then be covered with hotbed sash or shutters. The manure should be shaken evenly over the bed, packing it down with a fork, thus filling it up in thin, even layers spread over the surface. When a bed is filled, a gentle treading will benefit it, and when under the greenhouse benches, the desired result can be secured by beating it down with a brick, or wooden pounder. Unless thorough ventilation can be given, the surface of the bed should be covered with three or four inches of dry straw, as the moisture arising from the bed would be condensed upon the surface, and render it cold and wet.

A thermometer should now be inserted, that the temperature of the interior of the bed may be noted. If properly prepared, it will rise at first to 115 or 125 degrees, but it should not go much above this. Should the temperature reach 130 degrees, it is well to cool down the surface in some way, either by forking it over to the depth of three or four inches, or by ventilating, by making holes with a dibble. As soon as the excess of the heat has passed off, the bed should be again compacted, and the holes carefully filled. Should it happen that, owing to the use of partially rotten manure, the temperature does not get above 80 degrees, it will be well to strengthen the bed by adding a couple of inches of fresh droppings, which should be well worked in. A temperature of 75 or even 70 degrees, if proper material was used in the bed, will, however, suffice, and the bed will last longer than if a high temperature was secured. When the bed has cooled down to 85 degrees, the spawn may be inserted.

MUSHROOM SPAWN.

The term spawn is given to the white, threadlike network that makes up the real body of the fungus, while the mushroom, or edible portion, is merely the fruit stalk. The spawn, or mycelium, spreads through the soil and after gathering a sufficient amount of food, the fruit stalk is sent up, on which the spores or seeds of the fungus are developed. While the spores, under proper conditions, will develop the fungus, this method is not resorted to in practice, as the spawn used in starting new beds is secured by a process of division similar to the growing of flowering plants from cuttings. If portions of old mushroom beds, containing the spawn in the form of white threads, are placed in a dry place, they will preserve their vitality for several years, but should not be relied upon for spawning mushroom beds.

As generally used, however, mushroom spawn is in the form of bricks, or flakes, the former being known as English and the latter as French spawn. It is all imported, and the amount used is steadily increasing, the annual consumption being several hundred thousand pounds. The bricks (Fig. 79) are about eight inches long, five inches wide and one and one-fourth inches

FIG. 79. BRICK SPAWN.

thick. They are made by mixing two parts of fresh horse manure, one part cow manure and one part loam, and adding a little chopped straw. This is made of about the consistency of mortar, and after being worked over two or three times, at intervals of two days, it can be made into bricks with molds, or by cutting it with a spade; when first made, the usual size of a brick is nine by six by two inches. They should be set on edge and placed in the sun and air for a few days, and when about half dry a small piece of spawn should be placed in the center of each brick, carefully filling up the holes with fresh brick material. A mild hotbed is then made, upon which the bricks are stacked and covered with litter to hold the heat. If kept at about 60 degrees, the mycelium will soon run through the bricks; as soon as the white threads have run through the mass, and before the tubercles have formed, the bricks should be taken out and dried.

The French spawn (Fig. 80) is prepared by treating fresh horse manure in about the same way as if for a mushroom bed, except that chopped litter is used instead of loam. This may be spread in a layer about three inches deep, and after scattering over it some good

FIG. 80. FRENCH SPAWN.

spawn, it should be pounded down; two or three more layers of manure may then be added, with spawn upon each, and the bed then covered with loam to the depth of three or four inches. The bed should be kept rather dry, and at the end of about six or eight weeks the spawn will have run through the bed. This stage should be carefully looked for, and when reached the bed should be broken up and carefully dried. The French spawn will go about twice as far as the English in spawning the bed, but the mushrooms, as a rule, are not more than two-thirds as large, and the number is also considerably smaller.

SPAWNING THE BED.

The spawn should not be inserted until the temperature of the bed at two inches below the surface has fallen to 90 degrees. When bricks are used, they should be cut into twelve or fifteen pieces, and inserted in the bed at intervals of ten to twelve inches, so that they will be covered fully an inch. The flake spawn should be inserted in about the same way, using about one-half as much.

If grown in a cool place, or if there is danger from moisture, it is well to cover the bed, after spawning, with two or three inches of litter, if it is not to be molded at once. By molding is meant, covering the bed with loam to the depth of about two inches. This can be done immediately after spawning, but unless the conditions are particularly favorable, it will be safer to delay it until from the fifth to the tenth day, yet it should not be put off after the twelfth day from spawning. The loam used for this purpose should be about the same as for preparing the bed. Sod from an old pasture, garden soil or sandy loam, will answer, but any soil containing much clay or a considerable quantity of sand should be rejected. All clods and coarse material of all kinds should be thrown out, and it should then be placed over all exposed parts of the bed, to the depth of from one and one-half to two inches, and firmly packed down, particularly on the edges of the beds.

CARE OF THE BED.

The best results are obtained when the beds are in an atmosphere of about 58 degrees; this can vary four or five degrees each way, but if raised above 65 degrees a failure may be expected. On the other hand, the temperature of the air may fall several degrees below the freezing point, but if the bed is covered with several inches of litter, and the heat is kept in by means of mats and blankets, no harm will be done. For all temperatures under 45 degrees, covering should not be neglected. In warm rooms, and after the air becomes warm in summer, the mushrooms will be light and with long spindling stems, while the bed will soon be exhausted. When kept at 55 to 58 degrees, the mushrooms will appear in seven or eight weeks, according to the warmth of the bed, after spawning, while at 60 degrees, it may not be much over six weeks, but the crop will not last.

WATERING THE BEDS.

When properly prepared, especially if the bed is in a cellar, or in a shaded house, watering should not be necessary, but when artificial heat is used the beds quickly dry out, and should be watered, if the mushrooms have begun to form. The water should be at 90 to 100 degrees, and should be used in sufficient quantity to wet down the mulch. If clean, soft water is used, it may touch the small mushrooms without injuring them, and may be used in sufficient quantity to moisten the covering soil, but it *should not reach the manure.* As soon as the mushrooms are up, liquid manure or fresh urine may be used with good effect. If the air is not dried out by the heating pipes, a sufficient degree of moisture can be maintained by sprinkling the walks. Water should never be used at the time the spawn is beginning to run, as it may ruin the bed.

GATHERING THE CROP.

In England, where mushrooms are so commonly grown, they are distinguished according to their development, as "buttons," "cups" and "broilers." The "buttons" are the mushrooms gathered while quite small, and before the "veil," or the membrane which connects the cup with the stem, bursts; they are always gathered at this stage when used for soups, and if grown from French spawn.

The English mushrooms, if to be used for other purposes than in soups, may be gathered just after the frill breaks, when they are known as cups, or may be left until the cups begin to open out flat, when their use is indicated by the name that has been given them, broilers. Care should be taken to gather them before the gills turn brown, as they will lose their flavor and become tough and leathery. While broilers weigh considerably more than cups or buttons, they do not bring as much per pound, and as the bed will be exhausted much sooner when they are allowed to develop than if picked before the frill breaks, it is not always profitable to grow them to the largest size. The cup is the size most generally marketed, and they are gathered by giving them a sharp twist and pull, and placing in baskets with the stems down. Pulling will be found preferable to cutting, as none of the crop will then be wasted, and the mushrooms will keep fresh longer than if the stems are cut off.

When mushrooms are gathered, it is best to take all that will answer, and the picking should be at frequent intervals, that none may become too old. In packing the mushrooms, they should first be sorted into three sizes, and after removing all dirt with a soft brush, pack them carefully in the boxes or baskets provided for the purpose. If to be sent any distance, a shallow, wooden box will be desirable, but for local markets, light baskets holding from one to ten pounds, according to the wants of the customers, may be used. The mushrooms should be packed quite firmly, and if more than two layers are placed in the packages, they should be separated by soft paper. One-pound packages are most commonly used.

A well-made mushroom bed will remain in bearing about three months, and although if kept at too low a temperature it may continue to yield a crop for five or six months, the total weight will be no more than in the first case. The spawn can produce about so many mushrooms and will keep on, over a period varying with the surroundings, until it becomes exhausted. One pound per square foot is an excellent crop, while half that quantity is a good average, and mushrooms seldom sell for less than fifty cents per pound wholesale in the winter months. When the crop has been taken off, if the litter is removed, the bed moistened with lukewarm water, an inch or two of loam added and the litter replaced, a second crop can generally be obtained.

The mushrooms are attacked by a number of insects, and for description and remedies the reader is referred to the chapter treating on "Insects and Diseases."

A NEW MUSHROOM.

In the summer of 1891, Mr. Boulon, a market gardener on Long Island, New York, discovered a new form of mushroom, which gave such returns that he grew it largely the following year. In 1892, the same form came under the eye of Wm. Falconer, then editor of *Gardening*, who brought it to the attention of Prof. C. H. Peck, who pronounced it a new species and named it *Agaricus subrufescens*. It differs from our common mushroom in being larger and coarser, with a lighter yellow neck and white gills. The cap is broader and thinner and somewhat lighter in color. When grown out of doors, it has a coarse, mushroom-like appearance, but in the house, especially if in darkness, it seems to bleach out and lose its coarseness.

It is an excellent mushroom for growing in the summer, as it develops so rapidly that it almost escapes the maggot, and it does equally well in winter, provided it can be given a high temperature. Beds made underneath the benches, where under-bench **piping** is used, generally do well if covered with a thick mulch to retain the moisture. Besides requiring more heat than our common mushroom, it also needs much more moisture, and many of the failures that have been met with growing it can generally be traced to the lack of one or the other. As a rule, however, it has been found rather irregular in bearing, but when one learns its proper care, it is certainly promising as a winter mushroom, and very valuable for summer growing.

During the summer a hotbed has been found to answer well for growing this mushroom (Fig. 81).

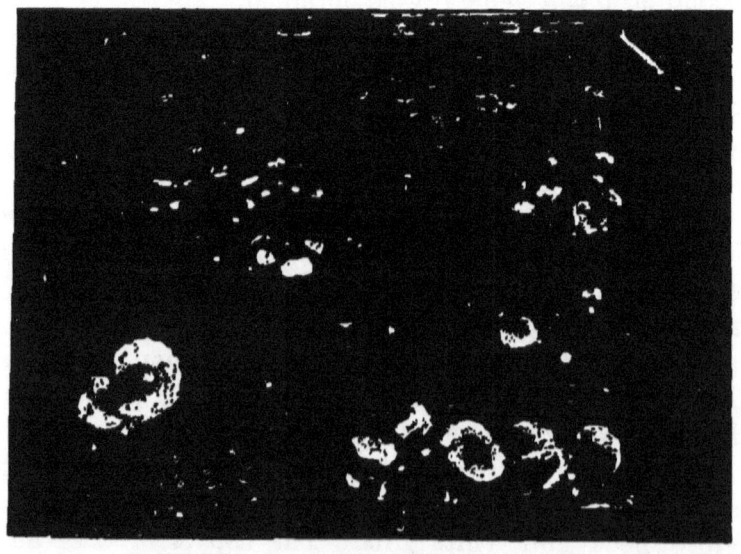

FIG. 81. THE NEW MUSHROOM (*Agaricus subrufescens*) IN A COLD FRAME.

After the bed is spawned some other crop may be put in and can be taken off before the mushroom will appear.

A CHEAP MUSHROOM HOUSE.

Many persons desire to grow mushrooms who perhaps have no greenhouse, or who have no place in it suitable for them. Aside from the needed heating apparatus, a house that will answer for the purpose can be constructed at a small cost.

A convenient form is built about the same as a narrow even-span greenhouse, except that there is but little glass in the roof and gables. Use posts about nine feet long, and having made an excavation three and one-half feet deep, twelve feet wide and of the desired length, set them around it about four feet apart, and so that they will be two feet in the ground. Double board upon the outside of the posts, and complete the gables and roof the same as if for a barn. A still cheaper roof can be constructed by using boards covered with hay. A small sash every fifteen feet along the roof will give all the light needed to handle the crop. Bank the excavated soil against the outside of the walls, up to the level of the plate. Constructed in this way there will be room for three beds, one above the other along each wall, with a three-foot walk in the center. The bottom tier of beds should be made on the floor, and if the others are placed thirty inches apart, it will give space for the making of the beds and caring for the crop. With the walls well banked, the necessary heat can be provided by four or five one and one-half-inch hot water pipes.

If a house twenty feet wide is preferred, it should, in addition to the three tiers of beds along each side, have three or four beds six feet wide in a rack through the center of the house.

CHAPTER XVI.

ASPARAGUS, RHUBARB AND CAULIFLOWER.

The forcing of these vegetables in the greenhouse is becoming an important industry with many florists, as nearly all the money obtained for them is clear gain; the space they occupy is not likely to be used for other purposes and there is no outlay except a small amount for labor, and this is paid for several fold by the returns from the crops.

ASPARAGUS FORCING.

The plants used for forcing asparagus are from old, out-of-door plantations, or they may be grown from seed to the age of three years, the seed being sown early in the spring in drills fifteen inches apart, upon rich and moderately heavy sandy loam. One pound of seed will be sufficient for 200 feet of drill. As the seed is slow to germinate, it is well to sow with it a few radish seeds, which will soon appear and will mark the line of the drill so that cultivation can begin at once. The seeds should be covered one inch or slightly more, and the soil compacted. The seeds need good cultivation the first year, and the following spring can be planted out to develop strength. As they will remain only two years, they can be placed quite thickly, if the soil is well enriched. A space of two and one-half by one foot for each plant will answer, although a little more is desirable. Here they are grown for two seasons, and can be dug just before the ground freezes, and used for forcing purposes. Since the sowing of the seed, a period of two years and six months has elapsed. The plants can be forced in almost any place where a temperature of fifty or sixty degrees can be secured, but the florist will generally utilize some of the space under his benches, or it may be he has a solid bed or even a raised bed for which he has no use for a season. The soil should be a rich, sandy loam with arrangements for thorough drainage.

For early cutting, they can be planted at the time of digging, about the middle of November, while the balance of the plants should be stored in a pit or cool cellar and brought in at intervals of four weeks, to give a succession. The plants should be set from six to twelve inches apart, each way, according to their size, and should be well wet down. For the first ten days after setting, they should be kept rather cool (45 to 50 degrees) and given a chance to establish themselves. Afterward, the temperature should be raised to 55 or 60 degrees, and if still higher it will aid in the forcing process and should be given, if needed, for other plants. During the day it can be run up as high as 80 to 85 degrees. The asparagus will use a large amount of water, but unless it has had the chill taken off, and ample means for drainage provided, it can do far more harm than good.

In setting out the asparagus in the house, the crowns should be covered about an inch, except in localities where a blanched article is required, in which case, unless they can be shut in from the light, additional soil should be added. In about six weeks from the time of planting, cutting can begin and will continue according to the temperature and the strength of the plants until they are exhausted. They can then be thrown out and the space filled with others. If care is taken to secure a succession, asparagus can be cut continually from Christmas until the field-grown article is offered in the spring.

Asparagus may also be grown in cold frames. The plants should be set about one foot each way, and at the end of two years a crop may be taken. In the fall, put up the frame and fill it with horse manure, banking up against the outside of the frame with the same material. Cover with sash and shutters to keep out the frost. Early in March, remove the manure over the plants, wet down the beds thoroughly, and handle the same as any cold frame.

WINTER RHUBARB.

With but few changes, the directions given for the forcing of asparagus will apply to rhubarb. The drills should be somewhat further apart, and a pound of seed will be sufficient for 300 feet of drill. In setting the plants in the field, they will need at least three and one-half by two feet, while in the greenhouse they should have a space of from fifteen to eighteen inches square, and if the roots are very strong twenty-four by eighteen will be none too much. Nothing will be gained by setting the plants before Jan. 1, or until they have had a period of rest. After the stalks are half grown, liquid manure can be applied to advantage once or twice a week. If the soil is properly drained, the plants can use large quantities, but it should not be used too copiously unless the chill has been taken off from the water, otherwise the growth might be checked. The Linnæus is an excellent forcing sort, but as with all other large varieties, the crop will need to be harvested when about half grown, if the plants are placed as thickly as recommended above. The crown of the plant is quite tender and care must be taken, when gathering the stalks, not to break it off.

For spring use, rhubarb may be grown in cold frames, the same as asparagus, except that the plants should be two or three feet apart each way.

THE FORCING OF CAULIFLOWERS.

While cauliflower is, to a considerable extent, forced in hotbeds for spring use, it has also come into popular favor as a winter vegetable. It can be very easily raised and there is no reason why, with a good market, it may not be a paying crop.

The seed of the first batch should be sown either in a flat or in a bed out of doors, about the first of September. The seedlings will be of a suitable size to prick out into other flats in about three weeks and can be set in the beds by the middle of October. The soil and the beds should be about the same as for radishes, except that the cauliflower requires a rather more nitrogenous soil.

They should have about the same temperature as lettuce and radishes, and the rules given for the watering and ventilating for those crops will answer for the cauliflower. The plants should be set about eighteen or twenty inches apart each way, and should be ready to market from the 18th to the 30th of January, according to the care they receive. Plants for a second crop should be sown about the first of November, and after having been pricked out and grown in a flat five or six weeks, they can be re-transplanted to other flats at four inches, or can be placed in four-inch pots to be grown until the first crop is out of the way, which should be by the early part of February. The plants at this time should be large and strong and will quickly make their growth,— perfecting marketable heads early in April. As with all forced crops, the plants should never be checked, but should be so handled that they will make a regular growth from the time the seed is sown until the crop is harvested. If space is available a continuous succession of cauliflowers can be obtained for the table or market, by making a sowing every two weeks.

The time allowed for the development of the heads does not allow them to reach full size, but when half grown they will bring nearly as much as if left two weeks longer, and it is best to cut them at the size of from four to six inches in diameter, as it allows the bed to be cleared for another crop. There is little difference between a good strain of Snowball cauliflower and any of the better strains of Early Dwarf Erfurt that are on the market under different names.

CHAPTER XVII.

RADISHES, CARROTS, BEETS AND BEANS.

FORCING RADISHES.

One of the first vegetables to be forced was the radish, and although it has perhaps held its own, there certainly has not been any marked increase in the amount raised for winter. The demand in the spring for hotbed and frame radishes has grown to large proportions. The crop can be easily raised in the winter, and there is no reason why the area of glass now devoted to it cannot readily be doubled.

The crop succeeds well on either a well-drained, solid bed or a deep, raised bench, filled with from four to six inches of rich, light loam; the greater depth should be used for the long-rooted varieties, while the bed can be more easily regulated, and as good results can be obtained, if the soil is not over four inches deep for the turnip-rooted sorts. The seed should be sown in drills, varying from five to six inches apart, according to the variety, as some kinds have small foliage that will enable the plants to grow close together, while other forcing sorts will need at least six inches. If the seed has been tested and known to be good, it could be scattered in drills half an inch deep, at intervals of three-fourths of an inch. It would be better, however, as some of the plants may be destroyed, to plant the seeds somewhat closer, say at intervals of half an inch. The seeds should be covered and the soil leveled off and pressed down. If the soil is moist, as it should be, one watering at the time of sowing will be all that is necessary until germination is completed.

During their entire growth, radishes need thorough ventilation and the air should be on at least for a short time each day, except in the most inclement weather. The night temperature should be about 50 degrees, with a minimum for best results of 45 degrees, although if it drops slightly below 40 degrees occasionally little harm will be done. With a full amount of air on, it will do no harm if on bright days the temperature of the house runs up, with sun heat, to 70 or 75 degrees, but as a radish grows best in a cool temperature, nothing over 60 or 65 degrees should be given, except by sun heat. When the second rough leaf begins to form, the plants should be thinned out so as to leave a plant every one and one-half or two inches in the rows.

While the plants are small, only a small amount of water is used by them and care must be taken not to saturate the bed. Syringing will be helpful on bright mornings. The first sowing should be made about the first of October and to secure a succession should be repeated every three weeks. The principal enemy of the radish in the forcing house is the green aphis, which can be kept in check by fumigating with tobacco twice a week. With proper conditions for growth and a clean house, they seldom appear. For spring use, the radishes should be sown in hotbeds about the 1st and 15th of March and in a cold frame on the 15th of April, after which they can be grown in the open air.

The best variety for winter forcing is a good strain of White-Tipped Scarlet Turnip, Cardinal, Globe or Scarlet Globe, although the Scarlet Turnip and French

Breakfast are still much used. Twenty Day Forcing and similar kinds are very early, but as a rule the small size more than offsets this advantage. Long Scarlet and Wood's Frame are among the best for hotbed and cold frame use.

CARROTS.

Carrots have not been largely grown in greenhouses, as they can readily be carried over winter from the previous summer. They should be sown in the same way, and require about the same care, as the radish, when grown either in the forcing house or hotbed. In the latter place and in the frame they are grown to a considerable extent. The Early French Forcing is the kind commonly used under glass.

BEETS.

This also is a profitable crop, either for the forcing house or hotbed. The best variety is the Eclipse, although the Egyptian is much used, as they are quick to develop and have small tops. The seed should be sown in drills twelve inches apart, and the plants should be thinned three or four inches in the rows when they have two leaves. A crop of lettuce or radishes can be grown between the rows and taken off before the beets need the room.

If given a high temperature, the plants run to tops, hence the house should be kept at 45 or 50 degrees, and given free ventilation.

FORCING BEANS.

While grown extensively for the winter markets of London, and Paris, the bean has not come into much prominence as a forced crop in this country. It requires a temperature of from 65 to 70 degrees for its successful growth and to maintain this requires a large consumption of fuel, so that the product must bring a high price to be remunerative. In connection with tomatoes or cucumbers, beans can, however, be grown as a catch crop. They can be grown either in the beds or in pots. If in the latter, five or six beans are sown in a seven- or eight-inch pot, and are grown without shifting, using liquid manure after the roots have matted. If to be grown in the bed, they can be sown in drills one foot apart and three inches in the row, and should be thinned to stand about six by twelve inches, or they can be started by sowing three or four beans in a four-inch pot, and as soon as the first two leaves have formed and before they become pot-bound, transplant to the bed, placing them one foot square, first removing all but two plants; in this way, the ground can be utilized to the best advantage and a succession can be maintained.

During the growth of the plants, the air should be kept rather moist, to keep down the red spider, but water should not touch the foliage. When they are in flower, in order to set well they should have good ventilation and the air must be kept rather dry. They can be aided in the fertilization of the ovules if they are hand pollinated. The Sion House and Osborne Forcing are generally used for this purpose, although Golden Wax and other early wax sorts are well suited for winter forcing.

CHAPTER XVIII.

GRAPE GROWING UNDER GLASS.

While the low price at which California grapes can be placed on our markets has rendered the raising of grapes in greenhouses, as a commercial venture, decidedly unprofitable, the vinery is likely to remain a part of private greenhouse establishments, and as there is a dearth of literature upon the subject, a brief statement as to the proper methods to pursue is here appended.

Writers upon this subject are generally very exact in their advice, but while much depends upon the character of the soil, and the amount of moisture and heat furnished in a forcing grapery, this exact treatment is not so necessary in a cold grapery. In fact, grapes have been grown with success in greenhouses with but little, if any, more care than should be given the hardy grapes in the open air. It is desirable, however, that a well prepared bed or border be furnished them, particularly as grapes under proper conditions will live for many years.

THE GRAPE BORDER.

In choosing a soil for grapes, the heavy clay as well as the light, sandy loams should not be selected. If nothing better can be secured, the former may be used, as mixed with sand it will be made friable, but the light sandy loams are not lasting enough to be used as the base for the vine compost. If turf can be obtained from an old pasture, that has a thick fibrous sod and a heavy sandy or light clay loam soil, it will be found to be well adapted for grape growing. This should be broken up, and for every five yards of sod, about one yard of lime rubbish, a small quantity of charcoal, broken bricks and calcined oyster shells, should be added. It will also be well to add one hundred pounds of broken up bones. If this compost is prepared in the fall and piled up so as to shed rain, it will be in shape to use the next spring, although if necessary it may be used at once.

As a rule, if the soil is fairly rich, no manure should be applied with the compost, but it can be added as a top-dressing whenever needed. In case the best turf that can be obtained is thin and growing upon exhausted soil, cut it to the depth of two inches and mix it with equal parts of rich garden soil and half decomposed strawy manure. A well drained, deep, moderately rich garden soil will give good results without preparing any special border, if properly top-dressed. As soon as the vines get to bearing, it is well to scrape off the surface soil, if it can be done without destroying the roots, and add a compost of equal parts of turf and stable manure.

The vine border should be as wide as the roof that is to be covered, and may be entirely within the houses, or half inside and half outside, with the roots passing out through arches in the wall. The border should be about two feet deep, but it need not be made to its full width at the time of planting. If five or six feet wide, it will suffice for the first year, and additions can be made until, by the beginning of the fourth year, the full width has been reached.

To provide the necessary fertility for the vines, mineral fertilizers are desirable, as they produce a firm and healthy growth that is less likely to be injured by unfavorable conditions than the soft, watery growth obtained from stable manure. If one peck of wood ashes, two pounds of ground bone and one-half pound of nitrate of soda are used to one hundred square feet of border, it will have an excellent effect. In addition to this application, an inch or so of finely rotted manure should be spread over the border, both to furnish food and to act as a mulch to prevent evaporation from the surface.

SELECTING THE PLANTS.

The best plants are grown from eye cuttings, and should be planted when one year old. These will make a stronger start than layers from old plants, or than plants two or three years old. In selecting the varieties, the method in which they are to be grown should be considered. The first choice will always be Black Hamburg, as this is easily grown and thrives in either a hot or cold vinery. As a rule, fully half of the vines should be of that variety, and for commercial purposes it will be as well, at least so far as the yield is concerned, if the other half are also of that sort.

For a cool house, 20x20 feet, the following varieties, in numbers as indicated by the figures in parentheses, could be used:

> Black Hamburg (6), medium. (Fig. 82.)
> Royal Muscadine (2), white, early.
> Buckland Sweetwater (2), white, medium.
> Alicante (1), black, late.
> Rose Chasselas (1), red, early.
> White Frontignan (1), white, medium.
> Golden Hamburg (1), greenish yellow, medium.
> Muscat of Alexandria (1), amber, late.
> Lady Downer (1), black, late.

A hot vinery of the same size could be filled with:

> Black Hamburg (5), black, medium.
> Royal Muscadine (1), white, early.
> Muscat Hamburg (1), black, medium.
> Syrian (1), white, late.
> Muscat of Alexandria (1), amber, late.
> Lady Downer (1) black, late.
> Rose Chasselas (1), red, early.
> Barbarossa (1), black, late, large.

Buckland Sweetwater (1), white, medium.
Grizzly Frontignan (1), dull red, medium.
Alicante (1), black, late.
Golden Hamburg (1), greenish yellow, medium.

If the plants have been grown in pots, so that the roots have matted, the balls should be broken up. At any rate, the roots should be carefully spread out in an excavation about nine inches deep, and covered with fine soil, each row of roots being covered separately. If the border is all inside the house, the plants should be placed about two feet from the wall, unless the heating pipes are next to the wall, when a distance of three or even four feet will be none too great; if part of the border is outside, they may be planted inside so that the roots can run out through the arch, or they may be planted outside, and brought in through the opening, at a a depth of five or six inches below the surface of the border.

About the first of May is a good time to plant the vines, although the time might be varied two or three weeks either way, depending upon the conditions in which the vines have been kept. The proper time to plant is after the buds begin to swell and before they burst. The custom is to plant the vines about three feet apart, although some prefer a greater distance.

CARE THE FIRST SEASON.

As soon as the vines are planted, they should be cut oack to a strong bud within a foot of the ground, and a single shoot from this should be trained to the trellis, rubbing off all side shoots that form on the lower half of the rafter, but after it has reached a hight of six or eight feet it may develop at will. This will enlarge the leaf surface and will make the lower portion of the stem much stronger than if the vine was only allowed to develop at the tip.

Many growers advise glazing the roof of the graperies, so as to leave half-inch cracks between the panes.

thus providing for ventilation and watering, as a sufficient amount of fresh air and rain for this purpose can enter through the openings. In this way, the grapes can be grown with much less care than in tight houses, and good results are often obtained in favorable seasons. On the other hand, if the summer is cold and wet, far

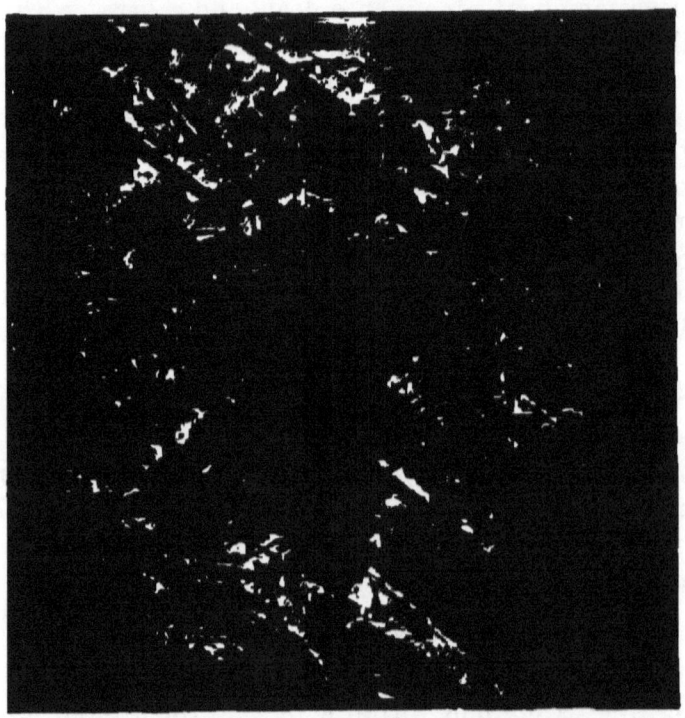

FIG. 82. BLACK HAMBURG GRAPES.

better returns will be received if the house is so arranged that the amount of ventilation and water can be regulated to suit the conditions.

In a cold grapery, the ventilation should be gradually increased, as the weather warms up, and after the middle of June the ventilators can be left wide open at night until the first of September, except in cold, wet weather, when they may be partly closed. Less ventilation should be given in a hot vinery, and the house should be closed at night and opened during the day, when it can be done without dropping the temperature below seventy degrees.

TRAINING AND PRUNING THE SECOND SEASON.

A vine that has been planted out one year and that has been trained as directed, should be cut back, a month or so after the leaves have fallen, leaving a stem from four to six feet long, according to the strength of the vine (Fig. 83). From this, a strong bud should be allowed to develop a leader, to extend the vine up the rafter, which should be treated in the same way as the leading shoot of the first year. All side buds should be rubbed off as they start, below the bottom of the rafter. If the vines are very strong, a few of the stronger side shoots, if grapes set upon them, may be allowed to ripen one bunch each. These laterals should be pinched off when they reach a length of twelve to fifteen inches. The simplest and one of the most satisfactory forms of trellis is made of No. 12 galvanized wire, stretched about one foot apart and fifteen inches from the glass.

Another method of training the vines, if they are strong, and of obtaining a little fruit the second season, is by layering the vine in a ten-inch pot four or five feet up the cane. This shoot may be allowed to set a few bunches, and the stem below will make about as good a growth as if it had not been layered. After ripening the grapes, the layer may be cut off at the lower end of the rafter, and may be used for planting out, or as a pot plant, while the main stem will be in good shape for its third season's growth.

A third and very good method of pruning the vine after being planted out one year, especially if its growth has not been strong, is to cut the cane back to the bot-

240   GREENHOUSE MANAGEMENT.

FIG. 83. A GRAPE HOUSE IN FRUIT.

tom of the rafter, and train the same as the first year, rubbing out all shoots that break for six feet above the rafter.

PRUNING AND TRAINING THE THIRD SEASON.

The vines should be cut back at the same time as the previous year, leaving about six feet of the main cane above the bottom of the rafters, or, if the cane was allowed to grow as first described, ten feet may be left. The buds upon this shoot should break into strong laterals, upon which the fruit is borne. Not over two bunches should be allowed, even upon the strongest shoots, and the laterals should be pinched after one or two leaves beyond the last bunch have formed. A leading shoot should be trained from the strong bud at the upper end of the main stem, from which all lateral shoots should be rubbed. When growth is over in the autumn and the leaves have fallen, the vines should be cut back for the fourth season. The laterals should be cut back to one bud and the leaves should be cut so as to allow about five feet of the stem to extend up the rafter. This is known as the spur system of pruning, and after the leader has reached the end of the rafter it merely consists in cutting the laterals back to one bud.

SUMMER PINCHING, DISBUDDING AND THINNING.

As soon as the buds break, all extra shoots should be rubbed out, and during the season the vines should be frequently examined and all superfluous shoots removed. As a rule, if large bunches are desired, only one should be left upon a spur, although two may be grown upon strong shoots. Each year, as soon as the fruit has set, the shoot should be pinched off, leaving one leaf beyond the last bunch, and if laterals start, they should be rubbed off. Not only should the surplus shoots and bunches be removed, but if large berries are desired the bunches themselves should be thinned out.

When the grapes are about the size of peas, the center of the bunches can be cut out with scissors, and when those on the outside have set in clusters of three, one or two of the berries can also be removed.

In forming the spurs upon the sides of the main shoots, it sometimes is necessary to remove some of the shoots that start. As a rule, the laterals should not be nearer than twelve or fifteen inches, and sometimes a distance even greater than this is desirable. The length to which the laterals may be allowed to grow before they are pinched in, is determined by the distance at which the vines are planted. If placed three feet apart, the laterals will interlace at eighteen or twenty inches and should be pinched back at the point of meeting. All superfluous bunches, and all tendrils at the same nodes with the remaining bunches, should be removed at the same time.

While it is desirable to pinch in some shoots and thin out others, to prevent the vines from becoming too thick upon the trellises, on the other hand, great harm can be done by thinning too much, as the leaves are the assimilating organs of the plant, and, up to the capacity of the plant and the trellis, the greater the amount of leaf surface, the greater will be the growth.

WATERING AND SYRINGING.

Grapes thrive best in a warm, moist atmosphere, which not only tends to keep the red spider in check, but promotes the growth of the plants. A proper degree of moisture should always be maintained in the border by watering whenever it shows signs of being dry, and in the air by wetting walks and syringing the plants. Syringing is particularly desirable at the time the vines are breaking, and on bright days should be performed two or three times, until the shoots have started and the flowers are opening, but it should then be discontinued, as the pollination is more perfect if the air is warm and dry. Fertilization is aided by giving the vines a thorough jarring. The pollen is generally shed in greatest abundance by the anthers during the forenoon of bright days, and its distribution can be assisted by giving thorough ventilation, which will remove all surplus moisture from the air.

As the bunches develop, the air should be kept moist by the free use of water upon the border, etc., but syringing the foliage at this time is not to be recommended, particularly with bearing vines. During the ripening period the air should again be dry, and water should be very sparingly used.

TEMPERATURE AND VENTILATION.

Ventilation is not only for the purpose of regulating the temperature of the houses during the day, but it serves to admit fresh air and also, to some extent, controls the moisture in the air. The air should be admitted on bright mornings as soon as the sun is well up, and the amount of ventilation should be gradually increased as the season advances. In pleasant weather, the ventilators may remain open at night, but, although grapes have been grown with success in houses where the ventilators are opened in the spring and not closed until fall, it is better to regulate them according to the weather, and in cold, wet spells, such as occur frequently, the houses will be better off if closed.

In the hot vinery, although the house should be opened to admit fresh air, the amount of ventilation desirable is considerably less than in cool graperies. When first started, the hot graperies should be given a temperature of about 50 degrees at night, with from 65 to 70 degrees during the day. This should be raised in three or four weeks to 60 degrees at night, and it may be 75 to 80 degress, or even more, during the day. On bright days in the spring, air may be given for three or four hours during the middle of the day, but it is well to close up early, in order that the heat from the sun may be trapped, and used to warm up the houses for the night.

FORCING GRAPES.

This term is now used in reference to several operations. In a strict sense, it applies to the starting of the vines by the aid of artificial heat, at any time from December to February or March, with the object of securing fruit in advance of the main crop. Forcing is also necessary with varieties that will not ripen without artificial heat, which may be used to start them earlier than would otherwise be possible, or it may be used to ripen them in the fall, or both. Another use of the hot vinery is to grow varieties that require a rather higher temperature than is afforded by our climate.

If vines are to be used for early forcing, they must be brought into this habit gradually, and by starting them one year by the first of March it will be possible to start them a few weeks earlier the next year, and by continuing this, the time at which they can be started will be carried back to January, or even December. It will take about five months for the early varieties to be brought to maturity in the forcing house.

Firing may begin about the first of March in the hot vinery, for the main crop, and should be regulated to give about the same temperature as in the forcing grapery proper. At the time the fruit sets, and as it ripens, rather more heat will be required, in order that ventilation may be given. If the season is cold and wet, the fire heat will do much to hasten the growth.

KEEPING THE FRUIT.

When thoroughly ripened, the fruit of some varieties will hang on the vines for a long time. By maintaining a temperature of about 45 degrees, and securing a dry atmosphere by thorough ventilation, some of the thick skinned sorts can be kept until March. An easier method, however, and one by which the grapes can be kept considerably later, is by cutting off the bunches with six or eight inches of cane attached, and placing the end of the shoot in a bottle of water; the bottles can be arranged in racks, in a dry, dark room, where the temperature is kept at 40 degrees, and where a close, dry atmosphere can be maintained. In this way there will be no trouble about keeping them fully a month longer than would be possible if kept upon the vines.

CARE OF THE VINES IN WINTER.

After the leaves have fallen, the vines should be pruned and prepared for winter. In the cold grapery, they should be laid down close to the wall, where they may be covered with sand or loam, or wrapped in mats. During bright days the house should be ventilated. If proper care is given to ventilation during the day, the hot vinery can be used for growing crops during the winter that need 45 degrees as a maximum temperature. The vines can be laid close to the wall and shut away from the interior of the house, by means of wooden shutters. Before they are taken out, if the interior of the house is sprayed with a solution of sixty grains of corrosive sublimate, or of copper sulphate, to one gallon of water, the spores and germs of the various diseases of the vine will be destroyed. It is also well to annually whitewash all of the brick and stone walls.

PROPAGATION.

Having obtained a stock of plants, it is frequently desirable to increase them, which can readily be done, either from eyes or short cuttings. Strong, well-ripened shoots, with large but firm buds, should be selected when the vines are pruned, and for eye cuttings (Fig. 84) make them into pieces one and one-half inches long, with a bud in the center, and after removing a shaving of wood from the underside, place them in the cutting boxes. These should be about three inches deep and have about two inches of rich potting soil in the bottom. Upon this place the cuttings, with the eyes up, and scatter on sand until the eyes have been covered about half an inch. Keep them moderately cool until Jan-

FIG. 84. EYE CUTTING OF GRAPE.

FIG. 85. SHORT CUTTING OF GRAPE.

uary, when they should be given bottom heat in a cool propagating house. Care should be given in watering not to saturate the soil; and to lessen the amount of evaporation it may be well to cover the sand with a thin layer of sifted sphagnum as a mulch.

The short cuttings (Fig. 85) are made in much the same way, except that the stem is cut off just above the bud and about an inch and one-half below it, making a cutting about two inches long. After removing a shaving of wood from the lower end, they are inserted vertically in the cutting boxes, which should contain three inches of sharp sand. As soon as roots have formed, the cuttings should be potted off and plunged in a mild bottom heat. By repotting as needed, plants can be grown to a hight of two and one-half feet by the middle of June, when, if carefully planted in the border, they will do equally as well as yearling plants. If not needed as permanent plants, they will be excellent for use as pot plants. Layering may also be resorted to.

POT PLANTS.

If well grown, the plants will be large enough to furnish fruit the following year, but, as a rule, they are cut back, repotted and grown for the second year before they are allowed to fruit. When at a fruiting size, they should be cut back to eight or ten buds and plunged in a narrow, low house, about the time the permanent vines are started. The vines may be trained to wire trellises, or three or four stakes may be placed in a pot around the edges, and the vine arranged in a spiral form around them. The pots should be mulched with half-decomposed manure, and after the fruit has set, liquid manure should be used freely. The same general rules as to pinching, watering, ventilating, etc., apply here, as with vines permanently planted.

If one does not have the means to erect a span roof, or even a lean-to grapery of the usual width, very good results can be obtained against the south side of a wall or fence, by erecting a wall about two feet high and three feet from the back wall, upon which common hotbed sash is placed upon end and leaning against the back wall. If a wooden framework eighteen inches wide is built out from the back wall to receive the sash, it will increase the size of the house and provide for top ventilation.

The most troublesome insect in the grapery is the red spider, which can be kept in check by syringing. If either of the mildews appear in a grapery, an application of the copper sulphate solution, or ammoniated copper carbonate, should be used (See Chapter on Insects and Diseases), or, if it is the powdery form, evaporated sulphur will be found effectual.

CHAPTER XIX.

STRAWBERRY GROWING UNDER GLASS.

When properly handled, few greenhouse crops will afford more interest and pleasure to the amateur, or more profit to the commercial grower, than the strawberry when grown as a winter crop under glass. The requirements are a well-lighted house, in which a temperature of 65 degrees can be maintained during February and March, and where the plants can be placed near the glass.

The plants should be obtained from plantations set early in the spring previous, or in July or August of the year before and not allowed to fruit, by layering the first runners that form in July, in two and one-half or three-inch pots that have been plunged near them. Unless the soil is a rich, sandy loam, the pots should be filled with good compost. In about two weeks the pots will be occupied by roots, and the plants should then be repotted into four-inch pots and placed in a cold frame. Here they should be kept during the fall, requiring careful attention in watering, and being repotted to five-inch and again to six-inch pots, which should be the fruiting size, as soon as the smaller sizes have become filled with roots. If, at any time, leaf blight or any other fungous disease appears upon them, the plants should be sprayed with Bordeaux mixture.

In order to force successfully, the plants must form strong crowns and harden them before winter comes on. As freezing weather approaches, the frames should be covered with glass, to prevent the breaking of the pots

STRAWBERRY GROWING UNDER GLASS. 249

FIG. 86. BENCH OF STRAWBERRY PLANTS, CORNELL EXPERIMENT STATION.

by frost. Plunging the pots in sand or coal ashes will also be desirable on the same account. The plants should be kept in the frame until about the first of January, after which short rest they can be brought into heat. If a succession is desired, only a part of the plants should be started at first and these should be placed in a room where a temperature of 40 to 45 degrees can be maintained at night, with thorough ventilation during the day. All dead and diseased leaves should be removed and the plants sprayed with a one to one

FIG. 87. THE CROP GATHERED.

thousand solution (one ounce to eight gallons of water) of copper sulphate, to destroy all spores of fungi Other lots should be brought in at intervals of two to four weeks.

In five or six weeks after growth starts, the plants will blossom and they should then be transferred to a warmer room, or the temperature must be raised to 65 or 70 degrees at night. The pollen will be shed most freely in a warm, dry room and these conditions must be secured in order to have the flowers properly fertilized. The pollen will, however, need to be transferred by hand from the stamens to the pistils, and it can be done best by means of a small camel's-hair brush, at the same time carrying along any surplus pollen that may be found, on a small spoon or wooden paddle. Care must be taken that pollen is conveyed to every pistil, or the fruits will be irregular in form. The pollinating should be repeated every pleasant morning. As soon as

FIG. 88. FRUITING STRAWBERRY PLANTS, CORNELL EXPERIMENT STATION.

the fruit has set, the application of liquid manure should commence, and should be repeated two or three times a week until the fruits begin to color.

If more than eight or ten fruits set upon a plant, the smaller and imperfect ones should be removed. The plants should never be allowed to suffer for want of water, and occasionally on warm, bright mornings the foliage should be syringed, but this is not advisable while the plants are in blossom, or after the fruit begins to color. In order to keep the fruit from the damp soil, where it will be likely to rot, some support must be provided. Mr. Hunn, of the Cornell Experiment Station, who has been quite successful in forcing strawberries, is well pleased with cork chips, and with fine netting placed upon the pots, as seen in Fig. 86. In about a month from the time the fruit sets, the berries will begin to ripen, and in ten days to two weeks the plants may be thrown out and replaced with others, which will need the same care, except that less attention need be paid to pollinating the flowers. The red spider and aphis may be troublesome, unless proper remedies are used.

The variety selected will have much to do with the results secured. For the best success, it should be an early sort, with rather short petioles and small leaves, that is little subject to disease. Unless other perfect flowering plants are grown to provide pollen for them, pistillate sorts should not be selected, although otherwise many of the imperfect-flowered varieties are well adapted for forcing. The Beder Wood, a perfect-flowered variety, is one of the best, its principal fault being the light color of the fruit. Among the later sorts Sharpless and Parker Earle are well adapted for forcing. Although the results will be less satisfactory, fruit may be obtained four or five weeks earlier, by shortening the period of rest.

In a good market, well-grown fruit (Fig. 87) will bring from two to four dollars per quart in February, and not over a dozen plants, which in six-inch pots will not occupy more than three or four square feet, will be required to furnish them, and they will not occupy the houses more than ten or twelve weeks. There is also a call for the plants, while in fruit, at prices that will be quite remunerative. A well-grown plant with a crop of fine fruit, as seen in Fig. 88, is a handsome ornament for a table.

CHAPTER XX.

FRUIT TREES UNDER GLASS.

In many sections of the country the climate is not adapted to the growing of such fruits as the peach, apricot and nectarine in the open air, and although these fruits can generally be obtained in the market in their season, as a rule the varieties are not of the best quality from the fact that the most desirable varieties, so far as quality is concerned, are generally lacking in hardiness and are consequently unproductive when grown in the open air. On this account there seems to be a growing interest in orchard houses and in the forcing of fruit under glass.

While a cheap lean-to house built against a wall will give good results, the form best adapted to the purpose is the even-span. If the expense can be afforded, the curvilinear roof is desirable, as it gives more room for the growth of the trees. While good results can be obtained without fire heat, it will be necessary if the fruit is to be forced, and may save a crop if the weather is cold or wet at the time the trees are in blossom, or while the fruit is setting, as a check at that time may prevent the setting of the fruit. Ample ventilation should be provided at the ridge and will be desirable in the side walls, that a good circulation of air may be procured.

The trees may be grown either in pots or tubs, or planted out in borders in the house. The former is desirable from the fact that the trees being portable can be placed close together during the winter, and the conditions can be controlled better, but on the other hand there is the disadvantage of requiring much more frequent attention regarding the watering of the trees, particularly during the summer months.

For the pear, a quince stock is desirable, and the Mahaleb is preferred for the cherry, but peach seedlings can be used as stocks for the peach, nectarine and apricot, although the myrobolan plum stock can be used for them as well as for the plum.

For pot culture, trees of pear, plum or cherry will require from ten-to fourteen-inch pots when three or four years old, and as they increase in size can be shifted to tubs. The peach and nectarine trees will require somewhat larger sizes. The soil for the plum and pear trees should have a liberal admixture of

FIG. 89. PEAR LOUISE BONNE GROWN IN A POT.

clay, while the cherry and peach trees will **do best in a** sandy loam soil. When first potted, about one **part of** decomposed manure to five parts of soil will be sufficient, but for repotting and top-dressing the amount of manure can be doubled. It will also be well to add for each bushel of soil a four-inch pot each of ground bone and wood ashes. The repotting should be done after the growth has ripened in the fall, but if the roots have not become matted it will not be necessary each year, as it will often suffice if the surface soil is removed and a top-dressing added.

When the buds begin to swell in the spring, the trees should be syringed on bright mornings, but they should be kept rather close and dry while they are in blossom, and

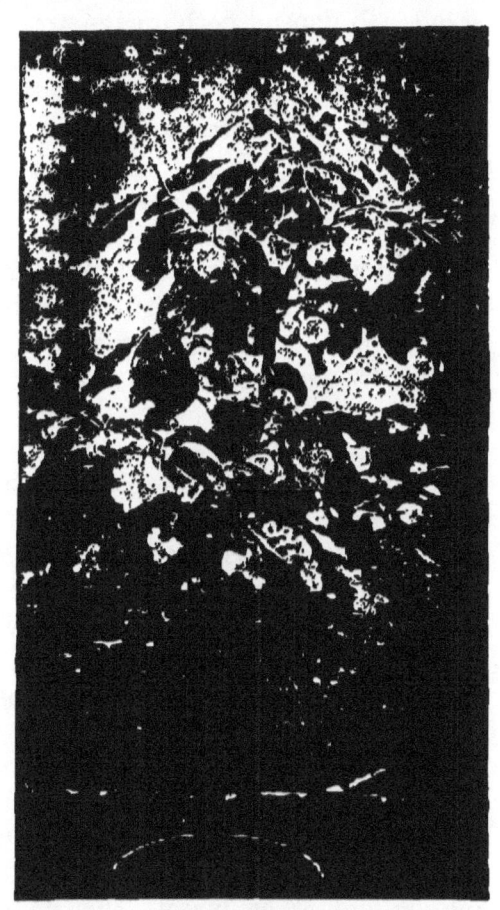

FIG. 90. EARLY TRANSPARENT GAGE FRUITING IN A POT.

particular care should be taken that they are not checked in their growth from any cause until after the fruit has begun to swell. After this time the trees **should be syringed in the morning and again in the after-**

noon of bright days. After the seeds begin to form it will be well to either top-dress the plants with horse or sheep manure or to apply liquid manure.

If the crop set is a large one, the surplus fruits should be removed. The distance at which they should be left will depend both on the growth of the plant and the number of fruits upon it, but except for the cherry and plum they should not be less than six inches apart, and if well distributed a single fruit upon a shoot or spur will be ample.

After the crop has been gathered and the end of the growing season approaches, water should be gradually withheld and all the ventilation possible should be given. This will aid the trees in ripening their growths and in securing firm fruit buds that will be less likely to be affected by changes of temperature during the winter, than when they are loose and open. If in pots it is often well to place the trees outside for a few weeks in the fall, but they should be returned to the houses before severe freezing weather comes. During the winter they may be packed closely together and the space that they occupied in the summer can then be used for some other crops. During the winter the trees should be pruned. This will consist in cutting the new growth back about three-fourths and the thinning out of surplus shoots. In the case of the peach and nectarine, especially, this should be thoroughly done. After they have been pruned, it will be well to spray the trees thoroughly with a strong solution of copper sulphate, and just before the buds start Bordeaux mixture can be used to advantage. For aphides and other insects that may appear, the usual remedies should be used.

While the labor of watering can be lessened by plunging the pots to their rim, during the summer, in a light litter of some kind, care must be taken that the roots are kept in the pots, and it will be desirable to have them rest upon a couple of bricks or some similar supports. While the pear, cherry and plum can be grown best in pots, the peach and nectarine should either be placed in large boxes, or planted out in a border. This should be prepared to the depth of two feet and its surface will need to be top-dressed once or twice each year. If in lean-to, or three-quarter span, houses the trees may be trained upon the north wall, or on trellises just beneath the glass if even-span, but as a rule the pyramidal form of tree will be preferable.

During the summer, after all danger of frost is over, no attention need be paid to ventilating the houses, the full air being left on, except when cold, chilly winds prevail. In the winter, after the trees have ripened, the sash should be handled with the idea of protecting the trees from extremes of temperature, ventilation being desirable on warm or bright days to prevent the swelling of the buds.

In selecting varieties of peach for forcing, only those of high quality should be taken, Early Rivers, George IV, Mountain Rose, Grosse Mignonne, Oldmixon, Early and Late Crawford, Foster and Elberta being among the best sorts for the purpose. Any of the better varieties of apricots and nectarines can be used, and any of the pears that succeed on dwarf stocks, such as Souvenir du Congres, Louise Bonne (Fig. 89), Angouleme and Anjou, will give satisfaction. Among the plums the choice should be made from among the Gage (Fig. 90) varieties and such other sorts as Diamond, Czar, Coe's Golden Drop, Grand Duke and Monarch.

CHAPTER XXI.

MANAGEMENT OF HOUSE PLANTS.

If one does not have even the simple form of veranda conservatory described in Greenhouse Construction, fairly good success can be obtained with a few house plants, with either a southern or western exposure. For most flowering plants the windows opening to the south are preferable, even to those with a western outlook, as, during the short days of winter, the plants in the latter will have but little sun, and then it will be too low down near the horizon. For a few plants, the windows looking to the east may be used, and for ferns and similar shade-loving sorts they are desirable. While the north windows may be used for some of that class of plants, it is not a desirable exposure.

In case a bay-window upon the south side of the living room can be obtained for flowers (Fig. 91), very good results can be secured. It should be separated from the room by glass doors, that can be thrown open or closed, at pleasure, but in case they are not to be had, much of the labor of keeping the plants in good condition can be saved if curtains are provided, to be used when sweeping. In addition to hooks for hanging baskets and bracket stands for pot plants, it will be well to have a shelf, from one to two feet in width, according to dimension of the window, upon which to arrange the smaller plants. This should have side pieces one to two inches high, and a zinc lining. The bottom could then be covered with coarse gravel or fine pebbles, and a much better growth could be secured, as the plants in small pots would then be less likely to dry out. A simple propagating bed can be very easily arranged by supplying the necessary clean sand, and a lamp to furnish bottom heat, unless heating pipes run along under the shelf, when they would only need to be boxed in. In case the lamp is used, it will be necessary to provide some sort of a shield to prevent it from setting fire to the wooden shelf. A shallow galvanized iron pan filled with plaster, suspended above the lamp and close to the bottom of the shelf, will answer the purpose.

If an ordinary window is to be used, it will be well to have a similar shelf, at the hight of the window sill. If made two or three feet longer than the window is wide, it will hold a considerable number of plants. For the bay window and the common window as well, if the size of the room admits of it, a plant stand with shelves in the form of stairs, or with a flat top, can be used to good advantage to display the larger plants.

By having it arranged with casters, if the plants that require a high temperature are kept upon it, on cold nights it will be an easy matter to roll it back away from the window and thus save the tender plants from becoming chilled.

SOIL FOR AND CARE OF HOUSE PLANTS.

In a general way, the directions given for greenhouse plants will apply to those grown in the dwelling. In the village or city, where it is difficult to obtain a suitable compost, the admixture of street sweepings with fresh garden loam will answer very well, although, if only a small amount is needed, it will be better to obtain some prepared compost from a florist. Unless new pots are used, they should be well soaked and scrubbed, to remove the mold that usually forms on them, and thus open the pores. A failure often results from using too large pots, as a small plant growing in a large quantity

260   GREENHOUSE MANAGEMENT.

FIG. 91. A WINDOW GARDEN, ARRANGED BY MRS. C. L. ALLEN, FLORAL PARK, N. Y.

of soil will not remove much of the water by transpiration, so that, unless great care is taken in watering, the soil will remain saturated most of the time and, the air being thus kept out, will become sour, and as a result only a weak, unhealthy growth can be secured. When a plant is found to be in this condition, it should be taken out, as much of the soil shaken off as is possible without seriously injuring the roots, and repotted in rich sandy compost, using a pot as small as will take in the roots without cramping them.

For the starting of cuttings, the saucer system, or the use of water alone, will generally be found better than the sand cutting-pan, as, if the latter is used, many plants will fail to root readily unless bottom heat is used.

POTTING AND REPOTTING.

While the florist uses pots not over two inches in diameter for his cuttings and his seedlings, a slightly larger size will be preferable for house plants, unless they are grown in a conservatory, as they will be less likely to be injured from drying out.

In potting off seedlings, or rooted cuttings, the pot is loosely filled with sifted soil, and a hole made in the center with the finger, in which the young plant is placed. The soil should then be pressed firmly into place and thoroughly watered. As soon as the roots begin to form a mat around the sides of the pot, they should be transferred to larger ones, using rich but light soil, in which a liberal amount of ground bone will be of value. To remove the plants from the pots, invert them in the palm of the hand, so that the stems of the plant will be between the second and third fingers, the pot being held by the thumb and fore-finger of the same hand. The edge of the pot can then be thumped against the table, and the plant will slip out. It is always well before repotting to remove from one-fourth to one-half inch of the surface soil, thus disposing of any weeds or slime that may be upon it. Then place from one-half inch to one inch of compost in the bottom of a pot, put in the plant, being careful to have it in the center, and add enough soil to fill the space between the pot and the ball of earth and furnish a slight covering over the surface. When all is completed the level of the soil should be from one-half inch to one inch below the edge of the pots. For sizes of pots up to four inches, a space of one-half inch will answer to hold the necessary water and secure the proper moistening of the soil, but above that one inch is preferable. Notice should be taken that the hole in the bottom of the pot is not clogged. This will provide the necessary drainage, in pots four inches in diameter or less, but for the larger sizes from one to two inches of pieces of broken pots should be placed in the bottom, and covered with a little sphagnum, or excelsior, to keep the soil from washing down and filling the spaces. Bits of charcoal or excelsior can be used instead of crocks. When large plants are repotted, a small rammer should be used to pack the soil well around the ball.

TOP-DRESSING.

In some cases, a plant does not make a satisfactory growth, from lack of sufficient plant food. If the pot is of the proper size and the roots have not become pot-bound, it will not be desirable to repot it, as that would give a needless check to the plant. Good results can generally be obtained if the surface soil is scraped away, down to the roots, and replaced with very rich soil containing 25 per cent of ground bone.

WATER AND LIQUID MANURE.

The rules given for florists will apply well here, but the home florist will need to take special pains to avoid both excessive and too little watering. When the plants have proper drainage, we should apply water until it runs through the pots and then wait until we can see, from the looks, feel or ring of the pot, that the supply has been exhausted and more water is needed.

As a rule, if the watering has not been too long delayed, when a space of one inch has been provided for the purpose, filling the pots to the brim will suffice. Too frequent watering is often a cause of failure with house plants, as the addition of a little water, at short intervals, wets the surface soil, and, keeping the air out, causes it to become sour, while it does not penetrate to the roots, where only it is of use to the plants. The chill should at least be taken off from the water, and if it is warmed to 90 or 100 degrees, all the better.

Liquid fertilizer made from stable manure will not be desirable in the house, but the soluble mineral fertilizers can be used, or ammonia water at the rate of a teaspoonful to a gallon of water used once a week will promote the growth and give a good color to the foliage.

INSECTS AND DISEASES.

While house plants are troubled with about the same pests as those of the greenhouse, as the conditions are even more unnatural, some of them are still more troublesome. As a rule, the air in a dwelling is dry and the conditions are particularly inviting to the red spider. To lessen the dryness, provision should be made in some way for the evaporation of water in the room and for the syringing of the foliage upon bright days. Some of the small hand sprinklers should at any rate be used. The thick-leaved plants will be benefited if they are occasionally sponged off with water containing whale-oil soap.

The same remedies as in the greenhouse will be efficacious here, but some of them, as tobacco smoke, cannot be used in the dwelling. Tobacco tea can, however, be employed for the green fly, either by spraying it over the plants or by dipping the stems into it. Pyrethrum, both as a powder and in water, and kerosene emulsion will be found invaluable remedies.

In addition to syringing and washing the foliage, much can be done to keep the plants healthy, if a little ventilation can be given on pleasant days. While plants do not like drafts of cold air, they are benefited if a fresh supply is frequently provided.

From the fact that the air in the living rooms is likely to be dry, the kitchen, with an atmosphere, during most of the day, charged with moisture, will be found best suited to plants, particularly while they are small. The fact that there is more direct and more frequent communication with the outer air from the kitchen than from the principal living rooms, thus affording ventilation and the access of fresh air, is another reason why plants grown in the kitchen of the cottage generally thrive better than in a bay window of the mansion.

One of the things that is sure to injure plants is coal gas, and whenever coal is used as fuel, whether in a furnace or stove, every precaution should be taken that it does not escape into the rooms and thus injure the plants, as well as the human occupants.

THE TEMPERATURE FOR HOUSE PLANTS.

The temperature which plants require in the dwelling is of course about the same as has been given for the greenhouse, but the growth, as a rule, is less soft and watery than in those grown in glass houses and they will generally be uninjured if the temperature drops a few degrees lower than the point where injury would ensue in the greenhouse. On cold nights, when there is liability that the temperature will fall below the danger point, it is well to spread newspapers in the window and draw the shades so as to prevent as much as possible the loss of heat. The plants themselves should be covered with papers, or, if possible, should be removed from close proximity to the windows. If placed in the center of the room, preferably upon tables, or at least raised well above the floor, they will often escape injury, while similar plants remaining in the window would be frosted and perhaps killed by cold.

As a rule, plants do best at a temperature ten or fifteen degrees colder than they need during the day, and most of the species commonly used as house plants do not need over 50 or 55 degrees at night and will not suffer if the temperature falls as low as 40 degrees, although if such a low temperature be continued for several days it will check the growth of most plants. In case plants have been frozen they should be slowly thawed out. While it will perhaps be impossible to save the foliage of tender tropical plants, the plants themselves, as well as the foliage of the hardier ones, can often be saved. They should be removed from the direct rays of the sun and kept at a temperature of 35 to 40 degrees until they have thawed, when it may be gradually raised. Cold water can also be used to advantage in thawing them out, but the temperature should be kept as low as 35 degrees so long as frost remains in the plant. Water used at 50 to 60 degrees will generally do more harm than to allow the plants to thaw out of themselves.

THE SELECTION OF PLANTS.

When plants are purchased from a florist, pains should be taken that they are in a suitable condition to give good results in the house. As a rule, it will be by far best to take young and vigorous plants, that have been in no way stunted in their growth, but by all means we should avoid using those grown at a high temperature and in a close atmosphere, as they will almost invariably be weak and spindling, and when removed to the dryer air of the dwelling they will be sure to disappoint one.

We should also avoid those that have been forced by the florist for the production of flowers, as they have been grown under unnatural conditions, and even though they have been given a period of rest, they are not likely to be satisfactory.

Much can be told regarding the fitness of a plant for growing in the house, by its structure and general appearance, and, as a rule, plants with thick leaves and a small glossy surface are but little affected by a dry temperature and can be readily washed, while plants with small thin leaves quickly dry up if neglected in any degree, and particularly if they have a rough hairy surface they hold the dust and cannot be readily washed.

Deciduous plants, particularly those that drop their leaves during the winter, should not be selected, as they will show only bare stems at the very time they should be in the best condition. While all plants should have a period of rest at some time during the year, there are long lists to select from that rest during the summer, and these should always be chosen.

Unless one is so situated that a minimum temperature of 60 degrees can be secured, the use of the tropical plants that need 65 to 70 degrees is not advisable, as a single cold night may greatly injure them. The selection should also be governed by the outlook, as influencing the amount of sunlight that can be given them. In partial shade, such plants as ferns, primroses, ivies, madeira vines, callas, bulbs, palms, begonias, *Ficus repens* and *F. elastica*, mahernia, achyranthes and similar plants can be grown with fair success, if conditions are favorable. Most of the other winter flowering plants do best if given southerly exposure, where they can have full sunlight.

PLANTS FOR GROWING IN THE HOUSE.

The choice of plants will depend somewhat upon the surroundings and the conditions under which they are to be grown, as kinds that would succeed well in a parlor conservatory, or that would be appropriate for the decoration of a drawing room, would not be desirable and might be out of place in the kitchen or sitting-room window of a cottage.

For the small window, and in a bay window conservatory, such well known plants as begonias, flowering and foliage; abutilons, white, red and yellow; callas; cyclamen; fuchsias; geraniums, zonal, scented and ivy; heliotrope, lantanas and oleanders, can always be used to advantage. In addition, we can add, for fall and early winter flowering, a sufficient number of chrysanthemums to afford a variety of colors, and in the spring the Chinese primrose, cinerarias and calceolarias, with their bright flowers, are always attractive. The azaleas do not thrive well during the winter in a dwelling, but when in bloom in the spring will be very ornamental if they can be added. Eupatoriums, stevias and ageratums are also excellent house plants.

Of the flowering bulbs, the hyacinth, tulip, crocus, narcissus, scilla, and lily of the valley, are most commonly grown and with but little attention add much to the effect. For house use, the hyacinth may be grown in water in hyacinth glasses. The oxalis, in some of its varieties, such as *Bowiei, cernua lutea,* or *versicolor,* is an excellent pot plant, while for basket purposes it has few equals.

The lilies are also very desirable for spring and summer blooming. *Lilium candidum* and *L. Harrisii* flower in March and April, or with *Lilium elegans, L. auratum* and *L. speciosum album* and *rubrum,* can be brought into flower during the summer months.

In addition to the above list, there are many flowers

that are readily grown from seeds, such as carnations, alyssum, candytuft, mignonette, nasturtiums, stocks, matricaria (feverfew), besides others used as bedding plants, as verbenas, petunias, pansies, pyrethrum, centaurea and dianthus, that are also often used as house plants.

While carnations, violets and roses are of value for furnishing cut flowers, they can seldom receive proper care in a dwelling and are seldom desirable as house plants, unless one has at least a small window conservatory in which proper conditions can be given them.

As plants for the decoration of a parlor, or to combine with others in a large window, the following are desirable, as they can be grown successfully with but little care: Palms, pandanus, aspidistras, rubber trees, *Cyperus alternifolius*, anthericum, dracænas and cordylines, araucarias and marantas, besides, in partial shade, ferns, lycopods, gloxinias, tuberous begonias, fancy leaved caladiums, and many others. As house plants among the palms, we may note as among the most valuable, *Howea (Kentia) Belmoreana*, and *H. Fosteriana, Areca lutescens, Rhapis humilis* and *R. flabelliformis, Livistona Chinensis (Latania Borbonica), Ptychosperma Cunninghamiana (Seaforthia elegans), Cocos Weddeliana, Livistona (Corypha) Australis*, and many others.

As plants for climbing or trailing, we may mention the ivies, English (*Hedera helix*), German, *Senecio mikanioides*, cape *S. macroglossus* and Kenilworth or coliseum (*Linaria Cymbalaria*), *Vinca minor*, var. madeira vine, moneywort (*Lysimachia nummularia*), *Mahernia odorata, Othonna crassifolia*, lobelias, musk plant (*Mimulus moschatus*), *Lygodium scandens*, wax plant (*Hoya carnosa*), *Cobæa scandens*, canary bird-flower (*Tropæolum peregrinum*), smilax (*Myrsiphyllum asparagoides*), maurandya, *Manettia bicolor* and *M. cordifolia* and cypress vine (*Ipomœa Quamoclit*). For training upon the walls or about the windows, nearly any of the climbers should be used, while the drooping vines are invaluable for use in hanging baskets and vases.

WINDOW BOXES.

Excellent results can often be obtained from boxes upon the window sills (Fig. 92). If made of the length of the sill, and as wide as will rest securely, with a depth of five or six inches, and with a lining of zinc, they can be filled with almost any of the small or medium sized plants, and with some of the more ornamental of the trailing vines they will present a very handsome appearance.

At the ends of the boxes, some of the stronger growing vines should be placed, and they will soon reach a size that will allow of their being trained about the window, as in this way a much better growth can be obtained than would be secured in small pots. The exterior of these boxes can be painted, or covered with oilcloth. In the summer time, these or similar boxes may be placed outside upon the window sill, and with a little care in watering will be very attractive. Equally good, if not better, results can be obtained from the use of rather larger boxes upon a veranda.

When designed for the decoration of the parlor or drawing room, the larger plants may be placed in jardinieres or in large ornamental flower pots. Some of the more simple forms of plant stands will be found very convenient and quite attractive, while for the decoration of the bay window, wire or earthen hanging baskets and plants upon brackets will serve to increase the apparent extent of the arrangement.

HANGING BASKETS.

There are few ways of arranging plants that give better satisfaction than in hanging baskets. If those made of wire are used, they should be lined with green moss, or sphagnum, from the swamp, and filled with a light, but rich soil. The glazed earthen pots are not porous, and the soil soon becomes sour, if the watering is not done very carefully; although less ornamental, the unglazed pots will be likely to give a better growth of plants. To hold the water, and prevent the baking of the surface, a thin layer of moss or sphagnum should be placed over it. From the fact that they are exposed at all times to drying influences, they need a copious supply of water. In case they dry out at any time, it will be well to dip them in a tub of water, as dry sphagnum takes up water very slowly. For the center of the basket, it is best to take some graceful, drooping plants, such as dracænas or cordylines, caladiums, begonias, ferns, small palms, pandanus, geraniums, and particularly ivy geraniums. Around these, if the basket is a large one, small upright or drooping plants, such as alyssums, lobelias, verbenas, anthericums, coleus, achyranthes, saxifrage, mikanias, mahernia, othonna, *Isolepis gracilis,* mimulus, nierembergia, mesembryanthemums, and other small plants may be used. In addition to the trailing plants mentioned, such others as Kenilworth (coliseum) ivy, moneywort and tradescantia, of various kinds. Tropæolums and variegated vincas will be desirable for hanging over the edge of the basket, while the German ivy, madeira vine, cypress vine, English ivy, and other climbers may be trained up the wires or chains, and festooned to some of the surrounding objects. While wire baskets or those made of earthenware, especially for this purpose, are best adapted, there is often about the house a variety of cast-off utensils that can be used as hanging baskets.

AQUARIUMS.

As an adjunct to the other floral decorations of the living room, these extremely interesting ornaments should not be overlooked. They can be stocked with foliage and flowering plants, fish, snails, and other animals, and with very little attention will be found extremely attractive.

The aquarium itself should be of some simple, yet tasteful design, and its beauty will be enhanced if its sides are of glass; while the framework may be of wood, it is preferably made of iron, with a slate bottom. In filling it, clean fine sand should be placed in the bottom and covered with a layer of gravel, over which ornamental shells, stones, etc., should be strewn. In the center, arches should be constructed of slag, or coral rocks. Of plants, for purifying the water, the *Sagittari natans* and *Anacharis Canadensis* are highly esteemed, although cel grass and parrot feather (*Myrsiophyllum asparagoides*) are valuable. The stems of these can be imbedded in the sand, and they will readily take root. Other plants in pots, such as callas and cyperus, can also be used in large aquariums.

In addition to small minnows, gold fish, sticklebacks and other fish, various kinds of snails, and if desired, lizards, frogs, etc., can be added. As soon as the plants have been arranged, the aquarium should be supplied nearly full of pure fresh water, and the animals added. In locating an aquarium, while it is desirable that it be where it can have sun for a short time each day, very much of the direct sunlight should be avoided, as it is injurious to the fish, as the water will soon fill with a green scum.

Aquariums need but very little care, as, if the glass is wiped off every week or two, using a swab at the end of a stick, and the contents taken out and the tank thoroughly cleaned once a year, little other attention need be given them.

The fish should be fed regularly once a day; while bread crumbs and similar food will answer, they will thrive best if fed upon earth worms, flies, or bits of raw meat. Care should be taken that no more is supplied than will readily be eaten by the fish, or other animals in the tanks. With the above attention, in a room at a temperature of from 60 to 70 degrees, there will be little trouble in keeping both animals and plants in a healthy condition, and much pleasure can be derived from them.

WARDIAN CASES.

When one desires to grow exotic ferns, and the more delicate plants, in the living rooms, some means must be employed to preserve an abundant, even supply of moisture, and to keep the dust from them. One of the simplest devices is known as a Wardian case. This consists of a shallow box, of any desired size, say 3 by 18 by 36 inches, lined with sheet lead or zinc, and covered either with a glass shade or a glass box of the same length and breadth as the base, and with a hight of perhaps eighteen inches. The framework for the glass can be of any light wood, fastened securely together. The cover itself should be removable, to provide for watering and ventilation. The bottom box can be made ornamental if one prefers, but the glass top will present the best appearance, if in some simple and neat style.

The soil for filling the box should contain a large amount of sand and leaf mold, and for some plants a generous supply of peat is advisable. If properly supplied with water when first filled, it will need but little more, as it condenses upon the glass and runs back to the soil. Among the best plants for a Wardian case are the more delicate of the tropical ferns and selaginellas, marantas, peperomias, dracænas, crotons and both foliage and flowering begonias. They will require little or no care in addition to an occasional watering, except to raise the glass for a short time each morning, to afford them a supply of fresh air, and to pick out the decayed leaves and flowers.

CHAPTER XXII.

THE GROWING OF BEDDING PLANTS.

In every greenhouse, whether public or private, some attention is given to the growing of plants for lawn decoration. A few years ago, the plants used on the ordinary lawn consisted of a few common varieties, grown from seeds, or "slips" taken from the plants grown for winter flowering.

Not only has the number of varieties used for this purpose increased, but within the last twenty years the attention given to carpet bedding and other lawn planting has increased many fold. For convenience, the plants used for this purpose may be divided into foliage plants, flowering plants, bulbs and ornamental grasses.

FOLIAGE PLANTS.

At the present time, the number of species of plants of this class in use is comparatively small, and yet perhaps they are used more extensively than all others combined. They are very easily and cheaply grown, and, unlike many of the flowering plants, are ornamental throughout the entire season.

Among the best-known and most useful plants of this class are the coleus, achyranthes (or, more properly, iresine) and alternanthera. The first two greatly resemble each other, and as they require about the same care, they may be considered together. The alternanthera, on the other hand, is a small, compact growing plant, seldom reaching a hight of more than six inches, while the others are from twelve to twenty.

These plants are grown from cuttings, those for the stock plants being made about the first of September. Sometimes the cuttings are not secured until the plants have been more or less cut back by frost, which will tend to weaken them considerably. The plants, as grown in the beds, require more or less pinching and trimming, and the portions cut off can be used for cuttings and will thus be secured and out of the way before the rush of housing the plants begins. As soon as rooted, they should be potted into two-inch pots and placed in a house, where they will have an average night temperature of 60 degrees. Considerable space can be saved if three or even four of the alternanthera cuttings are placed in one pot, and grown in this way until February, when they can be separated and each placed in a pot by itself.

The soil required for these plants during the winter should not be very rich, as it is desirable to hold them back until after the first of January. If they show signs of spindling, the terminal bud should be pinched off. When many cuttings are desired, the plants should be repotted about January 1, and started into growth. By the liberal use of liquid manure, several crops of cuttings can be obtained from the stock plants. These should be given the same treatment as was recommended for the stock plants, and by the first of May, if large plants are desired for planting out, they should be given a final shift into three or three and one-half-inch pots.

To harden them off for planting out, it is well to place the bedding plants in cold frames at this time, having it so that they can be covered in stormy weather and on cold nights. When to be used by the grower, it is very convenient to give them their final shift into deep flats, where. if placed four inches apart, they will do better than if left in pots, and require less care, besides being more convenient for handling.

The alternanthera requires a moist air and can be best propagated if the stock plants are placed in a good hotbed, also using it for striking the cuttings and growing the plants. The care necessary to winter and propagate coleus and achyranthes is about the same as for alternanthera, except that the cuttings are usually potted singly. If carefully watered and the temperature is kept at 60 degrees, they can be grown with little loss. Among the best varieties of coleus for bedding purposes are the Verschaffeltii, which is of a rich, dark maroon color and has been for years at the head of the list, and Golden Verschaffeltii, similar to the last in growth, but of a clear, bright yellow.

The varieties of achyranthes are either of some shade of red, or of yellow with a green ground. The best of the red leaved sorts are the Hoveyii, with dull, carmine leaves, which are broadly ovate in form and have whitish veins; Lindenii, with lanceolate, rich, blood-red leaves; Herbstii aurea-reticulata, with carmine stems, petioles and veins, while the leaves are green blotched with yellow. Among the others are Emersonii, a variety resembling Lindenii, and Gilsonii, which differs from aurea-reticulata principally in the shape of the leaves.

Among the better varieties of alternanthera are *A. amabilis*, *A. spectabilis*, *A. paronychioides*, *A. paronychioides major*, and *A. versicolor*, which have various shades of red, orange and bronze, or olive green. and *A. paronychioides major aurea*, with a foliage colored green and yellow. The latter, especially, is very useful for bedding purposes.

To contrast with the above dark colored foliage plants, a number with silver or yellow foliage are grown, the most common of which are the *Centaurea gymnocarpa* and *candidissima, Cineraria maritima,* and *Pyrethrum aureum.* These are all readily grown from seed, which should be sown in shallow flats during February. The seedlings should be transferred to small pots or flats as soon as the first true leaves appear, and with good care will be large enough by the middle of May to be planted out as borders for geraniums, dark-colored coleus and other bedding plants.

FLOWERING PLANTS.

Of the other bedding plants that are commonly grown from seed, we may mention petunias, phlox, verbenas, alyssum, candy-tuft, balsams, portulaca, asters, celosia, dianthus and ricinus. In a general way, these require about the same care as the other seedling annuals. There are also a large number of bedding plants valued principally for their flowers, which may be grown from seed, but which are usually propagated by means of cuttings, among them are ageratum, geranium, lantana, cuphea, while many of those grown from seeds could be propagated by means of cuttings, if it is desired to reproduce some choice variety.

SWEET PEAS.

While the sweet pea likes a cool, moist and rather heavy soil, it can be grown successfully in almost any place where the soil is not too dry and where the plants will not be too near large trees or in the shade of buildings. It is a good plan to prepare the soil the fall previous to planting by applying three or four inches of thoroughly decomposed manure, and working it into the soil to the depth of ten or twelve inches where the rows are to be. A liberal amount of wood ashes and ground bone can also be used to advantage. Another method is to dig a trench twelve inches deep and fourteen inches wide and place in the bottom six inches of composted manure, to which wood ashes and ground bone have been added. If the former method is used, drills for the seed are made six inches deep and ten inches apart, in which the seeds are sown as soon as the ground can be worked in the spring. They should be dropped in a scattering manner in the drills so that they will be two or three inches apart. Planted in this way, there will be ten or twelve plants in each foot of the double rows. When low-priced seed is used, twice as many may be planted and the surplus plants removed. If the bottom of the trench has been filled with compost, as was recommended above, a little soil should be sprinkled over it and the seeds sown. In either case they should not be covered with more than two inches of soil at first. If the weather is very cold after the seed is planted, it will be well to cover the rows with a light mulch or boards, removing them as the weather becomes warmer. After the plants appear above ground the trenches should be gradually filled, taking care not to cover the crowns. The danger of rot and blight will be lessened if the covering soil is sandy. If the ground is not ready when the seed should be sown, or in the case of choice varieties, the seed may be sown in some warm spot, or in boxes or pots in the house or cold frame, and the plants transplanted when one or two inches high. Unless sown in pots care should be taken in transplanting not to break the taproots.

When well grown, most of the stronger varieties will reach a hight of six feet and will need a substantial support. In some places bushy branches of trees may be used, but a neater and generally more satisfactory support can be obtained from either a twine, wire or wire-netting trellis. This should be from four to six feet high, upon strong, well-braced supports. It will be desirable to have a row of stakes for each row; they may either be vertical or inclined so that the tops touch. The strings may be run vertically, but it will be better if the wires are arranged either horizontally or diagonally. Whatever supports are to be used, they should be in place soon after the plants appear above ground, and care should be taken to have the bottom of the trellis at such a hight that the plants can readily reach it.

There should be a slight hollow where the rows are, so that rain water will be held, and to permit of the ready watering of the surface if the weather becomes dry. Sub-irrigation for sweet peas gives excellent results. It can be provided by laying three-inch drain tiles, into which water can be turned, along the rows, just below the surface of the ground. In order to prevent the loss of water by evaporation, the surface of the soil should be covered, as soon as the weather becomes dry, with two inches of fine grass, straw or other litter. If the flowers are not picked it is of the utmost importance that the seed pods be removed as soon as they form. If this is neglected, the plants will be likely to dry up by midsummer.

BULBS FOR THE LAWN.

Many of the bulbs used for the decoration of the lawn in summer are started in the greenhouse in the spring and are then transferred to the ground outside. Among them are the caladium, canna and dahlia.

The *Caladium esculentum*, which is the species most commonly used for lawn planting, should be dug after the leaves have been cut by frost, and after being dried should be packed away in some moderately warm, dry place. To prevent excessive drying, it is a good plan to place them in shallow boxes and pack dry soil or sand about them. In March or April the bulbs should be potted off singly in pots whose diameter is about twice that of the bulbs. They like a rich, light soil, and after being thoroughly watered should be placed in a warm room. If the potting has been delayed, they can be advanced by giving a strong bottom heat. After the leaves have appeared they will stand a considerable amount of water, provided the pots are well drained.

Cannas should be put away for the winter in about the same manner as caladiums, but will stand a somewhat lower temperature, although it should be kept well above 40 degrees. Many varieties do well if placed in pots or boxes, or planted out in beds, for several months in the fall, for supplying flowers and brightening up the greenhouse. It is also well to pot off some of the bulbs in the winter, after they have had a short rest, and thus secure flowers in the early spring. The usual plan has been to keep the bulbs in the cellar, or under the greenhouse benches, until danger of frost is over and then after dividing them so that there will be at least one strong bud on each piece, planting them in the open ground. Quicker and better results can be obtained, however, if they have been started in pots or boxes before they are transferred to the beds outside. With choice varieties it is possible to increase the rapidity of propagation if the bulbs are planted on beds in a greenhouse where they will have a brisk bottom heat about midwinter. In a short time new shoots will form, which can be taken off and in turn planted out to reproduce.

Several of the new sorts, such as Italia and Austria, seem to be well adapted for flowering in pots, but the texture of the petals is such that they do not succeed outside in most parts of the country unless they are planted in partial shade. For ordinary use, either on the lawn or in the house, there are few if any better sorts than the well-known Mme. Crozy. Florence Vaughan is perhaps the best yellow spotted variety. Among the other sorts that have been generally successful are

Alphonse Bouvier, Explorateur Crampbel, Egandale, Geoffrey St. Hilliare, J. D. Cabos, Paul Marquant and Pres. Carnot.

THE DAHLIA.

This old favorite is again becoming the fashion, and even now is usurping the attention that has for some years been given the sweet pea. The single sorts may be grown successfully from seed, but for the double varieties it is better to rely upon cuttings of the stem, or division of the roots. The cuttings root readily in sand, and if started early will give good results. In dividing the roots, it is necessary that there should be a bud at the end of each. The operation can be most readily performed if the stools are slightly started into growth before the division is made.

Dahlias like a deep, rich, moist and rather heavy soil, and in few plants will a little extra labor in the preparation of the soil be better repaid. An excess of nitrogenous manure should be avoided, as it will give a rank growth of leaves and few flowers, while a sandy soil is likely—owing to its usual deficiency in plant food and moisture—to give rather small plants upon a few small roots, and with undersized flowers. If moisture and plant food are provided, excellent results can be secured upon a sandy loam soil. The plants should be set in the beds as soon as danger of frost is over. They will be best in rows, if a large number are to be grown, and with a large collection it will be well to have them far enough apart to admit of cultivating them with a horse. Owing to their love of moisture, it is very desirable in dry summers that the surface of the soil be kept loose to the depth of two inches, to lessen the amount of evaporation.

As commonly grown, allowing them to form shoots freely, most varieties require staking to prevent the breaking down of the stems by high winds, but many of the new varieties have short stiff stems that make this unnecessary. A better way of training the plants, which will seldom require staking, is by pinching off the shoots after they have two nodes above ground and allowing four branches to form, all other shoots being removed. In this way four stout shoots will be secured which can be trained to single stems, if large flowers are desired, or they may be again pinched and thus made to form as many shoots as are wished. Another method, where large flowers are desired, is to allow but one main shoot to grow. This will become quite large and tree-like and will require staking.

When the tops have been killed by frost they should be cut and, if severe freezing weather is likely to follow, the roots should be dug; after the removal of most of the earth and partially drying them, if the soil is wet, they should be stored in some cool but frost-proof and moderately dry cellar.

The cactus dahlia is likely to become the favorite flower for late summer and early fall, and in the new varieties there are many handsome forms and brilliant colors. The original plant was carried from Mexico to Holland in 1872. It was named Dahlia Juarez, in honor of the President of Mexico. Instead of the quilled florets found in other forms those of the cactus dahlias are flat and strap-shaped.

The following list of varieties is recommended by the Cornell Experiment Station: Cactus, Mrs. A. Peart, white; Nymphæa, pink; Wm. Agnew, scarlet orange; Maid of Kent, scarlet and white; Black Prince, dark red; large flowered, Grand Duke Alexis, white; Ethel Vick, pink; Rev. C. W. Bolton, variegated, red and yellow; Fern Leaved Beauty, banded, red and white; pompon, Guiding Star, white, imbricated; Vivid, scarlet orange, and Ami Barillet, single, scarlet.

HARDY ORNAMENTAL GRASSES.

For planting on the lawn in connection with shrubbery and strong growing sub-tropical plants, there are many ornamental grasses that can be used with good effect. Although generally spoken of as hardy, most of them are greatly benefited by winter protection, and in many parts of the country even this is not sufficient. They delight in a rich and moist but well-drained soil, and in suitable locations present a handsome and striking appearance for three or four months in the year.

Among the most desirable are several species of Eulalia. Under favorable conditions *Eulalia Japonica Zebrina* will prove very attractive. It is a tall growing sort, with long, narrow leaves transversely marked with broad patches of yellow. In the fall its flower spikes form open, feathery plumes. It propagates readily by division of the clumps, and, if well mulched, will pass the winter in well-drained soil where the climate is not too severe, but where there is danger of winterkilling the clumps can be taken up in the fall and planted in pots or shallow boxes. Placed in a cool cellar or cold frame, they will require no care except an occasional moistening of the soil if it becomes dry. In the spring they can be started into growth and planted out after danger of frost is over. Of the other species, *Eulalia Japonica variegata*, which is the same as the above except that the stripes are narrow and longitudinal, and *E. gracillima univitata* are most desirable. The latter is six or eight feet high, with quite narrow leaves which bear a single longitudinal stripe. It is quite hardy and in most parts of the country will pass the winter in the open ground without protection.

Arundo Donax variegata is another strong-growing form which in most localities should be wintered in a cellar or cold frame. The Fountain grass, *Pennisetum longistylum* and its purple variety, *P. Ruppelianum*, are excellent as a border for other grasses and strong-growing plants of any kind. It is propagated from seed, which is freely produced, the seeds being sown in April and grown the same as other annuals.

In some sections the Pampas grass is also successfully grown and presents a very striking appearance. Several forms of bamboo can also be used to advantage for lawn planting, and in some localities can be wintered successfully in the open ground.

SUCCULENTS.

For bedding purposes, some of the succulents, such as Echeverias, are largely grown and their use for this purpose seems to be increasing in public favor, while the cacti proper, the aloes and agaves are so easy of cultivation, so interesting in habit and attractive in flower, that in every collection they are more or less numerous. Of the cotyledons (*Echeveria*) the form known as *secunda glauca* is most used for bedding. It propagates readily by means of offshoots from the parent plants, which only need to be separated and potted off, or by the use of leaf cuttings.

By the latter method, the leaves are separated—pulled off and not cut—from the parent plant, in the fall or spring, and after the end has callused over they are set in the cutting boxes, where they should have only enough water to keep them from shrivelling. Roots will soon form and the bud at the base of the leaves will start, and form a plant large enough to use the following season. Succulents of all kinds should be kept moderately dry during their resting period in the winter, but when growth starts in the spring water should be given in generous quantities, and, unless they have been recently repotted, liquid manure can be used to advantage. They delight in a sandy soil and thorough drainage. During the summer, the plants used for bedding purposes should have a fair amount of water, although they have few equals as bedding plants when the supply is short. During the winter they can be kept in a cool house (45 degrees).

Several forms, such as *Cotyledon gibbiflora metallica* (commonly called *Echeveria metallica*) are desirable for winter flowering and many of them, including several annuals, can be readily increased from seeds. The

FIG. 93. EPIPHYLLUM TRUNCATUM.

houseleeks, Mesembryanthemum, and similar forms, require much the same care.

Of the other succulents, the Cereus and the leaf cacti Phyllocactus and Epiphyllum (Fig. 93) are most commonly grown. The most desirable species of the first genus are *C. grandiflorus, C. Macdonaldi* and *C. triangularis* and the rat-tailed cactus (*C. flagelliformis*).

286 GREENHOUSE MANAGEMENT.

They are increased by cutting up the stems into pieces three inches long and rooting them under the same conditions as the Cotyledon. Soon after the growth starts, suckers and branches will be sent out. It will generally be best, in case an **old** stem was used for the cuttings, to cut these off and root them, which can be readily done. The Epiphyllums and other leaf

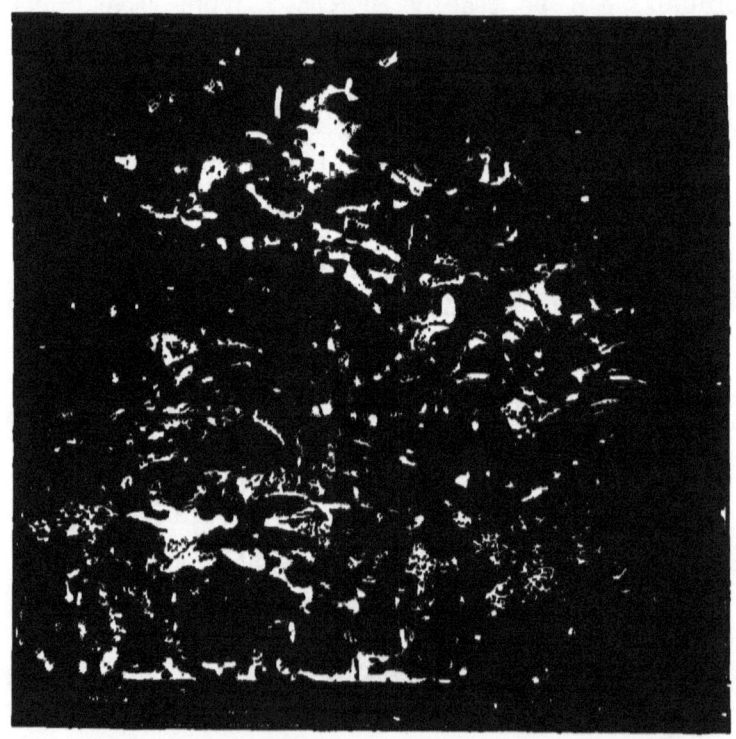

FIG. 94. A COLLECTION OF CACTI AND ALOES.

cacti are often grown as standards, by grafting them upon Pereskia stocks. The form of graft used is a modification of the cleft graft and is known as the saddle graft. Among the other desirable forms are the Opuntias, with their flattened leaf-like stems, the Mammillarias and Echinocactus, with their spherical forms, and a number of handsome species of aloes (Fig. 94).

CHAPTER XXIII.

PROPAGATION OF PLANTS BY SEEDS AND CUTTINGS.

In order to keep up a supply of plants and to multiply individuals of merit, some method of propagation must be employed, the one selected being that best suited to the particular species or variety. Many of our plants are known as annuals, from the fact that they will grow and mature seed in one season, after which they die. As a rule, such plants are reproduced the following year from the seeds, which are freely produced.

The methods of propagation known as grafting, budding and layering, are also sometimes employed in growing greenhouse plants, but a more common way is by means of sections of the plants, known as cuttings, which are removed and subjected to such influences as will induce them to throw out roots. Another method of division, used with plants that sucker freely, is the division of the roots, the plants being separated into two or more portions, each consisting of a piece of root surmounted by a stem, or at least bearing a bud. Whenever it can be used, this is one of the surest methods of multiplying plants, and some species can be increased very rapidly when other methods fail, or are, for some reason, unsatisfactory.

GROWING OF PLANTS FROM SEEDS.

Not only are our annual plants readily increased from seeds, but the method is also employed in multiplying many of our biennials and perennials, and is our only means, except in case of sports developed by bud variation, of obtaining new varieties. For the successful germination of seeds, certain conditions must be present; first, the seeds should be plump, well-ripened, and they must still possess their vitality unimpaired. The best results will be obtained if, after the seeds have been cleaned and properly dried, they are placed in paper sacks, or, better yet, in tin boxes or glass bottles, and kept in a dry room, at a temperature of 50 degrees. If they have been properly dried, few seeds will be injured even if the temperature falls below the freezing point, but vitality will be best preserved if they are kept at a moderate, even temperature; especially should a high temperature be avoided for oily seeds.

Second, the seeds must be exposed to a temperature suited to their needs, and a proper supply of moisture, with free access of air, must be afforded them. The temperature required for the germination of seeds is about the same as is needed by the plants, but germination will be hastened if it is some ten or fifteen degrees higher. When 45 to 50 degrees is suitable for the plants at night, the seeds should be given from 55 to 60 degrees, and if the excess can be in the form of bottom heat it will be even more beneficial; a similar increase will hasten the germination of the seeds of plants that need 60 to 70 degrees. After the seeds have been sown, they should not be allowed to become dry, and yet great care is necessary that the soil does not become saturated.

Particularly with small seeds that need but a thin covering, it is well to have them shaded, as well as to keep them covered, and thus prevent the rapid evaporation of the water, and the consequent drying out of the soil. If in the shade, the moisture can be retained by means of a pane of glass placed over the box or pan, but if so situated that the direct rays of the sun can fall upon them, it will be well to cover the glass with paper.

The glass should be slightly tilted to afford access of air. For holding the soil, shallow wooden boxes or flats answer every purpose, although some florists prefer unglazed, earthenware seed pans; in either case, thorough drainage must be provided by means of holes or cracks in the bottoms.

When only a few of a kind are to be sown, a shallow cigar box will answer for small seeds, and boxes with a depth of from one or one and one-half to two and one-half inches, according to the size of the seeds, are ample. In large establishments, the seed beds can, if desired, be made upon the greenhouse benches, thorough drainage being provided for.

The soil for the seed bed varies to some extent with the character of the plants, but, as a rule, the same soil as is used for potting will answer, although it will be improved by the addition of twenty-five per cent of sand, especially for covering the seeds. The depth of covering will vary with the size of the seed, but, under glass, it will be from three to five times their diameter, while in the open ground it will be about fifty per cent deeper, varying with the character of the soil. While seeds may be sown broadcast, it will generally be found best to have them in drills about one inch apart for small seeds, and two inches for the larger ones.

In filling the boxes with soil, pains should be taken to press it into the corners, and we must not forget the necessity of leaving the soil slightly below the edge, to prevent the water running off. The proper depth of soil for covering the seeds, when they need one-eighth of an inch or more, can be secured in various ways; one being by making shallow trenches across the seed beds, slightly deeper than the covering needed and, after sowing the seed, filling the trenches; while another is by filling the box so that, for seeds that require covering a quarter of an inch, when the soil has been leveled off and slightly pressed down, it will be about one-half inch below the edge of the box. After sowing the seeds, either broadcast or in rows upon the surface, fill up the box with light, prepared soil, strike it off and press it down. A wooden float of convenient size, with handle, will be useful in sowing seeds. In this way, a uniform depth of covering soil will be secured and the surface will be sufficiently pressed to hold the water. With a little practice, the depth can be adjusted for any size of seed.

When the sowing has been completed, the boxes should be thoroughly watered, after which, as with plants in pots, the seed boxes should not be watered until their appearance indicates the necessity, and then enough should be applied to thoroughly wet the soil. When the boxes can be placed for a few minutes in a water-tight bed, holding two inches of water, the soil will be moistened without danger of washing the seeds, or of causing the plants to damp off.

As soon as the first true leaves show, the seedlings should be pricked out, either in flats or small pots; for many plants, the flats will be preferable for the first transplanting.

THE FORMATION OF NEW VARIETIES.

While it is possible to obtain new varieties of many plants by merely growing seedlings, others almost invariably reproduce themselves, and with them we must resort to artificial crossing, or hybridizing. In fact, although some progress may be made in improving those of the first class, by selecting the more promising seedlings, far better results can be obtained if we control the parentage by artificial pollination.

For any desired improvements, we should select as parents two varieties that have the desired qualities well developed, and transfer pollen from the anthers of one to the stigmas of the other. To do this properly, precaution must be taken that no other pollen gains access to the stigmas. This can be done by first removing the anthers from all perfect flowers that are to be used as females, before the petals open, and covering them with small paper sacks. We have thus prevented them from being self fertilized, or crossed with pollen of unknown origin. The anthers may be pulled off with tweezers, or the corolla may be cut away, thus permitting their easy removal.

As soon as the stigmas have developed, the pollen from the other parent should be applied, using a toothpick for small flowers, while the anthers may be broken out from large ones with tweezers, and the pollen dusted over the surface of the stigmas. To secure the best results, a superabundance of pollen should be used. The bag should then be replaced and kept on four or five days. In this way, we may hope to secure seedlings some of which, if they do not surpass them, will possess to a high degree the good qualities of both parents.

PROPAGATION BY CUTTINGS.

Success with this method of propagation depends upon the condition of the plants, and the surroundings to which the cuttings are exposed. As a rule, most of our perennial greenhouse plants are grown from cuttings. In some cases, seeds are not readily obtained, and in others the seedlings do not make desirable plants, or they do not reproduce the variety. In a great majority of these cases, cuttings are readily obtained and rooted.

The plants from which cuttings are taken should be strong and vigorous; if stunted by insects or by improper surroundings of heat, light, temperature, or food, or weakened by excessive production of flowers, the results will be quite unsatisfactory, and it will be equally so if soft, watery growth, produced by a high temperature

and excess of nitrogenous food, is used. The use of cuttings from plants enfeebled by disease will be even more disastrous, as the plants produced will not only be susceptible to the attack of the same and other diseases, but they may even have the germs of the disease within them when severed from the parent plant.

On the other hand, it is always best to propagate from individual plants that, in their vigor, freedom from disease, prolificacy, or in the size, shape or color of their

FIG. 96. IMPROPER AND PROPER CONDITION OF STEM FOR CUTTINGS.

flowers or fruits, show unusual merit. If such plants are marked in some way (Fig. 95), cuttings can be made from them at the proper time and thus a strain of pedigree plants can be established.

Greenhouse plants are generally multiplied by what is known as soft cuttings of the stems. They are usually made from terminal shoots, although if cuttings lower down the stem can be obtained in the proper condition, they will readily root and make good plants.

While a soft, watery growth is not desirable, cuttings cannot, as a rule, be induced to root readily after they become woody, and the usual test is to reject all cuttings that when bent do not snap off, rather than crush down without breaking, the latter behavior indicating that the fibro-vascular bundles (woody fibers), have formed (Fig. 96). Cuttings made from stems in that condition root slowly and sparingly, and the plants will be weaker than when made from those in the proper condition. For a few plants like the rose, a firmer condition of the wood is desirable.

Soft cuttings should have a bud at the top, and from one to three inches of stem. Unless a cutting can be made three inches long and have its base in proper condition, it will be better to shorten it to one inch, and, if necessary, the length may be even less, its stem being principally of value to give a secure hold in the cutting bed. Cuttings of this kind should have at least one leaf, and sometimes from two to four are left. Those at the lower part of the stem should be removed, and the others shortened in (Fig. 97).

FIG. 97. SOFT CUTTING OF COLEUS.

In this way the amount of evaporation will be checked and the cuttings can be placed nearer together. Cuttings should be so handled that they will not wilt. It is well to use a sharp knife, and to cut off the stem at nearly right angles. Neither, however, is really necessary, and in many cases the cuttings can be broken off without the use of a knife. If in the proper condition, most cuttings will root readily from any part of the stem, but with others that root with difficulty, and especially if they have become too hard, it will be well to have a bud near the base of the cuttings, as roots are most readily sent out from near the nodes.

THE CUTTING BED.

Cuttings root readily in sand, but, although the silver sand that was a few years ago insisted upon is not a necessity, it should be free from organic matter. The sand should also be sharp, and of about medium fineness; if too fine, or too coarse, it should be rejected, as the one packs together and obstructs the entrance of air, while the other admits it too freely, and dries out too readily. The cutting bed should have sufficient drainage to let off any surplus water, and bottom heat should be provided in some way. A narrow span-roof house, or a lean-to to the north or east, makes a good propagating house. It should afford ample means of securing ventilation.

The sand should have a depth of about three inches, and, although not necessary, the best results will be obtained if it is renewed after each batch of cuttings is taken out. After the sand has been thoroughly wet down and has drained off, the cuttings may be inserted. They should be placed in straight rows across the bed, so that the leaves of the cuttings do not quite touch. It is a good plan, if space permits, to have the rows about twice as far apart as the plants are in the rows. Having made a narrow trench for the cuttings, they are inserted about one-half their length, the sand is pressed firmly about them and the bed is wet down.

For the first few days, it is well to give them at least partial shade from sun, either by placing lath or cloth screens over the glass, or by spreading paper or cloth over the cuttings. With a slight shading of the glass, the latter can generally be left off after the first week. While precaution must be taken against excessive watering, there is also danger from allowing the bed to dry out as, if they wilt, the cuttings are much injured. Especially on summer days, an occasional slight sprinkling will be beneficial. The ventilation should be carefully looked after, and the arrangement should be such as will prevent a draft over the cutting bed. As soon as the roots have reached a length of half an inch, the cuttings should be potted into small pots and will need careful watering and shading for a few days.

While the above instructions apply to most plants, there are a few that, owing to some peculiarity of construction or growth, need different treatment, and among them are our common Pelargoniums (geraniums), (Fig. 98), and many of the cacti and other succulent plants. These are more or less succulent, and if placed at once in a cutting bed and treated as above, are likely to rot off. After being made, it is well to spread them out and allow them to wilt for from one day to one week, and then place them in a rather dry cutting bed, or they may at once be potted off, using a soil containing at least one-half sand.

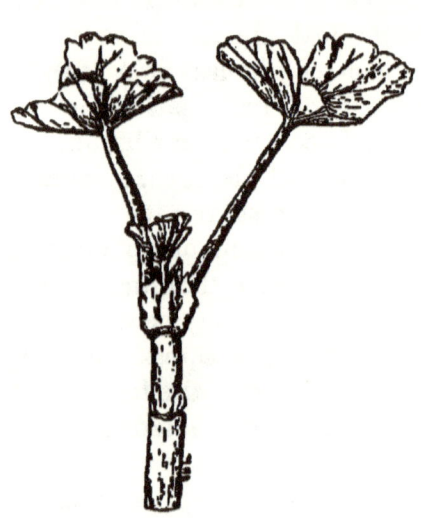

FIG. 98. GERANIUM CUTTING.

If, after giving them one thorough watering, water is withheld until they begin to wilt, cuttings handled in this way will often show smaller losses than when grown in a cutting bed. Many plants do not strike readily unless in a moist warm air, and for such a hand glass or propagating case must be used.

SAUCER PROPAGATION.

Another method of rooting cuttings that gives excellent results when bottom heat cannot be secured, is by placing them in earthenware pans of sand, two or three inches deep, which are kept constantly saturated with water. The other treatment, such as the making and setting of the cuttings, watering and ventilating, is exactly the same as for the cutting bed. Some of our common plants, like the oleander, root even better if placed in clear water than when in a cutting bed, or the saucer with its mud.

Any kind of glazed earthenware vessel, of a suitable size and depth, may be used, but if it is unglazed the water will need to be much more frequently added.

EYE CUTTINGS.

Many plants, such as the dracænas, cordylines, Dieffenbachias and others that form very few terminal shoots, have latent or adventitious buds upon their stems, and if these are cut into sections, about three inches long, and placed in a strong bottom heat in a propagating case, shoots will soon be sent out, which can then be taken off and rooted in sand. It is often beneficial to split the sections and place them in the sand with the rounded side uppermost. The eye cutting used in propagating the grape (Fig. 84) differs in having a thin shaving of bark removed from the side opposite the bud.

ROOT CUTTINGS.

It sometimes happens that it becomes necessary to multiply plants rapidly that do not grow readily from cuttings of the stems, and which either increase in number very slowly from the roots or fail to make good plants when grown in this way, and some other form of multiplication must be tried. If they have a tendency to sucker from the roots, we can use what are known as root cuttings. These are made by taking the roots of such plants and cutting them into pieces from one to three inches long. The pieces should be placed in flats, either on propagating benches or in hotbeds, and covered with about one inch of sandy soil. With bottom heat, they will soon callus and send out roots and one or more stems. The after-treatment is the same as for stem cuttings.

HARD CUTTINGS.

Some plants root readily from the wood of the previous year's growth, even after it has become hard, if made and callused while the stems are dormant, so that they will be ready to send out roots as the leaves appear. What are known as short cuttings need bottom heat to start readily, but with proper attention are excellent for the propagation of grapes and other deciduous plants that root readily. They are from two to three inches in length, with a strong bud near the top, and with a strip of bark and a little of the wood removed from one side for about an inch from the lower end (Fig. 85). They should be inserted in shallow boxes of sand with about an inch of rich compost in the bottom, so that the buds will be just covered. They need a cool room where they can have a little bottom heat, but the temperature should be low enough to retard the swelling of the buds until after the roots have appeared. While they must not be allowed to become dry, only a little water will be needed until the leaves appear, and an excess must be avoided. A layer of soil at the bottom of the box or propagating bed will permit of the cuttings remaining some considerable time in the sand, or they can be taken out at once after rooting, and boxed or potted off.

FIG. 99. CUTTING OF ARBOR VITÆ.

Many of our conifers, such as the improved varieties of arbor vitæ (Fig. 99), retinosporas, junipers and others, are readily propagated from cuttings of the ripened wood made in the winter. If they are in any way tender, it will be best to collect the wood in the fall and pack it away in moist sphagnum in a cool cellar, until the cuttings can be made up. In a general way, they are made in about the same way as soft cuttings, but are rooted and cared for more as the short, hard cuttings. In the spring they are planted out in nursery rows.

Long cuttings are from six to eleven inches long, with a bud at the bottom and another about one inch from the upper end (Fig. 100). It will be of advantage if a little of the bark is removed near the base, as was recommended for the short cuttings. These cuttings should be made in the fall, and packed away in a cool cellar or buried in some well drained spot out of doors. It is generally customary to place them in bundles with

FIG. 100. LONG CUTTING OF GRAPE.

the butts up and cover with about two inches of soil, over which enough straw or other rubbish is placed to keep out the frost. As soon as severe freezing weather is over, the mulch should be removed, and when they have callused the cuttings should be planted in drills twelve to fifteen inches apart, and one to two inches in the rows, with the buds just covered. This is a cheap way of propagating grapes, currants, gooseberries, willows, poplars, and many shrubs and vines.

HALF-HARD CUTTINGS.

Intermediate between the hard and soft cuttings are those sometimes called "half-hard," in which the woody fibers have begun to form. Such plants as the rose, and many of the shrubs, when used in a soft state, are likely to decay in the cutting bed, and with them a somewhat firm condition of the wood is desirable. They are made in about the same way as the soft cuttings and require the same care. With many of the shrubs, it is a good plan to secure a heel of the old wood, if possible, at the base of the cuttings.

LEAF CUTTINGS.

Several plants are most readily grown from what are known as leaf cuttings, among the plants propagated in this way are the rex begonias, gloxinias, and bryophyllum. If a leaf of bryophyllum be placed on a cutting bed, the buds along the margin will develop and send out stems and roots. The small plants can then be detached and potted. A rex begonia leaf can be made to develop buds from any of the larger veins. The leaves may be cut into strips of a fan shape an inch or so in width, severing as many of the main ribs as possible, and by inserting them edgewise in the cutting bed, small plants will soon form. Another way is to place the entire leaf upon the surface of the bed, severing the larger veins at intervals of two inches, and either pegging them down, or sprinkling a little sand over them. The gloxinia may be grown as above, or the entire leaf may be used as a cutting by inserting the end of the petiole in the sand.

CHAPTER XXIV.

PROPAGATION BY LAYERING, GRAFTING AND BUDDING.

Layers differ from cuttings only in being rooted while still attached to the plant. Many of the soft wooded plants that have long, slender branches can be readily rooted by pegging them down upon a propagating bed and covering the nodes with sand. Most of the climbing and trailing vines start readily in this way. The layering of hard wooded plants can be hastened by removing a ring of bark, or making a tongue upon the branch at the point where the roots are desired. The tongue should be an inch or a little more in length, pointing towards the main plant, and include something less than half the thickness of the stem, and may be on either the upper or the under side, the former being perhaps preferable, as there will be less danger of the breaking of the stem.

The old method of layering stems that were too stiff to bend down was to fasten a flower pot filled with sandy soil about them, but while this method is now somewhat used, a better way is to bind green sphagnum about the stem, after having partially girdled it, or pierced it to the center in a number of places with a knife. If the sphagnum is thoroughly moistened when bound on, and is frequently watered, roots will soon be sent out. It is a good plan to fasten around the sphagnum a strip of cloth, in such a way as to form a sort of saucer and thus prevent the water from running off. When a sufficient number of roots have formed, the layers should be cut off, and, after any loose sphagnum has been shaken off, carefully potted. Until the plant has established itself in the soil, it should be kept in a propagating case, or in a small room where the air can be kept moist, and all drafts of air avoided. Frequent sprinkling of the foliage will also be desirable.

GRAFTING.

A graft differs from a cutting mainly in forming a callus and, after thus joining itself to another plant, taking up its food through the roots of the host (the stock) rather than through roots which it formed for itself. This method of multiplying plants is practiced with many that cannot be readily grown from cuttings or layers, and for which seed cannot be used, either because they cannot be readily obtained, or because they do not reproduce the desired varieties.

Grafting is performed just as the growth of the stock is beginning, and while the cion is still dormant. The cions are made from the last season's growth, and are from three to four inches long, with a bud near the upper end. If in the right condition, for success in grafting we only need to bind the cion upon the stock in such a way that the cambium of one will at some point be in contact with that of the other, and cover the cut surface so that they will not suffer from evaporation.

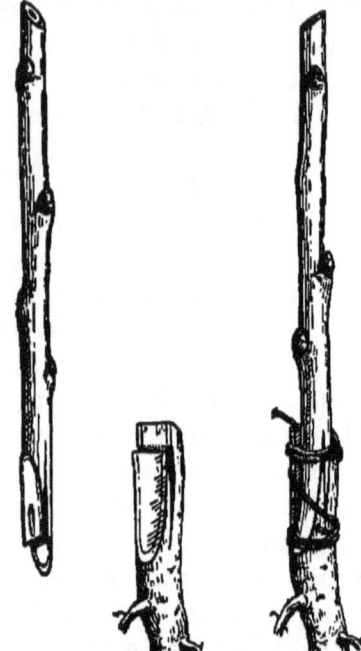

FIG. 101. TONGUE OR WHIP GRAFTING.

The more common kinds of grafting are, first, the splice, in which, as the name indicates, the stock and cion (which should be of about the same size) are cut at their ends with a long bevel, and are bound firmly together; second, the tongue or whip graft (Fig. 101), which differs from the splice only in having the ends so split as to form tongues, and they are then put together so that the tongues of one will be in the split in the other, and bound in place; third, the cleft graft, which is used upon large stocks, by inserting a cion with its lower end cut wedge shape, into a cleft in the middle of the top of the stock, which has been cut off at right angles, so that the bark at the outer edge of the cion will be in contact with the bark of the stock; if the stock is large, cions may be inserted upon both edges (Fig. 102).

For greenhouse work, the method known as side grafting (Fig. 103) is especially valuable. The stock is prepared by making a slanting downward cut about an inch long in the side of the stock; it should penetrate far enough towards the lower end to separate the cambium layer of wood. The cion should be cut about the same as for a cleft graft, except that the wedge should be about one-half longer on the inner side than on the outer. When pushed into place the tongue on the stock should cover the end of the cion and hold it in place. A modified form of this method of side grafting is known as veneer grafting, and while it is perhaps more likely to give a perfect union, it necessitates holding the cion in place while tying it. The cuts upon the stock are made just as in ordinary whip grafting, but the tongue is cut with a slanting stroke, so that it is only about one-fourth of an inch, or slightly less, in length. The lower end of the cion is cut off at an angle of 45 degrees, and the bark and a little of the cambium are removed for about one inch at the end of the longer side of the cion. The cion is then placed against the stock so that the tongue upon the stock will

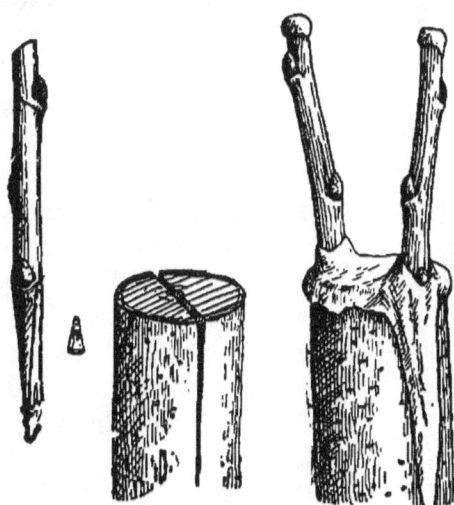

FIG. 102. CLEFT GRAFTING.

cover the end of the cion, and it is bound in place. Either of these methods of side grafting will be found particularly desirable for grafting the choice varieties of ornamental trees, both evergreen and deciduous. If the stocks are in pots they can be given a rest during the early winter and then started into growth so that they can be worked in January and February.

Many propagators have found difficulty in the drying out of the cions of conifers before the callus forms, but if they are placed on their sides upon a shallow bed of wet sphagnum, where they will have a little bottom heat, and the pots and grafts are then covered with the same material, the moisture will be retained and the failures will be very few. The same course can be pursued to advantage with choice deciduous trees. The stocks should be cut back to some extent at the time of grafting and as soon as growth has commenced the remaining portion may be cut away. Many other kinds of grafting have been practiced at various times and by different propagators, but none produce better results than the methods here described.

FIG. 103. SIDE GRAFTING.

In all cases except when large stocks are cleft grafted it will be necessary to wrap the graft with wax string, raffia, or yarn, in order to bind the cion and stock firmly together. Care should also be taken that all cuts are smooth and true, and a sharp knife with an even bevel from the back to the edge of the blade should be used.

GRAFTING WAX.

When the graft is made upon a stock at a point below the level of the soil, there will be no necessity of covering the cut surfaces with any other material, as the moist soil will answer the purpose. Whenever the graft is made at a point where it will not be covered by the soil, some preparation should be used to prevent the evaporation of water from the cut surfaces. For this purpose, nothing is better than grafting wax. There are many formulas for this mastic, most of which contain varying proportions of resin, beeswax and tallow, or linseed oil. As a cold wax to be used with the hands, a good proportion is, four parts resin, two parts beeswax and one part of tallow or linseed oil. After melting, it should be poured into water and left to cool until it can be held in the hands, which should be well oiled. It should then be pulled, the same as candy, until it takes on a light yellow color, after which it can be made into sticks of convenient size for use. This will be found of the right consistency for use in a warm room, or in warm weather outside. For use out of doors in cold weather, the wax should have one part less of resin (three parts resin, two of beeswax and one of tallow) and should be well worked before it is taken out.

As a thin mastic, to be applied with a brush, or the fingers, some of the alcoholic waxes may be used. They contain about 10 parts white resin, and one part beeswax (or one part tallow) melted together; after removing from the fire and partially cooling, stir in enough alcohol to give the right consistency. Keep in a tight bottle to prevent evaporation.

BUDDING.

Propagation by means of buds is only a modification of that by grafting, and in fact it is often called budgrafting, or shield grafting. It consists in the insertion of a piece of bark, containing a bud, under the bark of another plant of the same or a closely related species. The plant upon which the bud is placed is known as the stock and it should be in a growing condition, so that the bark will lift readily. The bud should be dormant, firm and well developed. In preparing the cion,

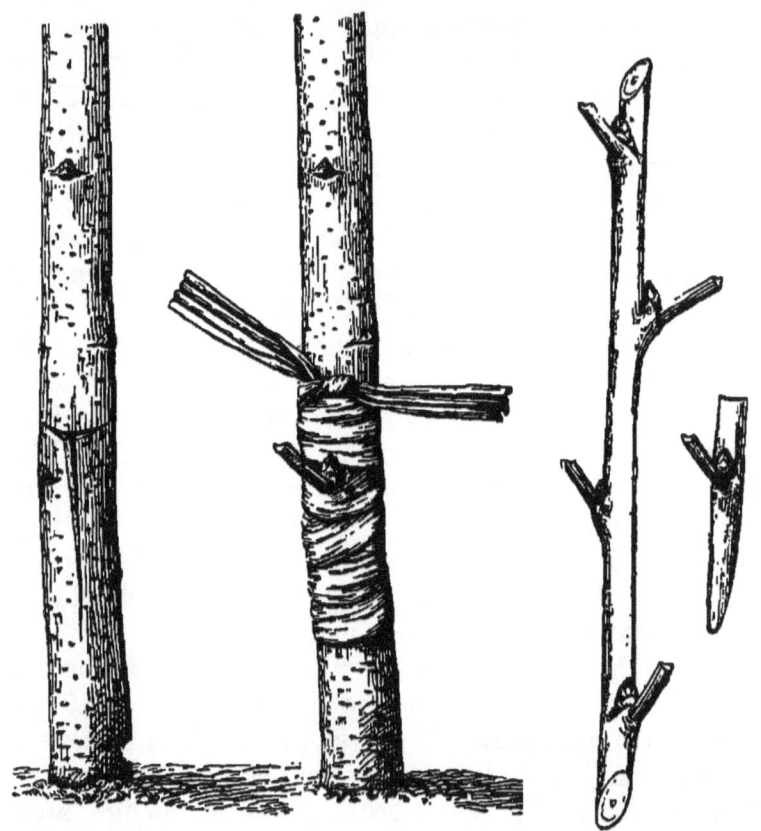

FIG. 104. BUDDING.

the leaves should be cut off about three-eighths of an inch from the bud, as shown in the illustration (Fig. 104).

In the open ground, budding is generally performed toward the end of the period of growth, the buds being those that have developed that season, but in the greenhouse it is done in the winter or early in the spring. The stocks are ripened off, and given a rest until January, when they are brought into growth and, as soon as the bark will slip, the budding is performed, using buds that have been kept dormant. A "T" shaped cut is made in the bark, generally as near the collar as possible, and the corners are lifted up so as to permit the insertion of the bud. In removing the bud from the cion, the cut is started about half an inch below the bud and is continued upward so as to take off a thin shaving of the wood until it is about half an inch above the bud, where the strip is cut off. The lower edge of the bark is inserted beneath the bark of the stock, and the bud is pushed down as far as it will readily go. For many plants it is fully as well, or better, to remove the shaving of wood from the bud before placing it in the stock. If, however, it cannot be done without injuring the bud, the wood should not be removed.

It should then be wrapped with raffia so as to press the bark of the stock firmly down around the bud. As a rule, two or three turns below and two above the bud will be sufficient; care should be taken in wrapping not to cover the bud, which should be in sight between the edges of the bark. A portion of the top of the stock should now be cut off, to check the growth and promote a union with the bud, and as soon as the bud has formed *l*eaves of its own, the remainder of the stock should be cut away. While almost any form of knife can be used for budding if it is sharp, the regular budding knives have thin blades and rounded points. Unless it has at the end of the handle a piece of ivory to be used in lifting the bark of the stock, the point of the blade can be arranged to serve for this purpose, by slightly rounding it.

CHAPTER XXV.

INSECTS OF THE GREENHOUSE.

Few of our greenhouse plants are free from the attack of insects, and many of them are greatly injured by parasitic fungi, so that constant watchfulness is necessary if they are to be kept in a healthy condition. In this chapter we shall describe some of those that are most troublesome, and give remedies for their destruction. It should be mentioned, however, that if proper care is given to the selection of the stock from which the plants are propagated, and if attention is paid to providing them with suitable soil, a congenial temperature and the necessary amount of water and fresh air, the plants will not only be more likely to escape attack, but will be much less injured if the insects and diseases appear.

It will be found that the fungicides are for the most part intended for use as preventives rather than cures, and to be effectual will need to be applied before the disease has any hold upon the plants. The same thing is true with many of the insecticides, to the extent that they are most effective before the insects have reached their full development. Another reason for the early application of the remedies against both insects and diseases is that they multiply very rapidly and if not checked at the start they may propagate and become so numerous that much harm may be done.

In making a choice of insecticides, we should be guided by the nature of the insect for which it is to be used. Thus against many insects that take their food by biting off and chewing the leaves, the arsenites, such as Paris green and London purple, will be found efficient, while for the sucking insects, which are more troublesome in the greenhouse, we shall need to rely upon kerosene emulsion, tobacco, whale-oil soap, pyrethrum and other remedies that act upon the exterior, or the breathing apparatus of the insects.

THE APHIS.

This insect and its allies embrace a great variety of forms, all of which may be included under the common name of plant lice or "fly." While most of them are of a green color, some forms, such as chrysanthemum aphis,

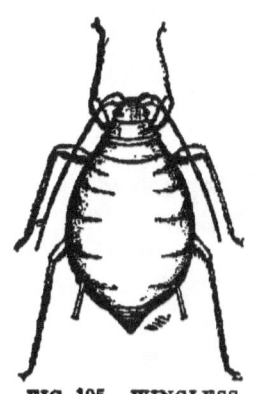

FIG. 105. WINGLESS FEMALE APHIS.

are black in color, and in some cases we find a blue aphis upon the roots of plants. They have long, slender antennæ or feelers, a small head, a full, round thorax or chest, and generally a very large, round abdomen. From near the end of the abdomen, two tubes project, from which the so-called honeydew exudes (Fig. 105). During the early part of the season, the female aphides give birth to living female young; these propagate very rapidly until, as fall approaches, when eight or ten broods have been produced, both males and females appear. This brood, only, has wings (Fig. 106). The eggs produced as a result of pairing serve to carry the species over winter. It has been estimated that from a single individual a quintillion could develop in one season.

Aphides seem to thrive, in particular, upon plants in partial shade and poor ventilation. The best way of destroying them is by means of tobacco smoke, extract, or tea. All of these should be used upon the first appearance of the aphides, as, if they are allowed to reach full size, they are hard to destroy. As a preventive, greenhouses should be fumigated once or twice a week if insects are troublesome. Kerosene emulsion, and buhach, either as a powder or in water, are also quite effectual. The black chrysanthemum aphides are even more difficult to destroy than the green fly, and tobacco will have but little effect, if they once get their growth; the remedies last given will, however, be found effectual.

The black aphis of the violet is quite troublesome in some sections, but can be readily destroyed with hy-

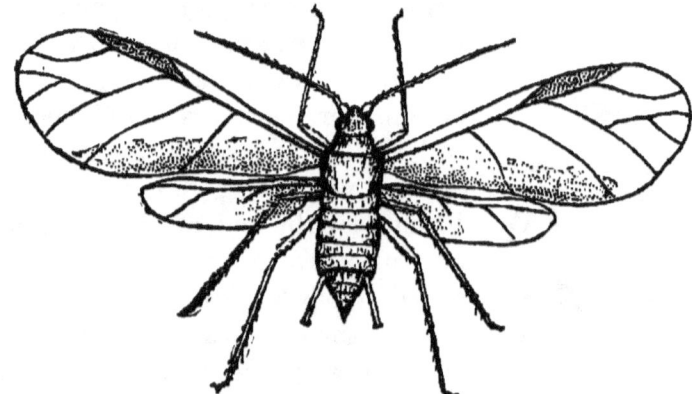

FIG. 106. WINGED MALE APHIS.

drocyanic acid gas, as can the gall fly which attacks the violet leaves.

The blue aphis sometimes appears upon the roots of plants that have in some way been stunted, particularly if they have been kept unduly dry. The plants should be shaken out, placed in whale-oil soap solution, and repotted in fresh soil.

PLANT BUGS.

When plants are housed in the fall some of the insects that have been working upon them out of doors may be housed with them. Among the most common are the Yellow-lined plant bug and the Tarnished plant bug. They feed upon a number of plants and sometimes do much harm by sucking the sap from the buds and tender shoots. To destroy them, use kerosene emulsion upon plants that will stand it, or in its place spray with whale-oil soap solution, or fir-tree oil.

ALEYRODES (*White Flies*).

Allied to the aphides are the Aleyrodes or "white flies," as they are usually called, which sometimes appear in large numbers in the greenhouse and do considerable injury. The perfect insects are winged in both sexes, but instead of being vertical, as in the aphis, their wings are outspread. In the larvæ and pupæ, there is a strong resemblance to young scale insects, and they injure the leaves by puncturing them and sucking the sap. The eggs can often be found in large numbers on the underside of the leaves. Soap is not entirely effectual, and it will be better to rely upon kerosene emulsion and similar remedies.

FULLER'S ROSE BEETLE (*Aramigus Fulleri*).

A few years ago great harm was done to roses in greenhouses by Fuller's Rose beetle (Fig. 107, *a*), which was often spoken of as "the rose bug." The mature

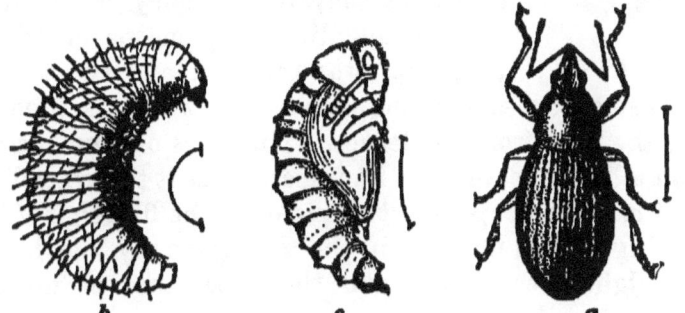

FIG. 107. FULLER'S ROSE BEETLE.
a, adult ; *b*, larva ; *c*, pupa.

insect is about half an inch in length, and of a gray color. It conceals itself upon the stem or under the leaves, from which it eats semi-circular pieces, and when its work is noticed, the beetles should be hunted and destroyed; in this way they can generally be held in check. The beetles deposit their eggs on the stems near the ground, and the larvæ pass down and feed on the roots, where they may become so numerous as to destroy the plants. The liberal use of wood ashes will do much to hold them in check, but the plants should be taken out and burned, the soil removed and the benches thoroughly whitewashed, if they become very numerous.

RED SPIDER (*Tetranychus telarius* Linn.)

Few insects seem to have so little choice in their host plants as the red spider (Fig. 108), as they not only attack plants in the greenhouse and garden, but also in the field and forest. They are very minute, being rather less than one-twentieth of an inch in length, and vary in color from green and yellow while immature, to dark red in their adult form, with small greenish spots upon their sides.

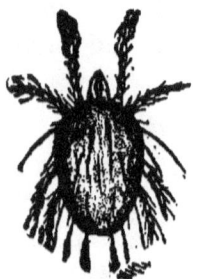

FIG. 108. RED SPIDER.

The red spider spins a fine web upon the leaves of plants, under the protection of which they feed. They have stout jaws or mandibles, by means of which they tear away the cuticle of the leaves, and also a barbed sucking apparatus, which is used to take the food from the leaves. Numbers of these insects upon a leaf, sucking out its juices, cause it to turn yellow and finally to drop from the plant. The first sign of the working of this insect is in the taking on by the leaves of a light green color, and the appearance of minute yellowish spots.

This insect thrives in a hot, dry atmosphere, and its appearance can generally be prevented if the houses are properly ventilated and syringed. If the spider does appear, steps should at once be taken to destroy it. If the ventilators are kept closed for awhile on bright mornings and the walks and plants thoroughly syringed, the conditions will be unfavorable to the red spider and the numbers can in this way be reduced. When the warm days of spring and summer come on, a similar treatment in the afternoon is often advisable. Another remedy that is entirely effectual and quite easy to use is evaporated sulphur. If this is applied thoroughly once or twice, it will rid the plants from these pests.

THE THRIPS.

The insects grouped under this name, although quite small in size, are often the source of considerable trouble in the greenhouse, as well as upon fruits and grains. They have long, slender bodies (Fig. 109) and generally four wings; these are also long and narrow and of nearly equal size and shape, with a fine hair-like fringe around their edges. In most cases the wings are without veins, except, perhaps, one or two longitudinal midribs. The antennæ are long and slender, with generally from seven to nine joints. In their mouth parts they resemble both the true bugs and the Orthoptera, or grasshopper group, as they are adapted for both biting and sucking. They resemble the adult in both the larval and pupal forms, and when full grown they are slightly less than one-tenth of an inch in length. They are sometimes light yellow, but are generally brown or black, with the extremity of the abdomen in some cases bright red. The antennæ and legs are usually light colored; as larvæ and pupæ most of the forms are of a yellowish-white.

FIG. 109. THRIPS.

Thrips do considerable injury in the greenhouse, as they eat holes in the leaves and flowers and suck the juices. They are especially injurious to the rose, carnation, lily and azalea. As a remedy, the hose should be used freely on bright days, and if this does not suffice, it is well to make free use of whale-oil soap, kerosene emulsion, or evaporated sulphur. The vapor of tobacco can also be used with good effect, as can Paris green. When they have become imbedded in the flowers, the buds should be picked off and burned. *Heliothrips hæmorrhoidis*, Bowd, is sometimes quite troublesome upon crotons, and *Coleothrips trifasciata*, Fitch, is another troublesome greenhouse species.

SCALE INSECTS.

Although at first these insects have but little resemblance to the aphides to which they are closely related, a careful comparison of the different organs will show that in many important particulars the resemblance is quite marked.

The simplest forms of these insects are the mealy bugs (Fig. 110), so-called from the fact that they cover themselves with a white cottony substance. The female mealy bug, one of the most common of which is *Dactylopius adonidum* (Linn.) Signoret, does not change its form, and except in size is much the same in appearance at all stages. When about to lay its eggs, it attaches itself by means of its beak to the surface of a leaf, or stem, secretes a mass of long, cottony, tuft-like particles of wax around the tip of the abdomen, beneath which the eggs are deposited. In addition to this, the antennæ, legs and each segment of the body have shorter appendages. From each lateral segment they appear as short bristles, while those at the rear end

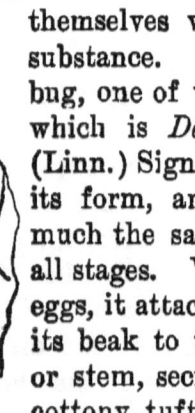

FIG. 110. MEALY BUG.

of the body are considerably elongated, often being as long as the body itself. The male undergoes a transformation, and covers itself with a thick cottony mass. It is of a brown color, with long grayish wings.

Another form, known as the Destructive mealy bug (*Dactylopius destructor*), of a yellowish-brown color, with seventeen short, stout, lateral appendages upon each side of its flattened body, with a very thin waxy covering. This form has been particularly destructive to orange trees. The form known as *D. longifilis* differs principally in having longer appendages, there being two in particular upon each side of the rear end of the abdomen that are as long as the entire body.

All of these forms of mealy bugs thrive in close, hot and dry air, and particularly like to conceal themselves in a corner or in a thick tangle of vines. The conditions that favor their development should be avoided, and where the plants can be reached a free use of the hose with a powerful spray will often blow them off from the leaves. Kerosene emulsion, where it can be brought in contact with the mealy bugs, is also a powerful insecticide, as is also fir tree oil and other commercial compounds. On many stove plants, with large delicate leaves, the use of a stiff brush and dilute kerosene emulsion, or whale-oil soap, is preferable.

The genus *Aspidiotus*, to which a large number of true scale insects belong, differs in lacking, in most species, the waxy covering. They are of a yellowish or brownish color. At first the larvæ are active, but soon they form a scale and fix themselves; after molting a number of times they reach full size, when they are covered with a thick, firm shell. Eggs are now deposited and, on hatching, the second brood starts on the road to development. In some cases there are as many as five broods a year.

Closely related to Aspidiotus, and often classed with it, are such other genera as *Diaspis, Chionaspis, Mytila-*

spis, Lecanium, and others which differ principally in the shape, or the markings of the scale. They are all sucking insects and must be killed by the use of kerosene emulsion and similar remedies. Using hydrocyanic acid gas is among the most effective methods of treating them. The males are nearly all winged, but the females have but little power of locomotion, being wingless and with but poorly developed legs. While often found upon plants that seem in perfect health, as a rule, weak, unhealthy plants are most likely to be attacked, and are most injured by them.

SLUGS, SNAILS AND SOW BUGS.

The damage done by the above-named animals is often very great, especially by the slugs, which seem to delight in eating off young seedlings. In modern well-built houses they are far less troublesome than in the old style of houses, that are generally damp, dark and with more or less of rotting wood. If flats, bits of board and other rubbish are not allowed to lie around under the benches, there will be little danger of their appearance in houses that are well lighted and properly ventilated. Neatness, then, should always be used as a preventive. If they make their appearance, they can often be held in check by sprinkling air-slaked lime over as well as under the benches. This will help both in drying up the surplus moisture and by its caustic action destroy or drive away the slugs and similar animals. "Traps" are also quite useful, as, by placing cabbage or lettuce leaves where they are numerous, the slugs and sow bugs will collect beneath them and if they are sprinkled with Paris green many of them will be killed. Sweetened bran also has an attraction, particularly for the slugs, and the addition of Paris green will soon clean them out. Bits of carrot poisoned with some arsenite are also good traps for sow bugs.

While we should always endeavor to make the surroundings uncongenial to them by keeping all rubbish and litter picked up, if they do make their appearance they can readily be brought under control by any of the methods given. What are commonly known as "Thousand Legged Worms" are often found with the above. They are Myriapods, and *Julus virgatus* is among the most common species. They feed, as a rule, upon decaying matter, but sometimes attack the roots, bulbs and fleshy stems of plants. They can generally be destroyed if baited with slices of poisoned vegetables.

EEL WORMS.

Florists have often found what they called "root galls" upon the roots of roses and other plants, but have not known what the real cause was. They are often due to the workings in the root of a microscopic worm called from its appearance an "eel worm." They luxuriate in warm, moist surroundings, and a rose house, especially if kept unnecessarily warm, and if the beds are overwatered, gives them the very conditions they prefer. In filling the beds, care should be taken that fresh soil is obtained, and the roots of the rose and other plants should be examined, to ascertain that they are free from galls. If they once get into a bed they will increase rapidly and the plants will take on an unhealthy appearance.

No satisfactory remedy is known, although air-slaked lime and kainit sprinkled over and worked into the beds have been used with fair success in some places. Care should be taken in applying kainit, but one pound per one hundred square feet can be used with safety upon roses. Frost is also valuable as a natural enemy of the eel worm. Various other plants, including the violet, tomato and carnation, are often seriously troubled by this pest.

MUSHROOM ENEMIES AND DISEASES.

The mushroom grower does not find it all smooth sailing, as his crops are attacked by a number of insects and other enemies, against many of which he has no remedy except to give the houses a scrupulous cleaning each summer. Little attention has been given to the scientific study of the enemies of this crop, and many may exist of which we have no knowledge. Most of the pests of which we know injure the mushrooms by eating holes in, or biting off small pieces from, the tender caps; among these are the sow bugs or wood lice, slugs, mice and other vermin.

One of the most troublesome of these pests is the mushroom maggot. It is about one-fourth of an inch long, and is the larval form of a fly. It burrows through the stems and caps of tender buttons, and in the full-sized mushrooms the brown lines running through the tissues are distinctly seen. The maggots appear in April, and make it impossible to grow the ordinary mushroom in the summer. It also attacks the new mushroom (*Agaricus rufescens*), but from the rapid growth of this species much less injury is done. If one has a cave or cool cellar, they can be grown later in the season than if the beds are in a warm place, but it is even then about impossible to escape their attack between April and October. No remedy that is now known will destroy them; insect powder, kainit, salt and other insecticides seem to have no effect upon them.

The so-called "black spot" shows itself as black or brown spots or streaks upon the top of the caps; it is also most troublesome during the summer months. The diseased appearance is caused by minute eel worms which enter the plants while they are quite small, and which generally infect all in one clump. They are most troublesome in old beds and seldom, if ever, appear in properly made new ones. As soon as they are through bearing, the old beds should be thrown out, and new ones made entirely from fresh materials. If the worms have been present, the walls and floor should be thoroughly whitewashed, and all decaying matter and diseased mushrooms should be removed at once. By the free use of lime and salt, the green mold in which they multiply can be kept down. Boiling water is also recommended for this purpose, to be applied to the walls, floors, boards, and sparingly to the surface of the beds, before the mushrooms appear.

One of the most common and troublesome diseases of the mushroom is known as "fogging off." It, however, seems to be a secondary trouble, as it as a rule only attacks mushrooms that have been injured in some way. If the bed is too wet, or too dry, or if the surface is disturbed in such a way as to loosen the young mushrooms, they will fog off, so that the disease seems to partake of a fungous as well as of a bacterial nature.

The so-called "flock" is even more to be dreaded. It is caused by one or more fungi that attack the gills of the mushrooms. They become thick and hard, and are often distorted. The conditions that favor the development of the disease are not understood and the only known treatment is to destroy the spawn upon which a diseased mushroom appears.

In growing mushrooms, much can be done to ward off the attacks of these various diseases and insects by keeping the house clean and free from litter and rubbish; the beds should be removed as soon as through bearing, and in the new beds only fresh material should be used.

If the atmosphere is too dry, mushrooms are sometimes injured by a species of mite, closely related to the "red spider," but as they are only troublesome under the above conditions, the way to prevent their appearance and of freeing the beds of their presence will be at once apparent.

FUMIGATION WITH HYDROCYANIC ACID GAS.

This is one of the most effective methods of destroying insects in the greenhouse and other places where the air can be confined, but it should be used with the greatest caution, as the fumes are fatal to all animal life. Every precaution should be taken against the possibility of anyone entering the house where the gas has been used, until it has been dissipated.

The gas treatment has for several years been used for scale insects in California, but it was not until 1896 that it was used to any extent in greenhouses. It was then tried experimentally, by Professor Galloway and his assistants of the United States Department of Agriculture, with very satisfactory results, as it cheaply and effectually destroyed all the insects in the houses, including several species that can be effectually reached in no other way, without injury to most plants. The treatment is, as yet, in its experimental stage, but it has progressed so far that for many plants the amount that can be used has been determined, and methods of producing the gas, with the least risk and to secure the best results, have been found.

The houses should be tight, and so arranged that the ventilators can be raised without entering the house. The gas is produced by the action of sulphuric acid upon cyanide of potassium in the presence of water. The experiments show that for violets, coleus, many of the ferns, *Ficus elastica,* crotons, etc., four ounces of chemically pure (98 per cent) potassium cyanide, six ounces of commercial sulphuric acid, and six ounces of water can be used for each 1,000 cubic feet of space. Roses, chrysanthemums and tomatoes are injured by this amount, and further experiments are required to determine the exact quantity that can be used with safety. It is also well to have a box in which cuttings and small plants can be placed for fumigation. If this is made to contain ten cubic feet, about one dram of the cyanide and one and one-half drams each of the sulphuric acid and water will be required.

For use in a greenhouse, it will be well to wet the glass, so as to close as many of the cracks as possible. Night should be selected, as the action of light and the usual high temperature of the daytime will increase the chance of injury to the plants, and lessen the injury to insects. The plants should be on the dry side, and the air moderately cool. At intervals of from thirty to forty feet, place in the walk a tall two-gallon earthen jar. Thus, for a house one hundred feet long, three jars will be required, unless it is very narrow, or very wide, when the number should be decreased or increased accordingly. In each jar place a proportionate part of the water required for the house, and then carefully add an equal amount of sulphuric acid. Care should be taken not to allow any of the acid to come in contact with the clothing, or person, as it is very acrid and will destroy anything that it touches.

The amount of cyanide of potassium required for each jar should be weighed out and placed in paper bags, and just before it is to be used it should be placed inside another larger bag, to prevent any danger of the bag giving way while preparations are being made. Screw eyes are then fastened in the woodwork directly over each jar, and through these stout cords are run to the end of the house near the door, where they are fastened. To the ends over the jars tie the bags of cyanide, so that, on the ends of the strings at the door being released, they will drop into the jars. When all is ready, close the ventilators, pass to the end of the house and carefully lower the bags into the jars and close the door. If any of the cyanide drops into the acid while in the house, hold the breath and get out of the house as soon

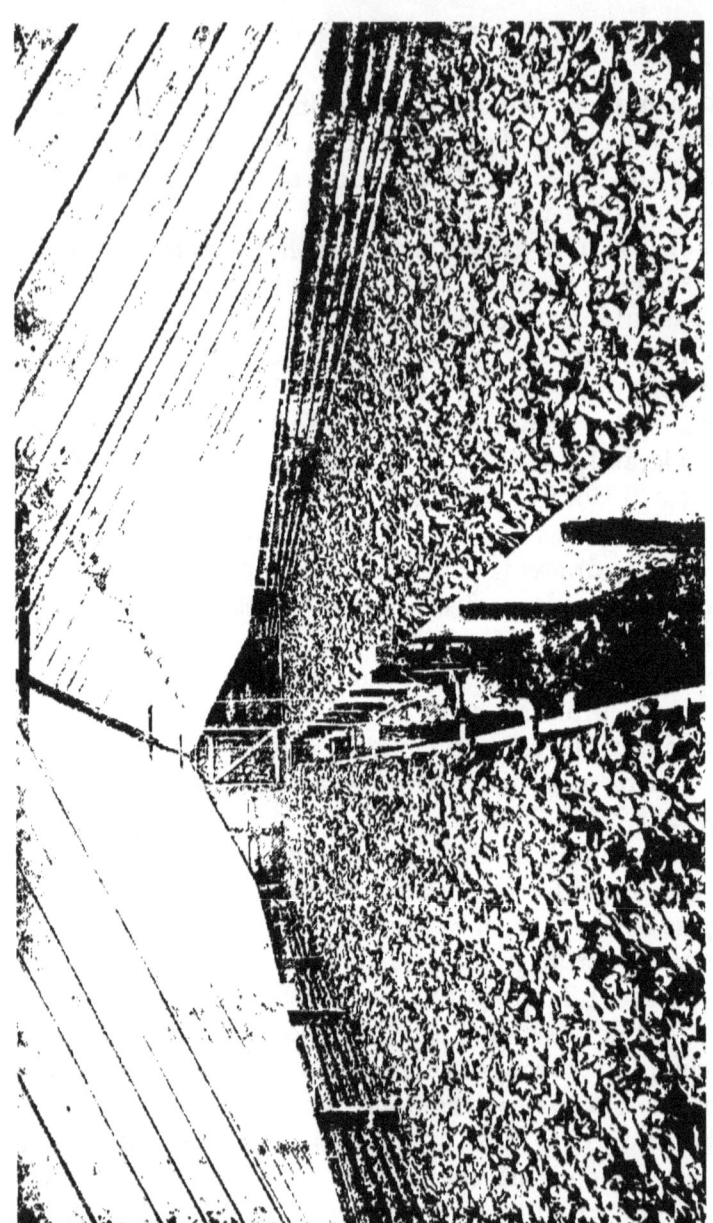

FIG. 111. FUMIGATING BY HYDROCYANIC ACID GAS.

as possible, as to inhale the gas is fatal. After twenty-five minutes, open the houses for at least half an hour, but do not enter even then unless obliged to, except with caution. At the usual price of pure cyanide of potassium, 30 to 35 cents per pound, and of commercial sulphuric acid, which can be bought in quantity at three or four cents per pound, the cost of fumigating a greenhouse will not be more than 12 to 15 cents per 1000 cubic feet. While it is very useful in destroying aphides, it is a particularly valuable remedy against insects and mealy bugs.

One of the first uses to which it was put was the destruction of white-tailed mealy bugs (*Orthezia insignis*) upon coleus, which had refused to yield to other remedies. Its next extensive use was for the black violet aphis, in the houses of Mr. W. G. Saltford, Poughkeepsie, N. Y. (Fig. 111), the results of which, as reported in The Florist's Exchange, were very satisfactory.

The same remedy is also much used upon nursery stock that has been dug for shipment. An air-tight shed arranged for ventilation is required. While in a dormant condition the trees will stand a stronger gas than will tender greenhouse plants. One ounce of the cyanide of potassium and one and one-half ounces each of water and sulphuric acid can be used with safety for each one hundred and fifty cubic feet. For the San Jose scale a second treatment will be desirable, but one application will suffice for all other insects. The same care about inhaling the fumes should be used here as in a greenhouse.

CHAPTER XXVI.

DISEASES OF GREENHOUSE PLANTS.

FUNGOUS DISEASES OF THE ROSE.—BLACK SPOT.

(*Actinonema rosæ*, Fr.).

This disease, which is the cause of the black spots that are so commonly seen upon the leaves of moss and hybrid roses in wet seasons, frequently invades the greenhouse and causes the leaves of the tea roses to take on an unhealthy appearance and finally to drop from the stems.

Its development here seems to be invited by the same conditions as in the open ground. If the bed is poorly drained, or has been over-watered, a drop in the temperature below 50 degrees is likely to cause the fungus to appear. The "spot" when first seen is of a dark brown color, with an irregular margin (Fig. 112); it rapidly enlarges and in a short time the portion of the leaf around the spot takes on a sickly yellow color and the leaf drops. A magnified section of the leaf is seen in Fig. 113. The dark bodies (A) are the outer layer of epidermal cells, the contents of which have been changed by the fungus into a dark brown granular substance, which can be seen through the transparent cuticle of the leaf, and gives it a brown or black appearance. The mycelium also penetrates the underlying cells and draws its nourishment from them, thus breaking down the tissues and causing the surrounding por-

FIG. 112. ROSE SPOT.

tions of the leaves to take on a brown color. The spores of the fungus are developed on the mycelium, just beneath the cuticle, and, as this finally bursts and rolls back, they appear as at B. When magnified 500 diameters, the spores are seen to be two-celled (B) and oblong in shape. If they fall upon a damp rose leaf they will germinate and cause another "spot" to form. For the destruction of this fungus, a perfect remedy is found in Bordeaux mixture, except for its giving the plants a whitewashed appearance. The copper carbonate solution is nearly as effectual and does not have this fault. Evaporated sulphur will also keep the disease in check. As in most other cases, prevention will be found the best cure, and to effect this have the beds well drained, avoid over-watering and maintain a regular temperature of from 56 to 60 degrees, according to the requirements of the variety.

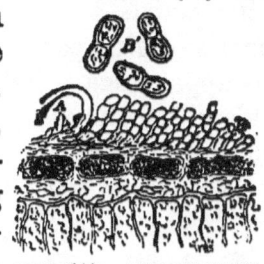

FIG. 113. BLACK SPOT, Section magnified.

POWDERY MILDEW OF THE ROSE (*Sphærotheca pannosa*.)

This common disease of the rose appears as a mealy or powdery covering upon the young leaves, and if the attack is severe they become twisted and distorted, and the disease even affects the stems. It develops rapidly upon the young leaves, its mycelium forming a fine cobweb from which the spore-bearing stalks are sent up. These stalks or hyphæ become constricted and break up into oval bodies—the spores, which are so numerous as to form a fine powder upon the leaves, whence the name of the fungus. This disease has another form of reproduction, the spores of which are formed in the fall and are designed to carry the disease through the winter. The spores are in sacs, which are themselves enclosed in a thick sac known as a theca. The winter spore covering has for its distinguishing feature short irregular threads that project from it.

Like many other diseases, this fungus is seldom troublesome unless there is some inducing weakness in the plants, and an excessive amount of water, an excess of nitrogenous matter in the soil and, particularly, cold drafts of air upon the plants, will hardly fail to induce its appearance. Being entirely superficial in its growth, this mildew is easily kept in check. The fumes of sulphur are fatal to it, and it is well to always paint the heating pipes with a sulphur wash; sulphur evaporated by means of an oil stove, or by the heat of the sun, will also be easy to use, as by the last method one has only to apply the sulphur to the plants with a bellows and allow the temperature to run up to 70 degrees before opening the ventilators; in airing the house after giving this treatment, it should be done gradually, so as to avoid cold drafts.

ROSE RUST (*Phragmidium mucronatum.* Winter).

Although this fungus sometimes attacks tea roses, it is principally troublesome upon hybrid perpetual and other hardy kinds. It first shows as light yellow spots on both sides of the leaves, or upon the stems. The epidermis is soon ruptured and granular pustules are formed. On the leaves these are generally quite small, but as they are very numerous and frequently coalesce, the leaves are often destroyed. When upon the veins, petioles or stems, the spots often extend themselves longitudinally and cover a considerable surface. In that case the stems and leaves become twisted and distorted.

At first the pustules are of an orange-yellow color, and the spores are spherical or slightly angular in form, and are arranged in chains. Each group is surrounded by elongated bodies called paraphyses, which form a cup shaped cavity in which the spores are formed. This constitutes what is known as the æcidio stage of the rust. Later in the season the pustules take on a reddish color, and spores that are then present are of about the same size and shape as the æcidio spores, but they are covered with minute spines and are arranged singly upon short stalks or basidia. Towards the end of summer, the reddish spots are replaced by minute black bristle-like tufts, in which the winter or teleutospores are found. These are compound, being separated by cross partitions into from five to ten cells, and are borne upon comparatively short stalks, which are thickened toward their base.

The æcidiospores and uredospores serve for the reproduction of the fungus during the summer. If the conditions are favorable, they germinate readily, but if kept dry for a few weeks they lose their power.

It is the function of the teleutospores, with their thick cell-walls, to carry the fungus through the winter, and in the spring they germinate, sending out thickened tubes which bear at their ends small globular bodies called sporidia, which are light and easily borne about by the wind, and thus serve for the dissemination of the fungus. If they fall upon rose leaves, they quickly germinate, and soon produce new rust spots.

If the disease appears upon a plant, the affected branch should be cut off and burned. By spraying with Bordeaux mixture and other copper compounds, the spread of the disease can be prevented. The so-called Rose Phragmidium (*P. speciosum*, Fries) is closely allied to the above, but differs in confining itself to the stems and seldom infecting the leaves. It forms its regular black masses of spores late in the season upon the stems. These spores (teleutospores) differ from those of the rose rust in having long, slender stalks. The spots frequently surround the stems, thus completely girdling them. The remedies will be the same as for the rose rust.

ANTHRACNOSE OF THE ROSE (*Glœosporium rosarum*).

Like many other plants, the rose has its anthracnose, which sometimes proves very troublesome. The spores, falling upon the young tender canes, germinate, and spreading through the tissues destroy the cells and even girdle the canes. The circulation is thus cut off to a greater or less extent, and many if not all of the leaves drop from the plant. The disease manifests itself at the exterior in the form of minute pimples in which the spores are formed. They are transferred to other plants in water. Other blotches can be found upon the leaves, particularly upon those that have fallen upon a damp surface.

The spores readily germinate, and as they are produced in great abundance, the disease may, under favorable conditions, spread very rapidly. The spread of the disease seems to be toward the tips of the branches, and frequently apparently healthy shoots appear at the base of diseased ones. As soon as the disease appears upon a plant, the infected portions should be cut off and burned. As the Bordeaux mixture and copper compounds are fatal to the spore development of fungi, the spread of the disease can be prevented by thoroughly spraying the plants. This disease is closely related to the anthracnose of the raspberry, and its development is both invited and hastened by such unfavorable conditions as poorly drained or exhausted soil.

FUNGOUS DISEASES OF THE CARNATION.

CARNATION RUST.

This destructive disease (*Uromyces caryophyllinus*), has long been known in Europe, but although it had undoubtedly appeared here previous to that time, its nature was not known in this country until the fall of

1890, when the writer received from a Michigan florist a number of diseased leaves, with an inquiry as to the nature of the fungus and a remedy for it. The plants had been recently received from Massachusetts, and recognizing the danger of spreading the disease, he was advised to destroy all plants that were badly infected, and to remove from the others all leaves that showed any pustules, carefully burning both plants and leaves, and then to spray the remaining plants with a fungicide. This fungus is closely related to the rust of grains and grasses, and seems to revel upon plants grown in poorly ventilated houses, or that have received a check in some way, particularly if the plants are syringed at such times as will allow the water to stand on the leaves and branches at night. It enters the plant and develops there without manifesting its presence, until a pustule is formed just beneath the epidermis. The spot takes on a grayish appearance, and the membrane soon becoming ruptured, the mass of brownish spores is seen. They are produced in great quantities and appear like fine, brown, dust-

FIG. 114. CARNATION RUST.

like particles. The pustules are often an eighth of an inch or even more in length, and are of an elliptical, oval, or sometimes of a crescent shape, and form on both sides of the leaves and even on the stems (Fig. 114).

The spores are of two kinds, one of which, the uredospores (Fig. 115 *a*), are round or elliptical, and show a few scattered spines under the miscroscope. They will germinate at once if they fall on a moist surface and if the moisture is on a carnation plant, the germ tubes will penetrate the epidermis, and work their way among the tissues, break down the cells, absorb the juices and, having made their growth, develop a new mass of spores, thus completing a cycle in perhaps two weeks. The other spores, known as teleutospores (Fig. 115, *b*), are somewhat darker in color than the others, and are more oval in shape, besides lacking the spines found upon the uredospores. Some varieties seem more subject to this disease than others, and plants with firm tissues are less likely to be attacked than others of the same variety with soft watery leaves. As water is required for the development of the fungus, syringing should only be done on sunny days and in the morning, that the plants may dry off before night. In damp weather, the ventilation should be thorough, and if moisture stands on the plants, the fire heat should be increased.

FIG. 115. SPORES OF CARNATION RUST.

To grow plants free from rust, they should be of a strong constitution and from a healthy stock. Preferably, as stated in the chapter upon carnation culture, they should be taken from plants that have not been long in flower, and that have not been grown in a high temperature.

When the cuttings are made, dip them in a solution of liver of sulphur (one ounce to three gallons), and root them in clean sand at a low temperature (48 or 50 degrees). Before potting off, spray them in the cutting bed with a solution of copper sulphate, using a fine spray that will cover both sides of all the leaves. If the disease is troublesome, it will be well to repeat the application every two weeks throughout the year, until the plants are thrown out. If one's stock has been free from rust it will only be necessary to watch it carefully and on the first appearance of the pustules to pick off and burn the infected leaves and thoroughly spray the plants, keeping it up at intervals, as above, until the disease has been checked.

The carnation has a leaf that will withstand the use of a much stronger application of copper sulphate than most other plants, and while we have kept the disease in check with a solution of one part of the copper sulphate in one thousand parts of water, if the disease has obtained a firm hold, it will be well to double the strength of the solution.

If the plants are grown on solid benches during the summer, and are thus saved the shock of transplanting, the chances of the appearance of the disease will be lessened. The fungicides can at best only prevent the spread of the disease, and if a plant is found to be badly diseased, it should be destroyed, and the diseased leaves removed from the others as soon as the pustules show.

SPOT OR BLIGHT OF CARNATIONS.
(*Septoria dianthi* Desm.)

Like many of the other fungous diseases of plants, the nature of this disease is not generally understood, and, although it is becoming quite commonly distributed, its presence is not recognized by florists. The spots are generally of a circular form, except when upon the edges of the leaves, when they are oblong or semi-circular. The centers of the spots are grayish-brown in color, with margins that have a purplish tinge (Fig. 116, *a*). Upon the light portion of the spots, minute black dots will soon appear; the mycelium of the fungus has developed within the leaf, and these points are projections from the flask-shaped conceptacles in which the spores are formed (Fig. 116, *d*). An enlarged spore case is shown at *b* and the spores themselves are seen at *c*. The spores are quite slender and, enclosed in a viscid substance, ooze out through the opening, to be dissolved in water and scattered to the neighboring plants, or they may be taken up by currents of air after the water has evaporated. The watering of the plants with a strong stream of water, through a hose, will be likely to scatter the spores, and if they fall in a drop of water on a carnation leaf, they will quickly germinate and cause other spots. If the flower stems are affected, the growth is likely to be checked and on the leaves the effect is to contract and weaken them, the spots turn brown and they become bent and twisted (Fig. 117).

FIG. 116. SPOT DISEASE OF CARNATIONS.

If taken in time, when the disease first appears, the application of fungicides will tend to keep it in check.

ANTHRACNOSE OF CARNATIONS (*Volutella dianthi*).

The nature of this disease was pointed out in 1891, by Dr. B. D. Halsted, who thought it to be *Colletotrichum dianthi*; the later investigations of Prof. Atkinson, however, would seem to show that it can more properly be referred to the genus *Volutella*. It causes a rapid decay of the affected portions and the warmth and damp of the cutting bench seem particularly favorable

FUNGOUS DISEASES OF THE CARNATION. 333

for its development and spread, as a spore will germinate, develop a mycelium and produce a crop of spores within three days.

While particularly injurious to cuttings, it often causes serious injury to the growing plants, where it is most commonly found upon the lower portions of the stems and the clasping bases of the leaves and leaf sheaths. The diseased portions shrivel, turn brown and

FIG. 117. EFFECT OF "SPOT" ON CARNATIONS.

at length are dotted with black, rosette-like clusters of spores (Fig. 118, *a*); these stools owe their color and general appearance to the development of a number of long, black bristles. Fig. 118, *b*, shows a section through one of these fruit clusters greatly magnified, the spores being much shorter than the bristles. The germinating spores still more magnified are shown at *c*.

The disease is most troublesome when the plants are grown in a poorly drained and over-watered soil, particularly if the stems and leaves form a dense mat at the base. While the fungus is generally confined to the stems and leaves that are upon or close to the damp soil, the effect is sometimes seen upon the upper leaves,

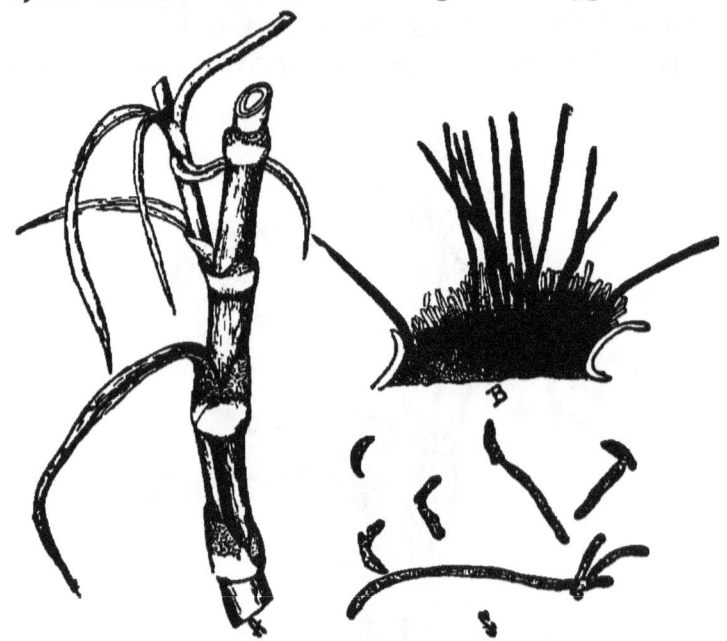

FIG. 118. ANTHRACNOSE OF THE CARNATION.
b Spores and bristles.   *c* Spores germinating.
(*a* natural size ; *b* and *c* greatly magnified.)

which will have a sickly appearance, and the stems will not develop flowers.

FAIRY RING SPOT OF CARNATIONS.

(*Heterosporium echinulatum* [Berk.] Cooke).

This disease was described and figured in the Gardener's Chronicle for 1870 by Mr. Berkeley, but it has only recently been observed in this country. The spores appear in concentric rings that develop centrifugally,

FUNGOUS DISEASES OF THE CARNATION.

much as does the well-known "fairy ring." The mycelium developing within the tissues causes them to take on a light yellow color. Just beneath the epidermis, dark brown swellings appear upon the mycelium, from which the fruiting threads (Fig. 119) are sent out through the cuticle. These are produced in great numbers from a single spot and gives it a dark brown appearance. A single spore (Fig. 120) is produced at the extremity of each thread; these are generally four-

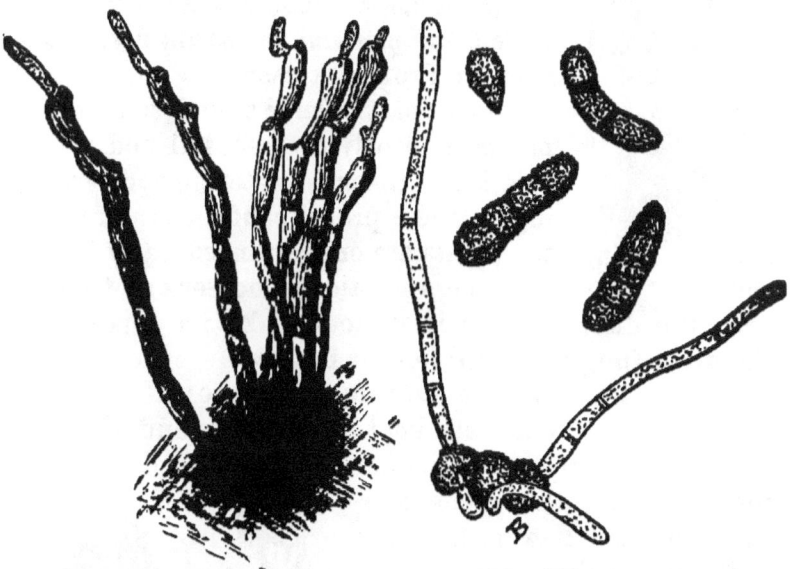

FIG. 119. FAIRY RING SPOT OF CARNATION, FRUITING THREADS. (Greatly magnified.)

FIG. 120. SPORES OF FAIRY SPOT. *b* Spores germinating (Greatly magnified.)

celled, but may vary from one to five, and are covered with minute spines. Germ tubes (Fig. 120, *B*) may be sent out from each cell of the spores. The mycelium continues its development and finally forms another set of fruiting hyphæ, generally in a circle around those first produced. In this way the disease can be distinguished from the carnation rust, with which a careless observer might confound it.

CARNATION LEAF MOLD (*Cladosporium* sp.).

This disease shows itself in minute circular spots, perhaps one-tenth of an inch in diameter, upon the leaves. They may become sufficiently numerous to destroy the leaves attacked. At first they are of a gray color and bear a dense growth of mold, consisting of fruiting threads, upon the extremities of which the spores are borne (Fig. 121).

These fall off and the spots become darker in color. The disease is thought to be *Cladosporium herbarum var. nodosum*, by Prof. Atkinson.

It is particularly troublesome upon plants in poorly drained soil and where care is not taken in watering and syringing. Under proper conditions and when the plants are only syringed early in the day, there should be no serious trouble from the disease, while if it does make its appearance the usual fungicides will hold it in check.

FIG. 121. CARNATION LEAF MOLD.

BOTRYTIS OR ROT OF CARNATIONS.

When the houses are kept quite warm and the soil and air are damp, the opening buds and the petals of the expanded flowers soften and turn yellow, and soon become covered with a slimy mold. This is the work of a fungus known as Botrytis (Fig. 122, *A*), which develops an immense number of spores (Fig. 122, *B*). The temperature and moisture should be regulated, all diseased portions should be destroyed, and the plants sprayed with cupram, or a solution of copper sulphate.

FIG. 122. BOTRYTIS OF CARNATIONS (*B* magnified).

BACTERIOSIS OF CARNATIONS.

Aside from the rust, no disease of the carnation is more to be dreaded. It appears upon the immature leaves as small, circular and slightly sunken yellowish-white spots; but before the spots appear, by holding the leaves up to the light, minute, translucent dots can be seen. Sometimes watery pimples form, but at any rate

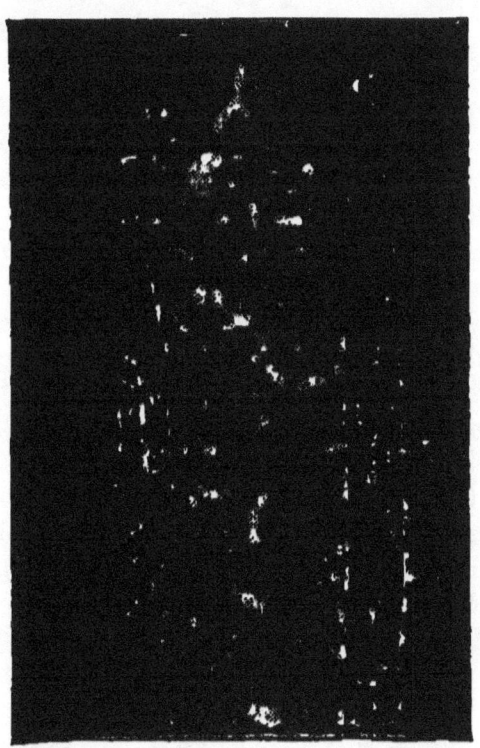

FIG. 123. BACTERIOSIS OF CARNATIONS.

the tissues affected soon dry out and sink beneath the surface of the leaf. The spots enlarge and the leaves wither (Fig. 123).

The "disease" was observed by Prof. Arthur of Purdue University in January, 1889, but it was not until more than a year later that he was able to announce what he considered to be the cause. From the **fact that** he found bacteria present it was thought to be of a bacterial nature, and the name "Bacteriosis" was given it.

The Division of Pathology of the National Department of Agriculture has recently proven that the bacteria are but a secondary cause of the disease, and that it will not appear if the plants are kept free from the attacks of aphides, thrips, and other insects through whose punctures the bacterial germs gain entrance.

FUNGOUS AND OTHER DISEASES OF VIOLETS.

The following notes were kindly prepared by Prof. Byron D. Halsted, of the New Jersey Experiment Station, who is an authority on the subject.

At the outset it may be said that there are more enemies to violets than most practical growers are at first willing to admit. Much has been published upon the general subject in the florists' journals and quite uniformly under the title of — The Violet Disease. There are enemies of all sorts and frequently the worst is man himself. In other words, lack of proper treatment of soil, of the watering can, of ventilation, of temperature, exposure to gases, cold winds, and many other things, can be charged with much of the lack of vigor of the plants and failure to produce profitable amounts of blooms. It is, however, not our purpose to treat of these things. There are several species of fungi that alone, or two or more working together, do much to destroy the crop. These will be briefly treated below, and it is hoped that light will be thrown upon the obscure subject that may possibly assist in the difficult labor of finding remedies that will check their ravages.

THE VIOLET LEAF SPOT (*Cercospora Violæ*, Sacc.).

This is one of the most conspicuous as well as common of the fungous diseases of the violet. As its name

FIG. 124. VIOLET LEAF SPOT (*Photographed by P. H. Dorsett*).

indicates, it produces spots upon the foliage which at first are not larger than the head of a pin, but increase in size until a third of a leaf may be included in a single spot. As there are other distinct species of fungi that produce leaf spots upon the violet foliage, it is necessary to place some stress upon the characteristics of the cercospora spot.

When the microscope is used upon the spots it is seen that the blanched surface of the leaf is covered with small tufts or rosettes of irregular brown threads. This fungus produces its spores outside of the infested tissue and the spores are thus in easy reach of any fungicide that may be applied to the surface. This Cercospora is closely related to the one upon the celery (*Cercospora apii*, Fv.) and no doubt can be controlled in the same way by the use of the compounds of copper.

VIOLET LEAF SPOT NO. 2 (*Phyllosticta Violæ*, Sacc.).

A second form of leaf spot of the violet can be distinguished by the naked eye. The spot is remarkably white and breaks near the margin, which consists of a ring of a cream color. Very often the central portion of the spot has disappeared, leaving the affected leaf with a number of holes. If viewed closely, the thin, white central portion of the spot is seen to contain a number of minute specks that are imbedded in the thin substance of the dead tissue. The spores, as the moisture dries away, are carried by the moving currents of air and falling upon healthy leaves produce, shortly, new spots of the disease. This fungus needs the same treatment as the Cercospora, and as they often grow together upon the same leaf, the spraying for the one will answer for the other.

VIOLET LEAF SPOT NO. 3 (*Ascochyta Violæ*, Sacc.).

Somewhat like the last described leaf spot is one that is caused by a species of Ascochyta. This is quite frequently met with, particularly upon specimens received from Massachusetts. The differences between this and the Phyllosticta are chiefly microscopic. The spores, for example, instead of consisting of one cavity, have a cross partition dividing them in two near the middle. The spore-bearing vessels (pycnidia) are pale pink colored and the hole upon the free side has a dark border. The diseased portion is a less well-defined spot than in previous cases, and is more like a brown patch.

VIOLET ANTHRACNOSE (*Glœosporium Violœ*, B. & M.).

A genuine anthracnose is met with upon the violet. This does not produce a spot, but the side of the leaf may be attacked and become brown and shrivelled, the trouble spreading over the whole leaf in the worst cases. When viewed under the microscope the surface of the diseased portion shows many patches where the spores are borne upon the surface. The fungus, after running in all directions through the tissue of the leaf, concentrates at certain points and there rupturing the skin produces large numbers of small spores upon the exposed surface.

A SECOND FORM OF ANTHRACNOSE (*Colletotrichum*).

Closely related to the last is a second species of anthracnose that belongs to the genus Colletotrichum. This causes a deadening of irregular patches in the leaf, and, owing to the numerous dark, stiff hairs, the affected parts may appear almost black.

There is a bacterial disease that causes the central portion (crown) of the plant to decay, and ruin is quickly effected. It frequently works in connection with the other fungous diseases and no satisfactory treatment is suggested for it.

But few satisfactory results have been obtained by treating the violets for fungous diseases. Several growers have been faithful in applying the ammoniacal carbonate of copper mixture, with fair results. But the beginning of the trouble is often below ground and quite out of the reach of fungicides, as shown below.

THE VIOLET EEL WORMS (*Root Galls*).

One of the serious pests of the violet is the eel worm or nematode. These are microscopic worms that multiply in the substance of the violet roots, and cause enlargements called galls, that may be very numerous and sometimes of considerable size. The worms enter the tender roots from the soil and there increase rapidly. Their presence seems to poison the tissue and induces an abnormal growth, similar to that which takes place upon many sorts of leaves when stung by gall flies and other insects. Many plants have their roots affected in this way, and the same species of nematode probably inhabits scores of kinds of plants.

So far as known, the gall trouble of roses is the same as that of the violet, and if this be true, it follows that the infection may pass from one kind of plant to another. It would not be well to grow violets in soil where roses had been galled, or *vice versa*.

There is no remedy for a plant that is badly infested, for nothing harmless to the plant can be used to kill the worms. The main point is to keep the nematodes out of the roots. The soil, therefore, should be free from them, and this is a difficult matter. The soil could be heated to a high temperature and the worms would be killed. Freezing would accomplish the same end; but either of these two extremes is not always possible. Lime water is said to kill them. The less manure used, the better, so far as the galls are concerned. Violets could probably be grown profitably with no manure. With the soil free from the worms, and the plants also, there ought to be no trouble in having violets, exempt from the nematodes. In setting out the plants, it is well to look at the roots and reject all with galls.

Underground troubles are the least readily investigated, but none the less fatal. If a plant looks pale and there is a drying of the edges of the leaf, it is always well to look for mischief at the roots.

THE BERMUDA LILY DISEASE.

For a number of years florists have been troubled by a disease that has attacked their Easter lilies. While *Lilium Harrisii* has been most commonly attacked, it

FIG. 125. PLANTS AFFECTED BY LILY DISEASE.

has also appeared on *L. longiflorum* and occasionally on *L. auratum* and *L. candidum*. It shows in the spotting of the leaves and of the bulbs themselves, and in the dwarfing and distorting of the leaves and flowers. Upon the leaves, where they show as yellowish-white sunken streaks, the spots are often quite numerous. These enlarge and finally the leaves severely attacked shrivel, and dry so that the plant is ruined (Fig. 125). The disease attacks the bulbs while growing in the field and is common not only in Bermuda, but in Holland, France and Japan.

The disease is due to the weakening of the plants by the attacks of various mites, fungi and bacteria, and its appearance is also undoubtedly induced, and the extent of the injury increased, by improper selection and propagation, as well as by the cutting of the flowers, and the harvesting of the bulbs before they are matured. In the greenhouse, the effect of the disease is increased and perhaps caused by the attack of aphides and mites upon the leaves and flowers, while the syringing of the plants, so that water will remain between the young leaves at night, may have its effect. From the above, which is the result of the investigations of the Department of Agriculture, it is evident that the condition of the bulbs at the time they are imported will have much to do with the extent to which they will be attacked while in the hands of the florist. Stunted and unripe bulbs should be avoided, and if they show the characteristic spots due to the work of the fungi and mites, they should be discarded. Before the bulbs are potted, they should be disinfected by dipping them into a solution of copper sulphate (one to one thousand) or of liver of sulphur (one to two hundred and fifty), and the mites and aphides should be destroyed by using strong tobacco-water or some other efficient insecticide.

In order that a close, firm texture may be secured, the chief reliance should be upon chemical manures, rather than animal manures, rich in nitrogen. Careful attention should be paid to the destruction of mites and aphides, and if any of the plants show signs of the disease, they should be isolated or at once destroyed, if the attack is a severe one. As will be seen from the above, the remedies are preventives rather than cures, and the most important thing is to secure strong, healthy bulbs.

DISEASES OF THE CHRYSANTHEMUM.

This plant is subject to the attack of several forms of what are commonly called "leaf-spot." In two of these forms, which the botanist calls *Septoria Chrysanthemi*, E. and D., and *Cylindrosporium Chrysanthemi*, E. and D., the first appearance is as small brown spots, which quickly enlarge until they cover considerable areas, when the leaves turn yellow and drop. In another form (*Phyllosticta Chrysanthemi*, E. and D.), the spots have more of a reddish color and seem quite velvety. If there are many of these spots upon a leaf, the portions between them turn yellow and the leaves droop.

The Bordeaux mixture is one of the most effectual remedies and if the disease appears when the plants are small, it should be used frequently. Although less effectual, if the use of a fungicide is necessary after the flowers open, cupram, or some of the other solutions, should be used instead. Infected leaves should be at once picked off and burned, and if the plants are badly injured it will be best to throw them out at once. Cuttings for a new stock should be selected only from healthy plants and should be frequently sprayed.

The chances of injury from these diseases will be greatly lessened, if mineral manures, such as wood ashes and ground bone, are freely used. Keeping the houses cool and well ventilated, and, if the plants are very thick, the removal of some of the lower leaves from plants growing closely in beds, will aid in keeping off the disease.

A MIGNONETTE DISEASE (*Cercospora Resedæ*).

In the *American Florist* for September, 1887, Professor Seymour figured and described a disease of the mignonette, which has become quite troublesome in some sections. The first sign of the disease is a reddish discoloration, which spreads over the leaf and is followed by the appearance of small, sunken spots with yellowish borders. The spots (Fig. 126) increase, and running together may destroy the entire leaf. They have a granular appearance caused by clusters of fungus threads (*B*) upon which the septate spores (*C*) are borne. The disease spreads very rapidly and may become quite troublesome. If taken in time, the disease may be kept in check by the use of the copper compounds. It will be well to remove all diseased portions and spray the plants with Bordeaux mixture.

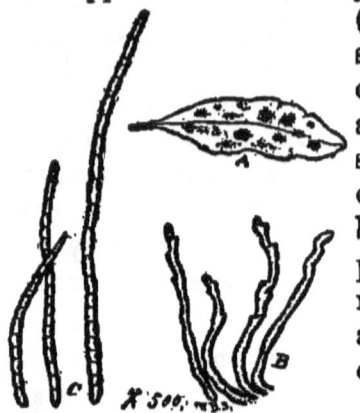

FIG. 126. LEAF BLIGHT OF MIGNONETTE. (*Cercospora Resedæ*.) B, Threads. C, Spores. (B and C magnified.)

LEAF BLIGHTS.

Nearly all plants are subject to the attack of certain fungi that are known as leaf blights. They belong to several species, but are alike in causing the appearance of yellow spots upon the leaves, which may spread until they assume large proportions, and if they are very numerous the leaves may be destroyed. Generally at the place where the spot first showed, a dark brown dot will later on appear; this is due to the development of a large number of spores, by which the disease will be scattered. When the spots first show, the leaves attacked should at once be removed and burned. Sometimes, there are but one or two spots upon large leaves, and it will be possible to cut off the portion of the leaf upon which the spot is situated, but to be effectual a considerable amount of the leaf should be taken off, as the mycelium of the fungus has probably spread to some distance beyond the margin of the discolored portion. Most of these fungi work within the tissues, and no surface application will stop their spread within the leaf, but by applying the Bordeaux mixture, or cupram, we will be able to destroy any spores that form on the outside of the leaves, and if the entire surface of the leaves is thus protected, any spores that may come in contact with the healthy leaves will be kept from germinating, and the spread of the disease will be prevented.

DISEASES OF LETTUCE.

If properly handled, there is little danger from the attack of any disease, but unless the soil, the temperature and moisture, are suited to the crop, one or more troubles may make their appearance, and greatly injure, if they do not entirely destroy it.

The one most to be feared is commonly known as "Rot." It attacks the under leaves in some cases and in others the inner leaves, causing them to rot off. If, when the lettuce is nearly grown, the air is too warm and close, especially if a large amount of water has been used, the disease is quite likely to appear. Heavy, compact soil that does not dry out, is also favorable to the appearance of the disease. The remedies will be entirely preveutive and will be merely to correct the conditions under which the plants are grown, by using a light, sandy soil, made very rich; keeping the temperature under 45 degrees at night for the cabbage varieties, and not allowing it to get to 50 for Grand Rapids and similar varieties; giving an abundance of fresh air during the day; and carefully regulating the amount of water supplied. If the disease has appeared, after correcting, so far as possible, the conditions that have brought about its appearance, the spores of the disease can be destroyed, and its further spread prevented by evaporating sulphur in the house, taking care that it does not take fire.

The fungus that causes the rot is known as *Botrytis vulgaris*, and as it can develop in decaying vegetable matter, care should be taken that the manure is well worked into the soil.

Another disease is the lettuce "Mildew." It is seldom troublesome, except in dark houses, where the plants are making little or no growth, on account of a cold, wet soil.

A third trouble is "Leaf-burn," which causes the edges of the leaves to turn brown. This is a common trouble with the head varieties, and greatly reduces the value of the crop. It is much less likely to appear in the variety known as Grand Rapids than in most other sorts. The usual cause of the trouble is growing the lettuce at too high a temperature, especially if the changes are sudden and extreme. A deficiency of water in the soil, especially if the air is hot and dry, will also lead to its appearance. In short, it may be attributed to anything that will cause the water to be given off from the tissues at the edges of the leaves faster than it can be supplied to them. If the soil is light, the roots will penetrate deeply and water will be supplied much more readily than if it is heavy.

DISEASES OF THE CUCUMBER AND MELON.

Both of these vines are attacked by a downy mildew (*Plasmopara Cubensis*, B. and C.), which first shows in the yellow color of the spots where the fungus is at work, followed by the appearance of the frost-like patches of spores on the underside of the leaves. In the case of the cucumber, the spores are of a violet color. This disease appears when the houses have been cold and damp, and unless a radical change can at once be made, the chance for a crop will soon be lost. The vines should at once be treated with Bordeaux mixture, after picking off all leaves that are affected and throwing out the plants that have been much injured.

CUCUMBER POWDERY MILDEW.

The cucumber, when grown under glass, especially if the air has been kept too dry, is sometimes attacked with a fungus that is thought to be *Erysiphe Cichora-*

cearum, D. C. It shows on the upper side of the leaves as small white patches, composed of a mass of fine threads and spores. This gives it a flour-like appearance, whence the common name. It also attacks the stems and even the fruits. The portions attacked soon turn brown, and, if the spots are numerous, the plant is soon killed. As a preventive, the temperature and moisture in the house should be carefully regulated, but as the disease lives upon the outside of the plants, it, like all powdery mildews, readily yields to treatment. Spraying with sulphide of potassium, or cupram, or evaporating sulphur in the house, will destroy it. If the disease has appeared in a house, during the summer everything should be cleaned out of the house, and a pound of sulphur should be burned for each 3,000 cubic feet. Care will be required, as this will be fatal to animals and plants, as well as to the spores of the fungus.

ANTHRACNOSE OF THE BEAN.

When grown under glass, the bean is very subject to the attack of this fungus, which appears on the stems and leaves, as well as on the pods, causing spots to form that quickly enlarge, until they cover a considerable area. Upon the stems and pods the tissues dry up and appear sunken. To succeed with this crop, the seed used must be free from disease. Although soaking the seed in copper sulphate solution may aid in destroying the spores, it is not entirely effectual. As soon as the first spot shows, the affected portions should be removed and burned, and the plants sprayed with Bordeaux mixture. After the pods form, some of the solutions should be used. We have had good results when using copper sulphate solution, 1 to 2,000, but others report failures with it.

DAMPING OFF.

Considerable losses often occur in the cutting bed and seed boxes from what is commonly known as "damping off," and the disease that causes the trouble is often spoken of as the "fungus of the cutting bed." Really, there are several fungi that may be the cause of the trouble, but the one that is most destructive has been named *Artotrogus debaryanus* (Hesse). Not only does it grow upon living plants, but it may subsist upon decaying vegetable matter; hence, one of the conditions that is likely to lead to its appearance in a bed of cuttings is the use of sand in which several batches of cuttings have been rooted. If we combine with this a high temperature and a close and moist atmosphere, the appearance of the trouble in a batch of cuttings will be more than probable. The same is true with seedlings, and for this reason clean sand forms the best seed bed in which to start plants that, like the cucumber, require a high temperature.

The remedy against this disease is self-evident, and, in addition to a frequent change of the sand in the cutting bed, we must avoid the conditions that have been mentioned as promoting its development. It has also been found that extremes of temperature and frequent sprinklings of the surface, thus keeping it wet while the soil beneath is comparatively dry, favor the appearance of the fungus. If the soil is too wet, it should be stirred, thus aiding its drying out.

The conditions that are mentioned as favoring the appearance of the fungus act in two ways, as they cause a soft, watery growth, thus making the cuttings or seedlings more subject to attack, and they are also favorable to the development of the spores and the growth of the fungus.

If it appears in a batch of seedlings, the healthy plants should at once be pricked out in a box of fresh soil, while in the cutting bed the sand should be thrown out, the boards coated with a thick wash of Bordeaux **mixture, and, if of a valuable variety, the healthy cut-**

tings may be replaced in fresh sand. If others can be readily obtained, however, it will generally be better to burn them up and make new ones.

Aside from the form mentioned above, "damping off" may be caused by one or more species of *Botrytis* and *Phyllosticta*, and upon beans by *Colletotricum Lindemuthianum*, which thrive under about the same conditions and which require the same treatment.

CHAPTER XXVII.

INSECTICIDES.

In selecting material for the destruction of insects, it is quite necessary that the nature of the insect to be treated should be understood. Frequently insecticides are applied without effect, when a little knowledge of the insect would have shown that the materials used were not adapted to the purpose.

ARSENITES.

While Paris green, London purple and other arsenites, hellebore, etc., are valuable when the insects EAT the flowers, foliage, or other external portions of the plants, they are in no way effective against the plant lice, scale, and similar insects.

If the above mentioned arsenites are mixed with one hundred parts (by weight) of plaster, and dusted over the plants when the foliage is wet, or used in water at the rate of a teaspoonful to twelve quarts, such insects as eat the portions to which they are applied will be destroyed. Hellebore can be diluted with five times its weight of plaster, or a teaspoonful can be used to a gallon of water.

Another class of insecticides, in order to be effectual, should be applied directly upon the insects, as they destroy by contact, and their effect is not lasting.

KEROSENE EMULSION.

Another remedy that is coming rapidly into favor for the destruction of aphides, scale, mealy bugs, and all other insects to which it can be directly applied, is known as kerosene emulsion. Various pumps and nozzles have been designed for the mixing of water with kerosene, but as yet the emulsion is safest to be used. It is prepared with either hard or soft soap, kerosene and water, as follows: Take a quart of soft soap that has been heated until it has become liquid (or two ounces of hard soap dissolved in a gallon of hot water), add one pint of kerosene and mix together until a thick, cream-like material is obtained. It can be best prepared by using a small force pump, such as is used in applying the mixture to the plants. Care should be taken to form a perfect emulsion that will not separate upon standing. Before using, the emulsion should be diluted with water, so that the kerosene will constitute one-sixteenth of the entire mixture, or, in other words, one pint of kerosene will make eight quarts of insecticide. This should be applied with considerable force and in a fine spray, covering every part of the plants, as it must come in contact with the insects, to be effectual. When properly prepared, this mixture can be used with safety upon nearly all plants. The cucumber and similar plants, and a few others with rough leaves, will, however, be injured by it. For the more tender plants, Professor Webster recommends one ounce of hard soap dissolved in two gallons of hot water, and mixing with it one ounce each of oil of cloves and kerosene. In this, while at a temperature of 125 degrees F., the plants are dipped.

PYRETHRUM.

Pyrethrum or buhach is another valuable insect destroyer. It contains a volatile oil that is supposed to act upon the insects through their breathing organs. It can be applied as a powder with a bellows, or in water with a force pump or a syringe, using a teaspoonful to a gallon. To be most effectual, it should be used in a closed room, but even then the liquid application will often succeed where the powder will fail. Care should be taken to have a fresh supply, and if it is to be kept any length of time, it should be placed in an airtight vessel.

TOBACCO.

For many insects, tobacco is an effective remedy. If the houses are filled with smoke from burning tobacco stems, the plant lice can be kept in check, provided they have not too much of a start. As in other cases, prevention is easier than cure, and if the houses are fumigated once or twice a week, no aphides will appear. The tobacco stems should be slightly dampened, and either placed in fumigating cans, made of galvanized sheet iron, with openings in the sides near the bottom to afford a draft, or in piles upon the cement or dirt walk. Shavings, paper, or better yet, a few live coals, may be used for kindling the stems. Care should be taken that the tobacco does not blaze. The amount of smoke that can be used will vary with the plants, but if so thick that one cannot see more than ten feet, it will generally answer. A strong tobacco tea sprayed upon the plants is also valuable as an insecticide, and in houses where fumigation cannot be relied upon, the sprinkling of tobacco dust or of tobacco stems about the plants will assist in keeping the insects in check. The stems give the house an untidy look and the dust is washed off in syringing.

Evaporated sulphur is also a valuable insecticide for red spider, scale and aphides.

Whale oil soap is a useful material for washing plants, or as a solution for spraying plants that cannot be readily washed, using one pound to eight or ten gallons of water for tender plants, and a pound to three or four gallons for the hardier ones. It is also much used in making kerosene emulsion, being preferable to common soap.

There is also a great variety of patent mixtures that are used as insect destroyers, among the most valuable of which is Hughes's fir tree oil, which can often be used to advantage upon plants that may be injured by the kerosene emulsion. At the rate of a half pint to a gallon of water, it is an effective and safe wash.

TOBACCO EXTRACT.

In large ranges of houses, where steam is used for heating or pumping, the application of the vapor of tobacco will be found easier, safer and more effective than the use of smoke. It can readily be applied by placing the stems in a barrel or tank and admitting steam through a steam pipe to the bottom. Three barrels will answer for a 100-foot house. Galvanized sheet iron pans may be placed upon the steam pipes and used for the evaporation of strong tobacco water. They are generally about forty inches long, four inches wide and nearly as deep, and if two are placed upon each side of a house 100 feet long, and the pans filled twice a week, it will generally keep the aphides in check. The commercial tobacco extract can be evaporated in the same way, but only a pint will be required for 4,000 square feet. The extract may also be used as a paint upon hot water pipes, applying it with a brush. It will soon dry on and in a day or so should be moistened with clear water. Another application of the extract should be made in a day or two, as is necessary.

If the extract is to be extensively used, it will pay to put in a specially arranged tank and piping for the purpose. This consists of a galvanized iron tank, in which a quart of the extract is placed for 8,000 feet of glass. The steam supply pipe enters at the top and extends nearly to the bottom. From this tank, the vapor is carried in pipes to the various houses, where there should be a vent every twenty-five feet. The size of the pipes should vary from one inch to one and one-half inches or larger, according to the amount to be treated. The pipes leading from the tank should have a downward slope, so that any condensed liquid will not collect. To prevent injury to the plants, the pipes should be carried in the walks or under the benches, and at each outlet there should be an ell and a valve, the former to turn the steam horizontally so that it will not reach the plants, and the valve to regulate and control the escape of the vapor. The piping and tank should be provided with drip cocks wherever necessary, and such valves as will be required to control the steam, and to permit the washing out of the tank and pipes.

As compared with tobacco stems, dust or tea, the concentrated extract, the one most commonly used being the "Rose leaf," is clean, easily and quickly applied and it has but little odor. For a house 200 by twenty feet, the cost is about twenty cents.

Aside from throwing the tobacco dust over the plants, it may be placed over an oil stove. The fumes should be slowly driven off, but the flame should be so regulated that it does not take fire. The burning of a pound of tobacco upon stoves, thirty feet apart in a house, will be effectual.

HOT WATER.

Especially for house plants, hot water forms a simple and effectual remedy, as nearly all insects are killed by water at 135 to 140 degrees, while tender plants will not be injured by water at 150 degrees, and many of the hardier species will withstand its use at 180 degrees. If the plants are small, they can readily be dipped quickly two or three times in the water, which should be from 150 to 175 degrees, or the water may be thrown over them. While a coarse stream could be used, it will hardly answer to apply it as a fine spray, as the water will be cooled before it reaches the plant.

CHAPTER XXVIII.

FUNGICIDES, THEIR PREPARATION AND USE.

Many of the diseases of plants are indirectly due to some unfavorable condition of temperature or moisture, that enfeebles them and provides surroundings that are particularly favorable to the development of the germs of disease. It has long been known that sulphur could be used for the destruction of some of the mildews, and various sulphur compounds are among the most valuable fungicides. Within the last ten years, several salts of copper have also come into use, and as the slightest trace will destroy the spores of fungi, they are employed as fungicides, to the almost entire exclusion of other forms. The following materials and methods of application are particularly worthy of mention:

Sulphur is a chief and simple remedy that is destructive, particularly to the powdery mildews. As flower of sulphur, it may be thrown upon the plants with a bellows, and if the temperature of the house is allowed to reach 90 degrees upon a bright morning, before ventilation is given, it will have a good effect. A more rapid evaporation of the sulphur can be secured if it is applied as a wash to the steam or hot water pipes. When made into a thick wash with an equal quantity of lime, it can be applied with a brush and its effects will be noticed for a week or more, according to the amount used and the temperature of the pipes.

Another method of obtaining evaporated sulphur is by the use of a small oil stove, over which the sulphur can be placed upon an iron dish. If sulphur is evaporated in this way about twice a week, until its presence can be detected by the eye, it will destroy many of the insects as well as fungi. Great care should be taken that the sulphur does not in any way become overturned or take fire, as that would destroy the plants. The latter danger will be lessened if an iron dish containing a half-inch of sand is placed beneath the dish containing the sulphur.

Liver of Sulphur, or sulphide of potassium, dissolved in water at the rate of two ounces to ten gallons of water, is also a valuable fungicide. Although its effects are less lasting than those of the copper compounds, it can be relied upon for the destruction of powdery mildew and other superficial fungi, and has the two strong points of being readily prepared, and of not discoloring the foliage.

COPPER COMPOUNDS.

During the past six or eight years, the use of various salts of copper as fungicides has rapidly increased. The simplest, cheapest, and most efficient form is a preparation of copper sulphate (blue vitriol) and lime, known as Bordeaux mixture. For some purposes, this fungicide is not desirable, as it leaves a coating of lime upon the plants, but when this is not objectionable, the effect of the application will be rendered more lasting by the adhesive qualities of the lime.

This mixture is made in various strengths, according to the severity of the disease and the nature of the plants. If the attack is widespread, and if the fungus is a difficult one to destroy, upon all plants where a thick coating of lime will not be objectionable the following mixture may be used: Four pounds of copper sulphate, three pounds of lime, forty gallons of water. Dissolve the copper sulphate in hot water (it can readily be done by placing it in a piece of burlap and suspending in a pail of water), and in another vessel slake the lime (also with hot water), pour together, and add the remainder of the water. This mixture should be strained, in order to remove all lumps that might clog the pump. It is well to test the mixture by adding a few drops of solution of ferrocyanide of potassium. If it turns the mixture brown, more lime should be added.

For the powdery mildews, and upon plants where the lime is not desirable, the mixture may be made half as strong as above, using two pounds of copper sulphate, two pounds of lime and forty gallons of water. The fungicide should be applied in a fine spray, covering every part of the plants. Except in cases where the disease has a firm foothold, the weaker mixture will generally answer.

For use when the lime mixtures are not desirable, the modified eau celeste, or the ammoniated copper carbonate, may be used: The former is made from 2 pounds copper sulphate, 1 1-2 pounds sal soda, 1 1-2 quarts ammonia water (FFFF), 32 gallons of water.

Dissolve the copper sulphate and sal soda in separate vessels, pour together and, when action has ceased, add the ammonia and dilute before using.

The ammonia solution of copper carbonate, or cupram, as it is called for short, is made by dissolving two ounces of precipitated copper carbonate in one quart of ammonia (FFFF), and diluting to thirty-two gallons. The last two preparations form clear, dark blue solutions and, although less effective than the Bordeaux mixture, will generally be preferred for use upon plants in the greenhouse, as they are less unsightly. Various other mixtures have been used for the destruction of fungous diseases, but none of them are as valuable as those described above. We have also had fair results from the use of a solution of copper sulphate, which is easily prepared and is quite inexpensive. We have used it at the rate of one to one thousand, or of one ounce to eight gallons of water, upon most plants, but in the case of the beet, bean, and other plants with smooth leaves, the strength should be reduced; for some plants, like the carnation, it can be doubled to advantage. To be effectual, soft water should be used in making the solution.

WHITE ARSENIC.

Good results from the use of a solution of arsenic, as a remedy for the rust of the carnation, are reported by E. G. Hill and others. If only a few plants are grown, it will be best to buy "Fowler's solution" of arsenic at a drug store, and use it at the rate of an ounce to eight gallons of water. With a little care, a solution can be readily made. The following formula is recommended: Take of arsenious acid C. P., 616 grains; bicarbonate of potash, 1236 grains; water, four ounces. Heat until a solution has been made and add enough water to make five ounces by measure. Use one ounce of the solution to eight gallons of water. Care should be taken not to inhale any of the vapor when making the solution. A thorough application seems to kill the spores and the body of the fungus, and at the same time causes the injured leaves to drop off, thus cleaning up the plants.

CHAPTER XXIX.

SOIL, MANURES AND WATERING.

Brief allusions have several times been made to the preparation of soil for various greenhouse crops, but a few words in a general way may not be amiss.

In the past, there has been great mystery thrown over the preparation of potting soil by the florist of the old school, whose recipes have been as exact and as complex as the physician's prescription. To-day, however, the veil has been thrown back, and the whole matter has been found to be simplicity itself. The materials that form the basis of the potting soil for nearly all greenhouse plants, are rotten pasture sods and cow, horse, or sheep manure, in the proportion of one of the latter to from two to five of the former. The sods should be cut in the spring or fall, several months before the soil will be needed, and should be obtained if possible from an old pasture that has a thick fibrous turf, the slice being made from two to four inches thick, according to the thickness of the sod. They should be piled up and decomposed manure added, using a layer of manure to two or three layers of sods. If the sods come from a clay soil, the addition of sharp sand will be of benefit and, for most crops, a portion at least of the manure should come from the horse stable. On the other hand, if the turf contains more or less sand, cow manure will be preferable and, if from a very light soil, the addition of a very small quantity of clay loam will be of value. As a rule, however, when the turf can be obtained from a moderately heavy, sandy loam soil, the addition of the manure alone is all that will be necessary. When the sods have become perhaps half rotted, the pile should be cut down and worked over. If this is done the first of May, the compost can be used for filling the benches, in three or four weeks, and by August it will be in good condition for potting. When it can be readily obtained, sheep manure is of value, either for mixing with soil for potting, as a top-dressing or for preparing liquid manure.

For seed pans and for potting cuttings, it is well to pass the compost through a coarse sieve, but for most purposes this will be an injury, as much of the fibrous portion of the compost will be removed. With a compost prepared as above, almost any kind of plants can be grown, but the intelligent florist will prefer to modify it to suit the wants of the different species.

For bulbs, in particular, and for cuttings of nearly all plants, the amount of sand can well be increased. Leaf mold is a valuable addition to a potting soil, but, for most plants, its use is not essential, and the same can be said of peat. Many of the stove plants, however, do best in a light, porous soil, and leaf mold and peat can be added to advantage, in the proportion of one part of each to eight of the compost.

SAND FOR THE CUTTING BENCH.

The use of "silver sand" has been insisted upon as necessary for success in growing cuttings, but florists now take no especial pains to obtain it, although it is desirable if it can be secured near at hand. The main thing is to use sharp sand of medium fineness, that is free from organic matter. Anything that partakes of a quicksand nature, where the angles of the grains have been worn off, will pack around the cuttings, and extremely fine sand has the same fault. Coarse sand, on the other hand, dries out too quickly, unless it is flooded, and admits air too freely to the cut surface of the cuttings. Soil containing organic matter is also to be avoided, as its fermentation will lead to the development of bacteria and fungi, which are likely to cause the decay of the cuttings. It is probable, too, that the presence of organic matter in the soil hinders the proper aeration of the cutting bed.

FERTILIZERS.

Although stable manure should be the principal reliance for plant food, some of the chemical manures can be used to advantage. Aside from their value in supplying plant food, they will, if judiciously applied, promote a firm, healthy growth of the plants, and improve the texture and keeping qualities of the flowers. Great care should be taken in the use of chemical fertilizers, as many of them are of a strong alkaline, while others are of an acid, nature, and if used to excess, they will have an injurious rather than a beneficial effect.

With the exception of ground bone, it is not safe to use any of them in seed pans, or in soil for cuttings or young seedlings. A large amount of water is given off from the surface of the soil by evaporation. The alkalies held in solution are deposited on the surface of the soil, and may be strong enough to destroy the tender plants. Even when used in small quantities in solution in water, if applied frequently, they may accumulate and become strong enough to injure the plants.

Ground bone is one of the most valuable mineral fertilizers, as it promotes a strong, yet firm and healthy, growth and can be used in almost an unlimited quantity, without danger of injuring the plants. Pure bone, only, should be used, and to produce the best effects it should be finely ground. Whatever the plants to be grown, bone meal can be added to the soil to advantage, taking the place of a part of the manure, and it will be found equally valuable whether they are in seed boxes, cuttings, or to be repotted. For plants grown either in shallow or in solid beds, the addition of bone meal to the soil, both at time of planting and at intervals during the season, will be of value. One quart of pure, fine ground bone to a bushel of soil will answer for this purpose, but two or three times as much can be used for seed boxes, or for repotting. Ground bone furnishes about twenty to twenty-five per cent phosphoric acid, of which less than one-half per cent is soluble, and about six per cent is reverted (available to plants). It also contains about four per cent of nitrogen. There is, however, a considerable variation in the amount of the constituents. Mildly acidulated bone, if used at all, should be first carefully tested.

Bone superphosphate is made by dissolving bones in sulphuric acid, thus rendering nearly all the phosphoric acid available to the plants. If used carefully, it is of value in the garden and for deep beds, but as the commercial brands generally contain some free acid and potash, its use by the florist in the greenhouse cannot be recommended.

Dissolved bone black consists of the refuse bone charcoal from sugar refineries and other sources, dissolved in acid, and ground. It is of varying strength, and contains all the way from fifteen to twenty-five per cent of phosphoric acid. The phosphorus is in a soluble form, and were it always free from sulphuric acid, it would be preferable to raw bone. It should be used with great care in pots or shallow beds, but when it can be thoroughly mixed with the soil in the garden or in deep beds, it forms a valuable source of phosphoric acid. When used in repotting soil, or in shallow beds, one pound to the bushel can generally be used with safety, while half that quantity will be as much as any crop will need. It is, however, particularly desirable as a top-dressing, using perhaps one pound to twenty square feet of bed, and in water, either alone or combined with other chemicals. Two or even three tablespoonfuls in a twelve-quart watering pot of water will be perfectly safe.

Sulphate and Muriate of Potash are the usual materials used as a source of potash, and when wood ashes cannot be obtained, are extremely valuable. The sulphate is the best form for greenhouse use, and may be applied either broadcasted and mixed with the soil, or in solution in water. They should never be used in seed boxes, or for young plants of any kind, but in repotting large plants or in shallow beds, a tablespoonful to a bushel of the soil can be used to advantage. In water, a tablespoonful to twelve quarts will be safe.

Kainit is a crude form of potash salts that is of value for supplying potash, and, on account of its strong alkaline nature, it is often used, about the same as the sulphate of potash, for the destruction of insects, worms, etc., in the soil.

Nitrate of Potash or saltpeter, is also used as a source for both nitrogen and potash. While its cost is an objection to its use in large quantities, it will be found valuable when dissolved in water at the rate of a tablespoonful in eight or ten quarts, and used as a liquid manure.

Nitrate of Soda is highly recommended for furnishing nitrogen for greenhouse crops, and has been tried by many florists. As a rule, however, it has been found a hindrance to the growth of the plants. This is owing to the fact that it has been used in too great strength. When thoroughly mixed with the soil, at the rate of a teaspoonful to a bushel, it will benefit large plants, or use one pound to 100 square feet of bench. As a liquid manure, it will be found safest, and at the rate of a teaspoonful to three gallons of water it will be useful. If used too frequently it may cause too rank a growth of the plants.

Sulphate of Ammonia is also used for its nitrogen, and is less likely to injure the plants than nitrate of soda. For all plants in which a large leaf development or rapid growth is desired, this chemical is a very valuable fertilizer. One pound to fifty square feet of bench, or a tablespoonful to a bushel of soil, or three gallons of water, can be safely used.

MIXED CHEMICAL MANURES.

Nearly every fertilizer manufacturer puts up a fertilizer prepared for greenhouse use, and, if purchased in large quantities, they can be obtained at rates but little above the market rates for the materials.

The following mixtures will be found useful to be added to the soil for nearly all greenhouse crops: Two hundred pounds pure ground bone, 30 pounds sulphate of potash, 50 pounds sulphate of ammonia, or 50 pounds of nitrate of soda; or 200 pounds ground bone and 50 pounds nitrate of potash. Either of the above can be used at the rate of one pound to twenty square feet of bench surface, or to two bushels of soil for repotting.

If desired for use as a liquid manure in water, dissolved bone black should be employed instead of ground bone, in the following proportions: One hundred pounds of dissolved bone black, 50 pounds sulphate of potash and 50 pounds nitrate of soda, or 50 pounds sulphate of ammonia. Or, 100 pounds dissolved bone black and 50 pounds nitrate of potash, used at the rate of a tablespoonful of either mixture to a gallon of water.

LIQUID MANURES.

In addition to the use of the above chemicals dissolved in water, every florist should employ at frequent intervals, especially during the summer, liquid fertilizers made from the animal manures, for which purpose the manure of the sheep, hen, pigeon, cow, or horse, may be used. A tank or barrel should be located at some convenient point, and in it should be placed about one foot of manure. If filled with water and allowed to stand a few hours, it will be ready for use. Plants of all kinds, either growing in beds or that have received their last shift in pots, and have filled the soil with their roots, should receive, during the growing season, an application of liquid manure, either animal or chemical, from once to three times a week.

To secure quick results and for application in solution, sixty pounds of nitrate of soda, twenty-five of nitrate of potash and fifteen of phosphate of ammonia, form a good mixture. A firmer, but less rapid, growth will be secured from fifty pounds nitrate of soda, thirty of nitrate of potash, and twenty of phosphate of ammonia. Elmer D. Smith of Adrian, Michigan, has been very successful in growing chrysanthemums with the above mixture, applying one pound in one hundred gallons of water for a house one hundred by eighteen feet, every five days until the flowers are half-open. Phosphate of potash is also used in place of the nitrate of potash and phosphate of ammonia.

FIG. 127. THE KINNEY PUMP.

Commercial brands are put up by several manufacturers, which give good results, but, like all concentrated fertilizers, they must be used with care.

For the application of liquid fertilizers the Kinney pump (Fig. 127), made by the Kingston (R. I.) Hose Connection Co., will be found very useful. It is attached to a hose and draws from a barrel or tank a strong solution and, after mingling it with the clear water, applies it to the plants with no more trouble than if the water alone is used. The rate of dilution can be readily varied.

JADOO FIBRE AND LIQUID.

These materials have been recently introduced as a potting soil and liquid manure. While rather expensive for general use, good plants can be grown in the fibre, and it is particularly valuable for decorative plants. It retains moisture and lessens the danger of injury from drying out of the plants. Professor Galloway, who has tested it thoroughly, recommends the fibre for hanging baskets, jardinieres, house pot-plants, palms, etc. Good results can also be obtained with the liquid, diluted with forty-eight parts of water.

WATERING.

In the past, the practice has been to apply water to the surface of the soil and allow it to soak in. While this method is still used for pot-plants, many persons are securing good results from the sub-irrigation of plants grown in beds. When plants are surface watered, unless one is familiar with the work, there is danger on the one hand of over-watering and, on the other, of keeping the soil too dry. When plants are watered, the amount applied should be sufficient to thoroughly moisten the soil, and no more water should be given them until they, in some way, manifest a need of it. An experienced florist can tell from the appearance of the plants, even before they begin to wilt, as to their need of further application of water. The appearance of the pots and soil should also be considered. While plants are at rest, or in the case of young plants before they have established themselves, especially if they are in large pots, little water will be required, and, unless withheld, there will be danger of injury. As a rule, the early morning is the best time for watering, but during the hot days of summer, the plants should be examined two or three times and should receive water, if they show the need of it. While cistern water can be used for most plants, it is desirable that the chill be taken from water brought directly from springs. For stove plants and others requiring a moderately high temperature, it will be necessary to provide some method for warming the water. This can generally be done by providing tanks through which steam or water pipes can pass.

SUB-IRRIGATION.

For several years, experiments have been carried on in watering plants growing in greenhouse beds, through subterranean pipes. In nearly every case good results have been obtained, as there was not only a larger and earlier development of the plants, but the labor of application was greatly reduced, and a smaller amount of water sufficed. In many cases, too, the danger from attack of various plant diseases was lessened. Among those who have had most experience with sub-irrigation in the greenhouse is Professor W. J. Green, of the Ohio Experiment Station, who has prepared the following notes:

SUB-IRRIGATION IN THE GREENHOUSE.

Sub-irrigation in the greenhouse grew out of the necessity of devising ways and means to prevent the lettuce rot. After several conversations on the subject, between Mr. W. J. Green, horticulturist of the Ohio Experiment Station, and Mr. W. S. Turner, assistant, the latter set some lettuce plants in a box in which a tile was so placed as to admit of watering without wetting the foliage. The subsequent development of the method is due to the combined efforts of W. J. Green, E. C. Green and W. S. Turner.

The experiments were begun in the winter of 1890-91, but in addition to some box trials a bed seven by ten feet was planted, and, giving satisfactory results, the work was extended the next season, when still better results were obtained. The third year nothing was done by the station, because of removal to Wooster, Wayne county, but the work was carried on at the university in Columbus, in the houses first used for the purpose, and along the same lines, but on a larger scale, under the management of Mr. Turner. The fourth season the experiments were extended and the scope widened, under favorable circumstances, in the four new houses built by the station at Wooster, Ohio.

The experiments, although not fully completed with all classes of plants which may be grown in the soil on greenhouse benches, show that all species do not respond in the same degree to the treatment, some being but slightly benefited, while with others the crop is often doubled. It is somewhat unexpected, but no plants, not even roses, have been injured by the treatment.

Thus far the experiments seem to show that the various classes of plants which have been tested are benefited by sub-irrigation in about the following order, beginning with those which show the greatest gain: Radishes, lettuce, cucumbers, cauliflower, beets, carnations, violets, smilax, roses, tomatoes. It is quite probable that further experiments will change the order, but the list is a provisional one simply, and is given for the general guidance of those who contemplate making a trial of the method. Radishes have generally shown more marked gains by sub-irrigation than any other crop, but in some trials lettuce has taken the first place. By this method radishes grow quicker, hence come to a marketable size earlier than by surface watering. It usually happens that marketable radishes will be found in both the surface and sub-irrigated beds at the same time, but the larger number in the latter, and of greater average weight. The following trial with French Breakfast illustrates the above:

	No. marketable Feb. 23.	Weight, ounces.
Sub-irrigated,	77	41
Surface irrigated,	40	18

The total number in each bed was 155, thus in the sub-irrigated bed about one-half were fit for the market at the first gathering, and four days later the remainder were marketable, whereas in the surface-watered bed but little more than one-fourth were ready on the 23d, and three pullings instead of two had to be made, and the average size was less. The market value of the sub-irrigated was more than double that of the others, even though earliness is not taken into account. The chief gain due to earlier maturity, however, is because of the fact that the beds may be cleared several days sooner, which is a matter worthy of consideration.

Lettuce is a much more profitable crop than radishes, and some of the results with it have been quite equal to the above. The following are some of the results with the Grand Rapids, taken at random from notes of recent experiments:

Experiment No. 1.

	No plants.	Weight.
Sub-irrigated,	55	17 lbs. 8 oz.
Surface irrigated,	55	9 lbs. 8 oz.

Experiment No. 2.

| Sub-irrigated, | 75 | 28 lbs. 15 oz. |
| Surface irrigated, | 75 | 18 lbs. 3 oz. |

Experiment No. 3.

| Sub-irrigated, | 50 | 14 lbs. 12 oz. |
| Surface irrigated, | 50 | 9 lbs. 13 oz. |

Some cases can be given where other varieties have shown even better results, and a number in which the crop has been more than doubled, by sub-irrigation. Fifty per cent is considered a fair average gain, and some cases have occurred where it has been as low as twenty. Several causes contribute to make the results vary so greatly. Generally it has been found that the gain by sub-irrigation is less in the early part of the winter than toward spring, owing largely to the comparative quantities of water required at these dates.

The character of the soil has something to do with the results also. Surface watering compacts the soil, but sub-irrigation does not, hence with a naturally heavy soil it is somewhat difficult to give the needed quantity of water when applied to the surface, without producing a water-logged condition, and there is danger also of inducing rot, no matter what the character of the soil. When the lettuce becomes so large as to cover the surface of the bed, the difficulty of watering on the surface is much increased, hence, uniform and thorough watering at this critical period requires much skill and patience. Care has been taken to give the surface-watered beds the best of attention, but it has not been possible to water them so thoroughly and well as by sub-irrigation, since by the latter method the watering can be done as easily at one period of growth as another, and the requisite quantity of water more certainly supplied.

The true explanation must await further experiments, but at present the opinion may be ventured that the amount of water and physical condition of the soil have much to do with the results, and are probably the most important factors. An important consideration in the case of lettuce is the fact that there is less rot among the plants on the sub-irrigated plots than where surface watering is practiced. There is a difference in waste in the way of trimmings, due both to rot and soiled lower leaves, ranging from ten to fifteen per cent in favor of the sub-irrigated. It should not be inferred, however, that rot will not occur where sub-irrigation is practiced, for it will appear if proper precautions are not taken in keeping the houses cool and in ventilating properly.

There is quite a marked difference in the quantity of bloom and size of flowers with carnations grown by the two methods, but no data can be given, as the experiments are incomplete. Since the plants do not shade the soil to any extent, it soon becomes quite hard where water is applied to the surface, which necessitates frequent digging. In the sub-irrigated beds, however, the soil does not become compacted, and the surface remains loose and friable, in a condition to be permeated by the air, even without digging. This physical effect upon the soil, of sub-irrigation, makes quite a difference in the amount of work required to care for a given space by the two methods of watering. The carnation is not an extreme case, but is a good example, as showing this difference.

Smilax and violets seem to respond well to this treatment, but comparative data cannot be given at present. The result of the experiment on roses has been lost because of nematodes, and it is worthy of note that this pest was less destructive upon the sub-irrigated than upon the surface-watered bed.

In speaking of lettuce, the fact was referred to, that less care and skill are required to water properly by sub-irrigation than by the ordinary method, and it may be further stated that the labor is less also. The water is applied quickly and it runs where it is needed. The gardener judges as to the amount required by the condition of both plants and soil, as by the old methods. Contrary to what might be inferred, he is less liable to over-water by the new than by the old plan, for with a loose, friable soil a water-logged condition is not liable to occur. In our experience it has never happened.

Do we syringe the foliage of sub-irrigated plants to destroy the red spider, and do we sprinkle the walks to supply moisture to the air? These questions are frequently asked, and seem to be uppermost in the minds of many. The answer to the first is, yes, of those that need it, and to the second, no. Lettuce, and most vegetables, in fact, need not be syringed, and never receive water on the foliage, except once at planting. Almost the entire houses are watered by sub-irrigation, but there is enough moisture in the air to keep the plants in a healthy growing condition, derived from transpiration through the foliage and evaporation from the soil. The necessity of supplying more moisture to the air than this, for the plants above named, is not recognized.

HOW SUB-IRRIGATION IS OPERATED.

With plants that are transplanted one or more times, sub-irrigation is begun as soon as the seed is sown. Flats sixteen by twenty-four inches, and two inches deep, with slatted bottoms, are used for seed sowing. As soon as the seed is sown the flats are placed in a shallow vat containing an inch or two of water, and allowed to stand until the moisture shows on top. They are then set in any convenient spot until water is again required, which is not so soon as when surface watering is practiced. This method of watering is followed until the plants are set in the beds, or benches. Probably this method of watering involves more labor than the old plan, but the plants do so much better and it is so much more satisfactory in every way, that it must be counted as an improvement. Referring to experiment No. 1, with lettuce, it will be seen that the results were better than in the other cases. The plants in this experiment were carried through from the beginning by the two methods. The sub-irrigated were watered in that manner from the time the seed was sown, while the surface-watered were treated in the old way throughout the experiment. In the other experiments the difference in treatment was begun when the plants were set in the benches.

By sub-irrigation, damping off is reduced, the soil does not harden, and less attention is required than when surface watering is practiced. It is particularly recommended for the first watering after the seed is sown, to prevent washing of the soil and baking of the surface.

In the benches sub-irrigation is accomplished by means of two and one-half or three-inch drain tile laid two feet apart on the bottom, either lengthwise or crosswise, and covered with soil to the ordinary depth. Gas pipe, with holes drilled at frequent intervals, may be employed, but the cost is greater. Our best results have been obtained with tile laid on a level, crosswise of the benches. Long runs of tile are not always satisfactory. If iron pipe is used the holes should not be more than two feet apart, and not larger than one-fourth inch. If long runs are used the pipe must be larger than for short runs, and in all cases the capacity of the pipe must be greater than the combined capacity of the small holes. The tile may be laid end to end closely, without cement, but ordinarily a more even flow is secured if the joints are lightly cemented and then broken just before hardening, so as to make cracks of uniform size.

The water may be introduced by boring holes through the side boards of the benches, or a T joint used, or, what is still better, a curved joint of sewer pipe of same size as the tile. When the beds are to be irrigated, water is introduced into the pipe or tile quickly, and allowed to run full length, when it soaks out uniformly through the adjacent soil.

Sub-irrigation pre-supposes a water-tight bench bottom. This may be constructed in various ways, but the cheapest plan is to use ordinary barn boards, with no shakes or loose knots. These are laid so as to nearly touch, and battened with lath, after which a coating of thin cement makes a water-tight bottom. Matched lumber, laid in white lead, answers the same purpose, but costs more. The best bottom is made of tile, either hexagonal, octagonal or flat, and covered with cement. Ordinary hexagonal (six-sided) tile laid on iron supports makes a very satisfactory bottom, and is as cheap as anything in the shape of tile. When cemented properly, this makes a durable and satisfactory bottom. Lumber may be used for the sides, but is not satisfactory, as it warps and springs away from the tile, causing leakage. Slate, seven or eight inches wide, is the best material, and this is held in place by galvanized iron strips at the top and bottom. These strips are cut two inches wide, and bent in the form of U-shaped troughs. The slate sets into the bottom trough, while the upper trough fits over the top of the slate, holding them together firmly. These slate sides rest on the iron supports to the tile, and are fastened to the iron gas pipes which support the purlins.

Thus it will be seen that to construct a bench for sub-irrigation adds but little to the cost over one equally durable made in the ordinary manner for surface watering. Where beds are on the ground, it might be necessary, in some cases, to make a water-tight bottom with cement, but not so if the subsoil is sufficiently retentive.

In conclusion, it might not be out of place to answer some theoretical objections urged against the plan because drainage is not provided for, and humidity of the air is not taken into account, but it is proposed to let facts stand in the place of arguments, and to place the whole matter in the hands of practical men for confirmation.

CHAPTER XXX.

FUEL—COAL, WOOD AND CRUDE OIL.

The location and extent of the establishment will have much to do in determining what kind of fuel will be most satisfactory and economical.

The use of hard wood, in localities where it is plentiful and where coal is dear, may be advisable, especially when flues are used, or in large establishments where a night fireman is employed. For small heaters in which coal is used, the nut anthracite will be preferable, and as the size of the heater increases, a choice must be made between the egg or pea sizes, and bituminous coal. Most of our modern heaters are made for either hard or soft coal, and the choice that is made will depend largely upon the cost of each. In large establishments some form of bituminous coal would probably be used.

When situated near the mines, some of the low-priced grades of pea or slack coal will make cheap fuel, but they are not worth more than two-thirds as much as good lump coal, and as the freight and handling make up the principal cost of the former, when they have to be transported any great distance, the latter will be the cheapest fuel.

CRUDE OIL AS FUEL.

Various devices have been invented for the burning of crude oil in greenhouse heaters. This material can only be used when steam under a moderately high pressure can be used to vaporize the oil. In order to use it in a hot water heater, a small steam boiler will also be needed as an auxiliary. One of the best of these burners

(Fig. 128) is that patented by James B. Moore, of Reading, Pa., which consists of an oil tube with a tapered nozzle, surrounded by a steam pipe also with a tapered nozzle. The combustion chamber is of solid metal and is placed in the ash pit, the grate having been taken out. The air for combustion is admitted through openings on three sides of the base of the boiler. The burner is inserted through a hole on the fourth side, and is surrounded by a conical tube through which the air for combustion enters.

The oil tube is connected with the oil tank, and the steam pipe with the steam dome, and also with an air

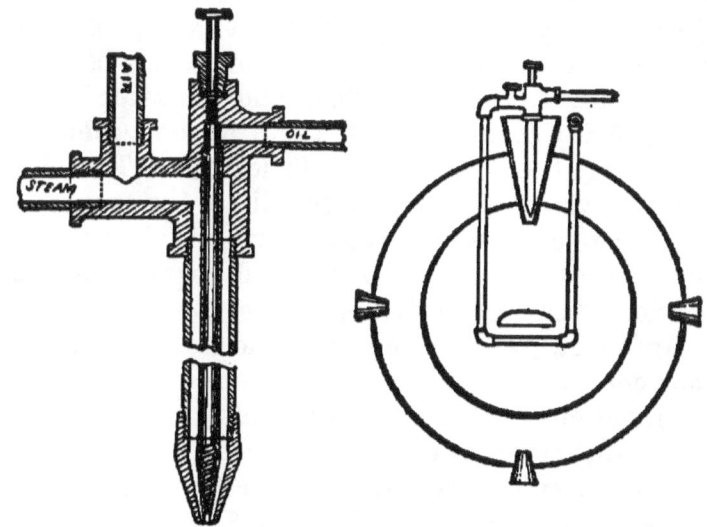

FIG. 128. CRUDE OIL BURNER.

pump, by which a blast is supplied while getting up steam. The steam pipe does not go directly from the dome to the burner, but first makes a circuit of the combustion chamber, and the steam is there superheated. In passing through the tube to the nozzle, the oil, being surrounded by the superheated steam, is considerably heated, and flowing through the spiral grooves in the valve escapes from the nozzle, but is at once vaporized by and mixed with the steam. It is thus carried into the combustion chamber, and may be scattered by a deflector. While a pressure of steam of from ten to fifteen pounds is desirable, the burner will give a perfect combustion of fuel with eight pounds, and even less.

In the past many persons have been prejudiced against the use of crude oil as fuel, on account of the offensive odor given off when it is handled, and from the many fires and explosions that have occurred from its use. Crude oil cannot be used to advantage unless a pipe can be run from the greenhouse to a large iron tank in which the oil is stored. This tank must be several hundred feet from any building, and so situated that it can be readily connected with a tank car on a side track. In this way there will be but little odor. The oil, by opening a valve, will run down hill to the greenhouse, and if the joints are all tight there will be no danger from explosions. The burners will require but little attention, there is no stoking to be done, no ashes to be carried out, and there will be no dirt and smoke to annoy one.

About one hundred gallons of oil will be equal to a ton of Anthracite pea coal, and making allowance for the extra labor required when coal is burned, it is generally estimated that with oil at $1.25 per barrel, it will be as cheap as soft coal at $1.80 per ton, and although the relative price may vary, the usual opinion is that with a good burner the oil is about twenty-five per cent cheaper than steam lump coal.

GAS AND GASOLINE.

Natural gas has been used with good results, but it cannot always be relied upon, and the supply is even now giving out in some places, while the limited territory in which it is found precludes its general use.

Water gas is found in many places to be an economical heating material. It costs only about twenty-five cents per thousand feet, and at that price is less than one-half as expensive as coal, and is regarded by many as cheaper than natural gas at current prices. While it may come into general use in cities, few florists are so situated that they can obtain it except at a considerable expense for the laying of mains, and it has not as yet been thoroughly tested for greenhouse heating. Gasoline can be readily handled, and florists are now looking to it as a valuable source of fuel. When a burner adapted for its use has been invented, it may revolutionize our present heating plants.

INDEX.

	Page
Achyranthes, varieties of	276
Aleyrodes (white flies)	311
Alocasias	180
Alternanthera, propagation of,	276
Andromeda, forcing of	141
Anthracnose of the bean	349
of carnations	332
of the rose	328
of violets	341
Anthuriums, propagation and care of	177
Aphis, the male and female	309
Aquariums	272
Aralias	166
Araucarias	166
Ardisias	138
Arsenites	351
Asparagus as a florist's green	158
winter forcing of	226
Aspidistras, propagation and uses of	168
Azaleas, potting and care of	131
Bacteriosis of carnations	337
Bean, anthracnose of the	349
Beans, the forcing of	232
Bedding plants, the growing of,	274
Beets for forcing	232
Begonias, tuberous, care of	103
Bermuda lily disease	343
Black spot of the rose	324
Bordeaux mixture as a fungicide	357
Budding, propagation by	305
Bugs, plant, and remedies for them	310
Bulbs and their culture	88
for the lawn	279
Cacti, care of	284
Caladium esculentum, treatment of	279
fancy	113
Calatheas	174
Calceolarias, growing the plants	143
Callas, how to grow	98
Cannas as greenhouse plants	108
propagation and care of	280
varieties of	109
Care of and soil for house plants	259
Carnation houses	32
rust	328

	Page
Carnations, care of the house for	48
disbudding	46
diseases of	328
growing plants in houses	34
history of	26
in beds and benches	36
planting out and cultivation	31
planting the houses	37
potting off	29
propagation of	27
soil for	30
staking and trellising	40
topdressing and manuring,	48
varieties of	49
watering and ventilating	39
Carrots, the forcing of	232
Cauliflower, forcing of	228
Cereus, night blooming, varieties of	285
Chemical manures and their effects	365
Chrysanthemums	60
care of the plants	57
diseases of	345
field culture	69
growing for cut flowers	57
history of	54
insects and diseases	76
liquid manure for	70
propagation by cuttings	56
propagation by seeds	55
single stem plants in pots,	66
specimen plants	67
staking the pot plants	70
standards	68
taking the buds and disbudding	63
varieties and their classification	70
Cinerarias, propagation and care of	146
Coal, hard and soft as fuel	376
Coleus, propagation and care of	276
Copper carbonate and its use	357
compounds as fungicides	358
Cordylines, propagation and care of	168
Crocuses, care of	93

380

Entry	Page
Crotons	170
Crude oil as fuel	376
Cucumber and melon, diseases of	348
as a winter crop	198
for forcing, varieties of	205
planting and training	201
pollination of	203
Cupram, its preparation and use	357
Cutting bed, the	295
bed fungus	350
Cuttings, propagation by	291
Cyanophyllums	173
Cyclamen, planting and care of	100
Cytisus	136
Dahlias, propagation and care	281
Damping off	350
Dieffenbachias, propagation and care of	177
Diseases and insects of house plants	263
of the carnation	328
of the rose	324
of violets	338
Dracænas, propagation and care of	168
Easter lilies, planting and care of	95
Eel worms	317
on violets	342
Electro culture of lettuce	194
Eulalias, propagation and care of	283
Extract of tobacco	354
Eye cuttings	297
Fairy ring spot of carnations	334
Ferns, propagation and care of	153
varieties of	154
Fertilizers, chemical	362
Flock in mushrooms	319
Flowering plants for bedding	277
Foliage plants, the growing of	274
Freesias, care of	95
Fruit trees under glass	253
Fuel—coal, wood and oil	376
Fumigation with hydrocyanic acid gas	320
Fungicides, their preparation and use	356
Fungous diseases of plants	324
Gardenias	139
Gas and gasoline as fuel	378
Gladiolus, forcing of	101
Grafting, propagation by	301
wax, preparation of	305
Grape growing in pots	246
growing under glass	234
Grapes, care of vines in winter	245
disbudding and thinning	241
keeping the fruit	244
propagating the plants	245
temperature and ventilation	243
the border for	234
the forcing of	244
Grapes, training and pruning	239
under glass, care of	237
varieties for forcing	236
watering and syringing	242
Gloxinias, growing of	109
Grasses, hardy ornamental	283
Ground bone as a fertilizer	362
Growing bedding plants	274
Half-hard cutting	299
Hanging baskets	271
Hard cuttings	298
Hardy plants, forcing of	140
Hotbeds for lettuce	195
Hot water as an insecticide	355
House plants, management of	258
plants, selection of	265
Hyacinth, the Roman	90
Hyacinths, Dutch and their care	91
planting and care of	88
water culture of	92
Hydrangeas, growing in the greenhouse	133
Hydrocyanic acid gas, fumigation with	320
Insecticides, their preparation and use	351
Insects and diseases of house plants	263
of the greenhouse	308
Intermediate orchids	121
Jadoo fiber and liquid	367
Kalmia, forcing of	141
Kerosene emulsion	352
Kinney pump, the	366
Layering, propagation by	300
Leaf cuttings	300
mold of carnations	336
spot of carnations	331
spot of violets	338
Lettuce, commercial growing of	186
diseases of	347
electro culture of	194
forcing of in greenhouses	182
growing, preparation and care of beds	189
houses for	184
in hotbeds	195
packing for market	192
pot culture of	188
varieties of	184
Lilacs, forcing of	141
Lilies, planting and care of	95
Lily of the valley, planting and care of	96
Liquid manure and its preparation	365
Liver of sulphur	357
Long cuttings	299
Manures, soil and watering	360
Marantas	174
Mealy bugs	315
Melons, forcing of	211
Mignonette, disease of	346
forcing of	149
Mildew of the cucumber	348
Mushroom, the new	223

Mushrooms, beds, care of	220
beds, spawning of	220
beds, watering of	221
enemies and diseases	318
house, a cheap	224
Mushrooms, culture of in greenhouses	211
gathering the crop	221
making the beds	216
preparation of material for beds	213
spawn for	217
Narcissus, planting and care of	88
Nepenthes	175
Oil as fuel	376
Orchids, care during growth	128
cool house	121
culture of	116
diseases and insects	130
for beginners	119
for intermediate houses	121
management while in bloom	129
the potting of	121
the watering of	127
treatment while resting	128
varieties of	120
Ornamental grasses	283
Oxalis, the cultivation of	99
Palms, propagation and care of	162
varieties of	164
Pandanus, how to grow	165
Peach culture under glass	254
Pear culture under glass	254
Pedigree plants	292
Plant bugs and remedies for them	310
Plants for the house	267
Plum culture under glass	254
Potash salts as fertilizers	364
Potting and repotting of house plants	261
Powdery mildew of the rose	325
Primulas, single and double	148
Propagation by layering, grafting and budding	300
by seeds and cuttings	287
of plants	287
Pyrethrum	353
Radishes, forcing	230
Red spider	312
Rhubarb, winter growing of	228
Root cuttings	297
galls of the violet	342
Rose beetle (Fuller's)	311
rust	326
Roses, diseases of	324
forcing hybrid perpetual	21
liquid manures and fertilizers	10
planting the houses	7
in pots and boxes	24
potting and care of plants	4
Roses, propagating the plants	1
soil for	4
solid beds vs. raised benches	6
staking and trellising	20
the forcing of	1
varieties for forcing	13
watering and ventilating	8
Rot of carnations	336
of lettuce	347
Rubber trees	172
Sand for the cutting bed	361
Saucer propagation	296
Scale insects and remedies	314
Seeds, propagation by	287
Slugs, snails and sowbugs	316
Smilax, planting and care of	157
Soft cuttings	293
Soil for and care of house plants	259
manures and watering	360
Sphærogynes	173
Spiræas, forcing of	141
Spot of carnations	331
Strawberries, forcing under glass	248
potting and care	249
varieties for forcing	252
Sub-irrigation in the greenhouse	368
Succulents, propagation and care of	284
Sulphur as a fungicide and insecticide	356
Sweet peas, cultivation of	277
Temperature for house plants	264
Thrips in the greenhouse	313
Tobacco as an insecticide	353
Tomatoes, forcing of	205
training and pruning	208
varieties for forcing	209
Topdressing house plants	262
Tuberose, planting and care	98
Tuberous begonias, care of	103
Tulips, planting and care of	88
varieties of	93
Violets, diseases of	338
growing plants in the house	85
houses for	78
propagation of	82
varieties, securing new	290
soil and planting out	83
varieties of	86
ventilation and care of the house	84
Wardian cases	273
Water and liquid manure for house plants	262
Watering, manures and soil plants	367
White arsenic as a fungicide	359
Window boxes	269
Window gardening	259

STANDARD BOOKS

PUBLISHED BY

ORANGE JUDD COMPANY

NEW YORK   CHICAGO
139-441 Lafayette Street   *Marquette Building*

BOOKS sent to all parts of the world for catalog price. Discounts for large quantities on application. Correspondence invited. Brief descriptive catalog free. Large illustrated catalog, six cents.

Soils

By CHARLES WILLIAM BURKETT, Director Kansas Agricultural Experiment Station. The most complete and popular work of the kind ever published. As a rule, a book of this sort is dry and uninteresting, but in this case it reads like a novel. The author has put into it his individuality. The story of the properties of the soils, their improvement and management, as well as a discussion of the problems of crop growing and crop feeding, make this book equally valuable to the farmer, student and teacher.

There are many illustrations of a practical character, each one suggesting some fundamental principle in soil management. 303 pages. 5½ x 8 inches. Cloth. $1.25

Insects Injurious to Vegetables

By Dr. F. H. CHITTENDEN, of the United States Department of Agriculture. A complete, practical work giving descriptions of the more important insects attacking vegetables of all kinds with simple and inexpensive remedies to check and destroy them, together with timely suggestions to prevent their recurrence. A ready reference book for truckers, market-gardeners, farmers as well as others who grow vegetables in a small way for home use; a valuable guide for college and experiment station workers, school-teachers and others interested in entomology of nature study. Profusely illustrated. 5½ x 8 inches. 300 pages. Cloth. $1.50

The Cereals in America

By THOMAS F. HUNT, M.S., D.Agri., Professor of Agronomy, Cornell University. If you raise five acres of any kind of grain you cannot afford to be without this book. It is in every way the best book on the subject that has ever been written. It treats of the cultivation and improvement of every grain crop raised in America in a thoroughly practical and accurate manner. The subject-matter includes a comprehensive and succinct treatise of wheat, maize, oats, barley, rye, rice, sorghum (kafir corn) and buckwheat, as related particularly to American conditions. First-hand knowledge has been the policy of the author in his work, and every crop treated is presented in the light of individual study of the plant. If you have this book you have the latest and best that has been written upon the subject. Illustrated. 450 pages. 5½ x 8 inches. Cloth. $1.75

The Forage and Fiber Crops in America

By THOMAS F. HUNT. This book is exactly what its title indicates. It is indispensable to the farmer, student and teacher who wishes all the latest and most important information on the subject of forage and fiber crops. Like its famous companion, "The Cereals in America," by the same author, it treats of the cultivation and improvement of every one of the forage and fiber crops. With this book in hand, you have the latest and most up-to-date information available. Illustrated. 428 pages. 5½ x 8 inches. Cloth. $1.75

The Book of Alfalfa

History, Cultivation and Merits. Its Uses as a Forage and Fertilizer. The appearance of the Hon. F. D. COBURN's little book on Alfalfa a few years ago has been a profit revelation to thousands of farmers throughout the country, and the increasing demand for still more information on the subject has induced the author to prepare the present volume, which is by far the most authoritative, complete and valuable work on this forage crop published anywhere. It is printed on fine paper and illustrated with many full-page photographs that were taken with the especial view of their relation to the text. 336 pages. 6½ x 9 inches. Bound in cloth, with gold stamping. It is unquestionably the handsomest agricultural reference book that has ever been issued. Price, postpaid . . . $2.00

Clean Milk

By S. D. BELCHER, M.D. In this book the author sets forth practical methods for the exclusion of bacteria from milk, and how to prevent contamination of milk from the stable to the consumer. Illustrated. 5 x 7 inches. 146 pages. Cloth. $1.00

Bean Culture

By GLENN C. SEVEY, B.S. A practical treatise on the production and marketing of beans. It includes the manner of growth, soils and fertilizers adapted, best varieties, seed selection and breeding, planting, harvesting, insects and fungous pests, composition and feeding value; with a special chapter on markets by Albert W. Fulton. A practical book for the grower and student alike. Illustrated. 144 pages. 5 x 7 inches. Cloth. $0.50

Celery Culture

By W. R. BEATTIE. A practical guide for beginners and a standard reference of great interest to persons already engaged in celery growing. It contains many illustrations giving a clear conception of the practical side of celery culture. The work is complete in every detail, from sowing a few seeds in a window-box in the house for early plants, to the handling and marketing of celery in carload lots. Fully illustrated. 150 pages. 5 x 7 inches. Cloth. $0.50

Tomato Culture

By WILL W. TRACY. The author has rounded up in this book the most complete account of tomato culture in all its phases that has ever been gotten together. It is no secondhand work of reference, but a complete story of the practical experiences of the best posted expert on tomatoes in the world. No gardener or farmer can afford to be without the book. Whether grown for home use or commercial purposes, the reader has here suggestions and information nowhere else available. Illustrated. 150 pages. 5 x 7 inches. Cloth. $0.50

The Potato

By SAMUEL FRASER. This book is destined to rank as a standard work upon Potato Culture. While the practical side has been emphasized, the scientific part has not been neglected, and the information given is of value, both to the grower and the student. Taken all in all, it is the most complete, reliable and authoritative book on the potato ever published in America. Illustrated. 200 pages. 5 x 7 inches. Cloth. $0.75

Dwarf Fruit Trees

By F. A. WAUGH. This interesting book describes in detail the several varieties of dwarf fruit trees, their propagation, planting, pruning, care and general management. Where there is a limited amount of ground to be devoted to orchard purposes, and where quick results are desired, this book will meet with a warm welcome. Illustrated. 112 pages. 5 x 7 inches. Cloth. $0.50

Cabbage, Cauliflower and Allied Vegetables

By C. L. ALLEN. A practical treatise on the various types and varieties of cabbage, cauliflower, broccoli, Brussels sprouts, kale, collards and kohl-rabi. An explanation is given of the requirements, conditions, cultivation and general management pertaining to the entire cabbage group. After this each class is treated separately and in detail. The chapter on seed raising is probably the most authoritative treatise on this subject ever published. Insects and fungi attacking this class of vegetables are given due attention. Illustrated. 126 pages. 5 x 7 inches. Cloth. $0.50

Asparagus

By F. M. HEXAMER. This is the first book published in America which is exclusively devoted to the raising of asparagus for home use as well as for market. It is a practical and reliable treatise on the saving of the seed, raising of the plants, selection and preparation of the soil, planting, cultivation, manuring, cutting, bunching, packing, marketing, canning and drying insect enemies, fungous diseases and every requirement to successful asparagus culture, special emphasis being given to the importance of asparagus as a farm and money crop. Illustrated. 174 pages. 5 x 7 inches. Cloth. $0.50

The New Onion Culture

By T. GREINER. Rewritten, greatly enlarged and brought up to date. A new method of growing onions of largest size and yield, on less land, than can be raised by the old plan. Thousands of farmers and gardeners and many experiment stations have given it practical trials which have proved a success. A complete guide in growing onions with the greatest profit, explaining the whys and wherefores. Illustrated. 5 x 7 inches. 140 pages. Cloth. $0.50

The New Rhubarb Culture

A complete guide to dark forcing and field culture. Part I—By J. E. MORSE, the well-known Michigan trucker and originator of the now famous and extremely profitable new methods of dark forcing and field culture. Part II—Compiled by G. B. FISKE. Other methods practiced by the most experienced market gardeners, greenhouse men and experimenters in all parts of America. Illustrated. 130 pages. 5 x 7 inches. Cloth. $0.50

Alfalfa

By F. D. Coburn. Its growth, uses and feeding value. The fact that alfalfa thrives in almost any soil; that without reseeding it goes on yielding two, three, four and sometimes five cuttings annually for five, ten or perhaps 100 years; and that either green or cured it is one of the most nutritious forage plants known, makes reliable information upon its production and uses of unusual interest. Such information is given in this volume for every part of America, by the highest authority. Illustrated. 164 pages. 5 x 7 inches. Cloth. $0.50

Ginseng, Its Cultivation, Harvesting, Marketing and Market Value

By Maurice G. Kains, with a short account of its history and botany. It discusses in a practical way how to begin with either seed or roots, soil, climate and location, preparation, planting and maintenance of the beds, artificial propagation, manures, enemies, selection for market and for improvement, preparation for sale, and the profits that may be expected. This booklet is concisely written, well and profusely illustrated, and should be in the hands of all who expect to grow this drug to supply the export trade, and to add a new and profitable industry to their farms and gardens without interfering with the regular work. New edition. Revised and enlarged. Illustrated. 5 x 7 inches. Cloth. . . . $0.50

Landscape Gardening

By F. A. Waugh, professor of horticulture, University of Vermont. A treatise on the general principles governing outdoor art; with sundry suggestions for their application in the commoner problems of gardening. Every paragraph is short, terse and to the point, giving perfect clearness to the discussions at all points. In spite of the natural difficulty of presenting abstract principles the whole matter is made entirely plain even to the inexperienced reader. Illustrated. 152 pages. 5 x 7 inches. Cloth. $0.50

Hedges, Windbreaks, Shelters and Live Fences

By E. P. Powell. A treatise on the planting, growth and management of hedge plants for country and suburban homes. It gives accurate directions concerning hedges; how to plant and how to treat them; and especially concerning windbreaks and shelters. It includes the whole art of making a delightful home, giving directions for nooks and balconies, for bird culture and for human comfort. Illustrated. 140 pages. 5 x 7 inches. Cloth. $0.50

Farm Grasses of the United States of America

By WILLIAM JASPER SPILLMAN. A practical treatise on the grass crop, seeding and management of meadows and pastures, description of the best varieties, the seed and its impurities, grasses for special conditions, lawns and lawn grasses, etc., etc. In preparing this volume the author's object has been to present, in connected form, the main facts concerning the grasses grown on American farms. Every phase of the subject is viewed from the farmer's standpoint. Illustrated. 248 pages. 5 x 7 inches. Cloth. . . $1.00

The Book of Corn

By HERBERT MYRICK, assisted by A. D. SHAMEL, E. A. BURNETT, ALBERT W. FULTON, B. W. SNOW and other most capable specialists. A complete treatise on the culture, marketing and uses of maize in America and elsewhere, for farmers, dealers and others. Illustrated. 372 pages. 5 x 7 inches. Cloth. $1.50

The Hop—It's Culture and Care, Marketing and Manufacture

By HERBERT MYRICK. A practical handbook on the most approved methods in growing, harvesting, curing and selling hops, and on the use and manufacture of hops. The result of years of research and observation, it is a volume destined to be an authority on this crop for many years to come. It takes up every detail from preparing the soil and laying out the yard to curing and selling the crop. Every line represents the ripest judgment and experience of experts. Size, 5 x 8; pages, 300; illustrations, nearly 150; bound in cloth and gold; price, postpaid, ... $1.50

Tobacco Leaf

By J. B. KILLEBREW and HERBERT MYRICK. Its Culture and Cure, Marketing and Manufacture. A practical handbook on the most approved methods in growing, harvesting, curing, packing and selling tobacco, with an account of the operations in every department of tobacco manufacture. The contents of this book are based on actual experiments in field, curing barn, packing house, factory and laboratory. It is the only work of the kind in existence, and is destined to be the standard practical and scientific authority on the whole subject of tobacco for many years. 506 pages and 150 original engravings. 5 x 7 inches. Cloth. $2.00

Bulbs and Tuberous-Rooted Plants

By C. L. ALLEN. A complete treatise on the history, description, methods of propagation and full directions for the successful culture of bulbs in the garden, dwelling and greenhouse. The author of this book has for many years made bulb growing a specialty, and is a recognized authority on their cultivation and management. The cultural directions are plainly stated, practical and to the point. The illustrations which embellish this work have been drawn from nature and have been engraved especially for this book. 312 pages. 5 x 7 inches. Cloth. . . . $1.50

Fumigation Methods

By WILLIS G. JOHNSON. A timely up-to-date book on the practical application of the new methods for destroying insects with hydrocyanic acid gas and carbon bisulphid, the most powerful insecticides ever discovered. It is an indispensable book for farmers, fruit growers, nurserymen, gardeners, florists, millers, grain dealers, transportation companies, college and experiment station workers, etc. Illustrated. 313 pages. 5 x 7 inches. Cloth. $1.00

Diseases of Swine

By Dr. R. A. CRAIG, Professor of Veterinary Medicine at the Purdue University. A concise, practical and popular guide to the prevention and treatment of the diseases of swine. With the discussions on each disease are given its causes, symptoms, treatment and means of prevention. Every part of the book impresses the reader with the fact that its writer is thoroughly and practically familiar with all the details upon which he treats. All technical and strictly scientific terms are avoided, so far as feasible, thus making the work at once available to the practical stock raiser as well as to the teacher and student. Illustrated. 5 x 7 inches. 190 pages. Cloth. $0.75

Spraying Crops—Why, When and How

By CLARENCE M. WEED, D. Sc. The present fourth edition has been rewritten and reset throughout to bring it thoroughly up to date, so that it embodies the latest practical information gleaned by fruit growers and experiment station workers. So much new information has come to light since the third edition was published that this is practically a new book, needed by those who have utilized the earlier editions, as well as by fruit growers and farmers generally. Illustrated. 136 pages. 5 x 7 inches. Cloth. $0.50

Farmer's Cyclopedia of Agriculture

A Compendium of Agricultural Science and Practice on Farm, Orchard and Garden Crops, and the Feeding and Diseases of Farm Animals

By EARLEY VERNON WILCOX, Ph. D and CLARENCE BEAMAN SMITH, M. S

Associate Editors in the Office of Experiment Stations, United States Department of Agriculture.

THIS is a new, practical and complete presentation of the whole subject of agriculture in its broadest sense. It is designed for the use of agriculturists who desire up-to-date, reliable information on all matters pertaining to crops and stock, but more particularly for the actual farmer. The volume contains

Detailed directions for the culture of every important field, orchard, and garden crop

grown in America, together with descriptions of their chief insect pests and fungous diseases, and remedies for their control. It contains an account of modern methods in feeding and handling all farm stock, including poultry. The diseases which affect different farm animals and poultry are described, and the most recent remedies suggested for controlling them.

Every bit of this vast mass of new and useful information is authoritative, practical, and easily found, and no effort has been spared to include all desirable details. There are between 6,000 and 7,000 topics covered in these references, and it contains 700 royal 8vo pages and nearly 500 superb halftone and other original illustrations, making the most perfect Cyclopedia of Agriculture ever attempted.

Handsomely bound in cloth, $3.50; half morocco (very sumptuous), $4.50, postpaid

ORANGE JUDD COMPANY, 439-441 Lafayette Street, New York, N. Y.
Marquette Building, Chicago, Ill.

www.ingramcontent.com/pod-product-compliance
Lightning Source LLC
Chambersburg PA
CBHW030424300426
44112CB00009B/839